# Graham Geraghty
# MISUNDERSTOOD

*With*

*Justin Doyle*

**BLACKWATER PRESS**

Editor
*Antoinette Walker*

Design & Layout
*Paula Byrne*

Cover Design
*Melanie Gradtke*

ISBN
1 84131 631 8

Produced in Ireland by Blackwater Press, c/o Folens Publishers, Hibernian Industrial Estate, Greenhills Road, Tallaght, Dublin 24

For permission to reproduce articles and extracts in this book, the authors and Publishers gratefully acknowledge *The Meath Chronicle*, Liam Cahill of An Fear Rua website, *The Irish Times* and the *Irish Independent*. Photographs are reproduced courtesy of the Geraghty family, John Quirke Photography, mike shaughnessy photographer, Inpho Photography and Sportsfile.

*To my wife Amanda, children Sophia and Lauren and also remembering Leslie Crinion, RIP*

# Acknowledgements

Each and every one of these people deserves a gold medal – and for those not mentioned it is not the winning, but the participation that counts.

Thanks to John O'Connor at Blackwater Press for taking on this book and showing so much enthusiasm; his very skilful editor Antoinette Walker along with Margaret Burns and all the rest of the Blackwater staff.

Brendan Cummins former PRO with the Meath County Board trawled his way through many match programmes; Fergal Lynch, *The Meath Chronicle*'s expert Gaelic games writer, was also a huge help. Others who chipped in with the vital facts were Siobhan Brady in Croke Park's Statistics Office; Anne Harrington of the Athletics Association of Ireland and Brenda Timmons of *Ireland on Sunday*.

The people of Athboy towed in with Mick Connell from Martinstown providing videotapes of important matches.

A huge debt of gratitude is owed to Anne Marie Doyle and Mary Carley. Finally, a really special word of thanks goes to Paula Ward from Mount Temple Comprehensive School whose help and support were invaluable.

# Contents

# 1 *Bred to Be a Winner*

From what I've been told, it was one of the few occasions in my life when I did not cause a stir. The date to be exact was 17 May 1973 when the maternity staff at Our Lady of Lourdes Hospital in Drogheda, Co Louth delivered me into this world. Born at approximately 20 minutes to three in the morning, and weighing in at 7 lbs 15 oz, I was the second child born to my mother, Gene, a housewife, and my father, Ger, a construction worker. Taking a line from a well-known Irish film, you could say that I was a small turkey but a big baby! Two years earlier, my parents had had their first child – my sister Sandra. Later, two more females would be added to the family home in Kentstown, just outside Navan in Co Meath. Karen was born a year after me and then following a seven-year itch, Lisa arrived.

I have been surrounded by women for almost my entire life, a fact that only recently dawned on me. Growing up as a young boy, and while my father was out working hard on the building sites, I was at home in the company of my mother and sisters. And now as a married man, I share my life with my wife, Amanda, and our two daughters, Sophia and Lauren. That is all a world away from when I'm out on the green sod in competitive action. On those occasions 29 mean and hungry males, all of whom have just one purpose – to get their hands on a white leather ball – usually encircle me. And that is not to mention the mostly male crowds who can shout all sorts of obscenities in your direction!

Looking back on my childhood, I am blessed that I can remember as far back as to when I was just two-years-old. Those memories are mostly of myself and my sister Sandra waiting for Dad to come in from work in the evenings. It had nothing to do with us missing him all day but perhaps more to do with the little bag of sweets he frequently brought home to us.

Even though times were hard and unemployment was the scourge of the country, Dad worked very hard and still always managed to find time for us. I therefore had a very happy childhood. And as is the case with most young fellas, the first time I ever touched a ball was in gentle kickabouts with my father. Of course, it helped enormously that he was a very good footballer in his own right. He started out playing with Duleek and then transferred to Seneschalstown around the time I was born. He won an Intermediate title with Duleek and, although he never managed to go as far up the ladder as I did, he did line out in a few challenge matches for Meath at Senior level. My father played in the half-forward or corner-forward positions. Several of my uncles also played. There were five of them in all and I am led to believe that a certain Eugene Geraghty was a very good player at Minor level!

Not to be left out or forgotten in any way, my mother also played Gaelic football. She played with the Kentstown Ladies' team. So if you are a student of the form-book, then I suppose you could say that being 'by' a footballer and 'out' of a footballer, I was destined to become a thoroughbred of the sport! Naturally then as a youngster, a lot of time, especially on Sundays, was spent travelling from match to match with my parents. Not only was football in my blood from such a young age, it was also in my whole being. Football socks, togs, jerseys and mucky boots would lie strewn around the house – especially with devious imps like myself about.

My first trip to Croke Park did not come about until 1984. I will never forget the whole occasion. It was the Centenary Cup Final, a once-off competition in football and hurling to celebrate the 100th anniversary of the founding of the GAA. In the football final, Meath played Monaghan and won by 0–10 to 0–8. I cannot emphasise enough the huge impact that day had on me. Prior to that occasion, I had only *heard* about Croke Park. But the more I listened to my father and uncles and so many others talk about it, I could not wait to see it for myself. Seeing it for the very first time was just breathtaking. It was a stadium the like of which I had only ever seen on television. Everything about my first time at GAA headquarters impressed me – from the amount of cars travelling up and back to the display of colour, the huge crowds and the tremendous atmosphere it all generated.

After that first experience, I hardly ever missed a day out to Croke Park when Meath were playing. Even now, after all the experience I have gained from playing there, nothing beats attending matches as a youngster. It really stood me in good stead for the future. It helped to instil in me a great sense of experiencing the big occasion and there is simply no substitute for experience. For any young lad who harbours dreams of playing for his county, it is invaluable.

By this time, trips away had become very common for me. I was also involved in a number of other sports. As well as football, I also played soccer and basketball. But my main sport, and my favourite outside the football circle, was athletics. I joined Seneschalstown Athletic Club and in doing so, I found myself representing them at running events all over Ireland. My longest journey with the club was to the Mardyke in Cork, where one of my proudest moments running for Seneschalstown came in 1981. I competed in the 50 metres and 200 metres as well as the long jump. At U-8 level, I happened to set a national record that still stands today.

Running in the 50 metres, I came home the winner in a time of 7.16 seconds. That was an official national record and it stood until 1990. In that year, the event was extended to 60 metres in line with international standards. Therefore the 50 metres is no longer in existence, so it looks like I will hold that record for a very long time! I'm very proud of that feat. It is nice to be able to tell people that I am the fastest ever under 8 to run the 50 metres in this country. Although I was never a winner at the Community Games in Mosney, I did compete there but only in the U-8s and U-10s relay events. To this day I feel that the pace and speed that I have shown on the field of play all sprang from my experiences in athletics as a boy.

Inevitably, schooling took a back seat with all the sport on offer. One thing which I recall most, and which I greatly enjoyed during my early education at Kentstown National School, was the storytelling. The headmaster, Mr McGillick, was a great man for telling stories. I would always look forward to Fridays, not just because it was the end of the week, but it was the day when we all sat around with mouths gaping open listening to his stories. Not surprisingly, physical education was my favourite subject. Another thing I always remember is the remark which Mr McGillick usually made on our way to PE class. As we all rushed in, eager to take part, he would constantly shout to us: 'Okay boys, last one in is a bag of snots.'

Mr McGillick was a good teacher but could be fairly hard on us as well. Back then, when corporal punishment was allowed, I felt the lashes of his cane on more than one occasion. Like a lot of young boys, I would have been a little 'hyper' and up to all sorts of horseplay, so a lash of the stick would have certainly quietened me down. It did me no harm and they could do with bringing it back today. Kids now feel they can get away with anything, safe in the knowledge that they will not be punished.

If I was a little headstrong and troublesome at school, then at home I was a little bit of a devil. One Christmas I remember Santa left me a Mecano set and a toy JCB. I was thrilled as it was the best present I received as a young lad and just what I had wanted. But when I grew tired of driving the JCB around and making shapes and things with Mecano, I somehow worked out that the JCB could be taken apart. My parents were none too happy.

A much more painful experience befell me when I was around eight-years-old. My best friend Kevin Clarke and I were out playing on our housing estate when we noticed some machinery working on the roads. After the men had finished their work for the day, we decided to take a closer look. We climbed up on the machines and then disaster struck. I was fooling around and as I was swinging on part of a machine, I fell awkwardly and ended up breaking my leg. The pain was unbelievable and my screams obviously frightened Clarkey so much that he fled to my house to raise the alarm. I was brought to Navan Hospital, where my leg was bound in a cast and I was left to hobble around for what seemed like months.

The switch from national to secondary school was no problem for me. Going to Navan Community School, now Beaufort College, was just like going into a higher class as I already knew most of the lads going there. I was also very tall for my age, so I was not in the least bit intimidated or fearful of any of the other lads. In fact, during my time in First Year, I was actually playing football for the U-16s.

Playing sports was everything to me and study came a very poor second. The more I could get of football, athletics, basketball and soccer, so much the better as it kept me out of classes. Cathal Brugha McDevitt was the principal of the school and Mick Lavelle the vice-principal, but my favourite teachers were Bartley Curran and Tom Lynch. They would get me out of various classes so I could play in a match, or after a match had finished, they would let me off home early. There were other ways of getting off classes as well as, for example, mitching. Quite often, a few of us would mitch off school or a particular class we detested. We would go off down to a well-known area of Navan called the 'the Ramparts' or hang around Navan Shopping Centre.

My best friend in secondary school was Leslie Crinion. We hung around and went everywhere together. Many years later, Leslie was to lose his life in a tragic accident. Another guy who became a very good friend of mine in the strangest of circumstances was Paddy McGarry. About a week before starting secondary school, I lined out for Seneschalstown in an underage football game against Gibbstown. I was sent off for fighting in that match and had forgotten all about it until I was reminded about it a few weeks later. Hanging around with a few lads in school one day, one of them, namely McGarry, told me it was him whom I had been fighting with in that match! Stranger still is the fact that Paddy now lives just down the road from my house in Athboy. It gets even better. Paddy's wife, Niamh Higgins, has been the best friend of my wife Amanda since childhood. Incidentally, Paddy is also Tommy Dowd's brother-in-law as Tommy married Paddy's sister, Geraldine.

I think that I must have been in trouble a few times at school. On one memorable occasion, I was down at the Ramparts with a few lads. Then suddenly, and without us spotting it, a green-coloured school bus pulled up. Trying not to get caught, I scampered off as quickly as possible and breathed a sigh of relief thinking that I had got away. Later, while I was sitting at my desk back at school, an announcement rang out over the intercom: 'Would Graham Geraghty please come to the office immediately.' In the office I had to stand there and explain what I was doing out of school. But it was all to no avail. My blond hair had given me away. As a result, I was suspended for a few days and, once again, my parents were not at all amused.

Another incident, but more humorous, occurred when myself and Kenneth Lynch hid under the teacher's desk at the top of the class! When the teacher came into the room we remained where we were. The teacher then began the lesson and amid much laughter from the rest of the class, Kenneth was found out. I remained under the desk and when I was eventually told to come out, I was promptly sent down to the office once more.

When the lads and myself were together, inevitably the subject of girls would come up. Nothing really happened during the week but all that changed when it came to discos at the weekend. Believe it or not but I was just 13 when I attended my first disco! My older sister Sandra was going to a disco one night so I secretly planned to meet her and tag along. My plans all worked out and then the funniest thing happened. As we approached the entrance to the disco at the Ardboyne Hotel in Navan, the bouncers stepped aside to let me through. But when I looked back, they were refusing to allow Sandra in! I did not know what to do. I was in two minds to go on or go back to Sandra. But having come that far I decided not to jeopardise my big moment by pleading Sandra's case. In the event, everything worked out well as later on I saw Sandra with her friends at the disco.

In those early teenage years, you tend to try all sorts of new and exciting things. I was no different from any other fella. While so many guys and girls seemed to be trying smoking, it never ever appealed to me. I have never smoked cigarettes but I will always remember my first drink. On the way home from the Meath Minor trials in 1989, Meath Minor chairman, Pat O'Neill brought a few of us into Bermingham's Pub in Navan. Hugh Carolan and Neil Cooney from St Colmcille's Club in Laytown were with me. We were standing there like lame ducks when Pat turned to the three of us and asked: 'So what will ye have, lads?' 'A shandy please, Pat,' came the reply from the two lads so I decided to have the same When I took a sip, I felt like getting sick. When they said shandy, I thought they meant a rock shandy!

About the same time, when I was 16, the temptation to drive my father's car was really eating at me. Not before long an opportunity presented itself. On Friday nights, my parents used to play cards in various houses in Kentstown. One particular night they went off to play cards and they left the car and car keys behind. With no time to waste, Kevin Clarke and myself let the handbrake off and pushed the car out onto the road. Then we hopped in and I drove it up and down the road in our estate. Next morning, Dad gave me a right telling off. When he arrived home in the early hours, he had noticed that the car had not been put back or parked properly. After that episode, he would only let me drive a little in his presence. Nonetheless, it was all thanks to him that I was well and truly able to drive by the time I was 18.

Academically, I achieved mixed results. I did fairly well in the Intermediate Cert, receiving seven honours and two passes. But that was because of the challenge of the early years in secondary school. It was a whole new way of learning. But then it all became monotonous and boring and as sport began to take over, my attention to study went into freefall and decline. The year before the Leaving Cert, i.e. Fifth Year, is seen by many to be a real 'doss' year. You can take it fairly easy and pack everything into the last and all-important year. That is not the case, however, with the student who keeps up with the studies and never ceases to fall behind. For those who take a relaxed attitude, it is generally a case of much work and much catching up to do in the final year. In my case, I only really realised the importance and seriousness of the Leaving Cert when it was all too late. You simply cannot cram two years of work into the last couple of months of your school life. Because of that, I failed the exam. However, I did go back to repeat it and passed the following year.

In those last two years at school, and like so many students, I was constantly asked what career I wished to pursue or what I wanted to do when I left school. I had no idea what I wanted to do. When push came to shove, I remember telling people that I would like to do recreational management or something in the line of coaching. In truth, all I ever wanted to do was play football. Therefore, how fitting that when I left Navan Community College, I left them a reminder of my days spent there. It was a very proud moment for them and me when I captained the school to win the Vocational Schools Leinster Cup in 1991. We beat Tullow from Carlow in the final and only lost the All-Ireland semi-final by a point.

Perhaps all my misdemeanours and my poor results in the classroom were forgiven by my efforts out on the field. I know it was a very proud moment for me when I captained that team to victory. More importantly, it was a very proud moment and a huge landmark in the history of the school.

******

## A Major Minor

Since the age of 13, I had been playing with Meath underage sides. The Minor Board chairman, Pat O'Neill, and the manager, Pat Kenny, had taken me up from U-14 and U-16 level. So I was hoping to make further progress when I went for the Meath Minor trials in 1989. The trials were run on a sort of league-like basis involving different areas of Meath like east Meath, north Meath and even counties further north like Louth. I think this system is still in use today. We would play a series of friendly matches against each other that involved heavy training schedules.

Most of the trial matches took place in Stamullen, a few miles outside Navan. Training took place at Páirc Tailteann, Navan, the home of Meath football. I was very excited going to the trials. I was also very determined to succeed because it was every young lad's dream to play at Croke Park. Since I had experienced the atmosphere there on big match days, I desperately wanted to play there in front of a huge crowd.

Attending these trials along with the chairman and manager were the selectors. The selectors I can remember who were almost always present were Johnny Sullivan, Patsy Duff, Benny Gartland, Oliver 'Spudler' Harding and Jimmy Cooney from Ballinabrackey, which is dangerously close to the Westmeath border! Spudler and Jimmy Cooney had perhaps the hardest job of all. It was their responsibility to go around collecting lads and then drop them off home again. Sometimes this involved bringing fellas on 400-mile round trips from counties like Limerick! These trips were not without incident or accident and I can recall Spudler's crazy driving.

On the first occasion we were playing a trial match in the North. Travelling up there, we came around a sharp bend off a by-road and before we or should I say Spudler knew it, we met a main road. Instead of stopping, he kept on going and all we could hear was loud screeching and a car horn blaring. Spudler slammed on the brakes and we ended up missing another car by about three inches. What a near miss and our hearts were in our mouths!

I used to get phone calls from the men overlooking the trials, so I thought everything was going well. Then the phone calls suddenly stopped and I knew then that I was not to be part of the 1989 Minor side. To say I was disappointed was an understatement. I was gutted especially after all the effort I put in. I had turned up for all the trials and all the training sessions and naturally it was hard to stomach rejection.

However, this made me even more determined and a year later, all was forgiven. I was selected for the Meath Minor team of 1990 and I could not hide my delight. It was not as if I had suddenly knuckled down. I did not work any harder the following year. In fact, I think I learned from the experience of the previous year. In 1990, I just applied myself to the task better. I gave more attention to things. The previous year I had been a little too tentative, too much in awe of the game. I stood back mouth-gaping and starry-eyed, looking at what was going on rather than concentrating on my own game. I was playing in the backs at the time and one of my strengths was going forward running with the ball. But instead of doing that, I was looking around and admiring the skills of players and play I had not seen before. At school and at local club level you come across a lot of average players and you tend to see the same style of play over and over again. But here, I was looking at the cream of the crop from all over Meath. In 1989, I was really just standing still at the trials and not going forward or becoming involved, as I should have been. Instead I was leaving it to the lads around me while I stood back just 'ball-watching' and admiring players like Tony Byrne from Dunboyne. Tony played half-forward and he was very quick. In fact, he was such a good player that he was voted Minor Player of the Year.

So everything went well in the trials of 1990. I played my game and generally expressed myself. We had a very special and talented bunch of players that year. I think we played in around 20 trial matches and challenges against all sorts of teams from North Leinster and the North. We were actually unbeaten and we won most, if not all of them, fairly comfortably. It just goes to show what a good job the selectors did. They can get lots of hassle – especially from people accusing them of favouring certain players – but in truth they have hard choices to make.

Things were so different when it came to our early-round matches in Leinster. From whipping teams in practice, we began to struggle and were actually very shaky. We beat Longford 2–16 to 2–9 in Navan, but then in my first ever competitive game in Croke Park, we conceded three goals in the first 15 minutes against Laois. That was a disaster and it looked like it was all going to end in tears. Amazingly, we managed to re-group and grab a hold of things. Thanks to Terry O'Connor's last gasp point, we ended up winning by the narrowest of margins. The 1–11 to 3–4 scoreline was a real wake-up call for us. We knew that we had to improve a great deal to have any chance against Kildare in the Leinster final. We did at least show a great trait of all Meath sides at all levels – our never-say-die fighting spirit.

Another thing going for us was our togetherness. We were a very close bunch of lads and that was largely due to the way we travelled to and from games. I mentioned earlier about my first drink and the two lads from Laytown who were with me. They were with me on that occasion too, but I would get to know so many new faces in the coming years, as it was rare to travel in the same car with the same people and players. We were always travelling in different cars and picking up different players.

On the morning of the Leinster final, Spudler picked up David Dillon, Conor Macken and myself at Kentstown church. We had breakfast in Ashbourne House and then travelled on to Croke Park where we joined up with the rest of the Meath team in the dressing-rooms. Back then, the dressing-rooms were situated under the old Hogan Stand. Kildare had Glenn Ryan playing for them, but at that time he and the rest of the Kildare side meant little or nothing to us. After listening to Paul Kenny's pep talk, heightened by him kicking and banging some tables, we just wanted to get out there and win. As we ran out onto the pitch, we were so revved up and raring to go that it was going to take a mighty effort from any team to get the better of us.

Paul Kenny's pre-match lecture certainly had the desired effect. We were in control of the match right from the start. The bad memories of the near disaster against Laois were well and truly banished as we thrashed Kildare, 1–19 to 1–6. I had a particularly good game and was voted Man of the Match. I remember getting a lot of ball and this boosted my confidence. The longer the game went on and the more ball I received, the more assured I became. It also helped that I was playing in front of, not only a big crowd, but also the television cameras. A special moment I remember well from that game was going on a long run up the field and finishing with a point. It was my only score of the match but it must have been a good one as next day the papers said I had soloed over 70 yards.

That Minor side, as well as being very close and skilful, were also a very confident side as a result. Thirteen of the 15 players were almost automatically picked. There were really only one or two positions to be fought for. Conor Macken was always on the fringe and it was a toss up between him and Cathal Sheridan with Sheridan getting the nod. So you could say that Conor was one of those unlucky players to miss out.

In contrast, and at the other end of the scale, you had a player who was so talented that he came straight into the side at the Leinster final stage! David Martin must have been the envy of every other player on the panel but in truth we all knew how multi-talented he was. David was to become a very good friend of mine and was affectionately known as 'Scobey' among us. He was small and stocky but very strong for someone so young. An all-round sportsman, Scobey also played soccer and was in the Meath Senior hurling team as well. But I think it says it all that in that Minor final, his first full involvement, he scored a whopping 10 points!

It is also worth mentioning the Meath team that lined out in that final. In goals was Conor Martin; the full-backs were Vinnie Ryan, Enda McManus and Noel Collier; the half-backs were Ronan McGrath, Tommy Hanley and myself. In midfield we had John McCarthy and Jason Hendrick; up front in the half-forward line were Brendan Kealy, Tony Byrne and David Martin; and the full-forwards were Hugh Carolan, the hero Terry O'Connor from Ballivor and Cathal Sheridan.

Celebrations went on well into the early hours and did not end there. On the following Monday, Scobey and I, along with Glenn Ryan from Kildare and Derek Duggan from Roscommon, were invited to attend trials of a different kind. Carlton, an Australian

Rules football side from Melbourne, were on a scouting mission in Ireland and invited us to take part in some trial matches. Seeing that the trials were held in Portmarnock, we were given accommodation in the Grand Hotel, Malahide, for four days. Nothing came out of the trials, which is probably no surprise after all the exertions from the Kildare match and the post-match celebrations. Even then, however, the trials did not stop us from enjoying ourselves further.

After one trial had finished, the four of us made our way to a well-known Malahide pub, Gibneys. I was never a great drinker and so was concerned about lasting the pace! I need not have worried, as it was Derek Duggan who keeled over first. While all this was happening, Scobey, who always had 'a way with women', was trying his luck with a couple of ladies! So I went over to see how he was getting on and soon afterwards the two of us, accompanying the women, went for a nice romantic stroll along the beach. I cannot speak for Scobey, but the only thing I remember about 'my' lady friend was that she was not Irish.

Scobey will not mind me telling this story because he has heard it all before. But as regards his football career it is true that he wasted the great talent he had. He was a young and gifted player who was also on the Meath Senior hurling panel as a teenager – he was the Meath goalkeeper at 15 years of age! To be very fair to him, however, it was not entirely his own fault. Had he been guided better, I have no doubt in my mind that David 'Scobey' Martin would have been a household name in Gaelic football – if not throughout Ireland, then most certainly in Meath.

On 19 August 1990, we faced Derry in the All-Ireland Minor semi-final. This was hyped up in favour of Derry. They were the favourites before the Championship began and a lot of people wrote us off because of that. We were also informed of the fact that they had no less than six of their 1989 winning team in the side. For Minors, they were very tall, very well built and of course they had the experience of winning the All-Ireland the previous year. I was marking a 'giant' by the name of Oliver Collins. When we were taking up our positions on the pitch and I saw Collins, I just remember thinking to myself, 'Jaysus!' He was 6 ft 3 or 4 in, which is phenomenal for that level. Certainly there would be very few Senior players at that height.

Reputations can add extra pressure to a side that carries the favourite tag. It was also a very wet day which seemed to suit us better. So when we got off to a flying start again, and knowing our confidence, it was always going to be extremely difficult for them to peg us back. We had them at sixes and sevens and by the end they were in tatters. We triumphed by 3–8 to 1–3 and I was very happy with my own performance having scored some nice points in the process.

The Meath Seniors were playing Donegal that day and after we had beaten Derry, we went up into the Hogan Stand to shout on the Senior team. There were always seats reserved for us after we had finished playing. It was great because after all the hard work was done, there was no better feeling than to sit back and shout on your beloved Meath.

Weather conditions were awful but after both sides had triumphed to reach their respective All-Ireland finals, spirits were high as we headed home to Navan. First off we were to stop at the County Club in Dunshaughlin for a few celebratory drinks and a bite to eat. Spudler was as excited as we were as he drove us out of Croke Park. He was delighted with Meath's successes and was full of talk, looking back at us while driving. A few minutes later, as he looked back, the traffic lights began to change. We shouted at him and he slammed on the brakes but the road surface was so slippy that his Fiat Ritmo went skidding into the back of the car ahead of us. Thankfully, the car in front belonged to Pat O'Neill who did not even bother to get out. We all laughed and drove on only stopping to survey the damage when we eventually arrived in Dunshaughlin!

******

Kerry were to be our All-Ireland final opponents. But whether it was Derry in the semi-finals or Kerry, we just did not care about the other team labelled as favourites. As I mentioned earlier, we were a very confident outfit and Paul Kenny certainly drilled us to such an extent in the pre-match build-ups that we were actually more afraid of him than we were of the opposition! We knew in advance that this Kerry side had a very potent and dangerous forward line. They had a very good full-forward by the name of Jason Wieboldt, whose father was German, if memory serves me correct. Jason did some serious damage to other sides earlier in the competition. He was definitely one we had to watch closely. They also had several other very good players, most notably Seamus Moynihan and Billy O'Shea both of whom went on to become household names in Kerry.

It was a very tight final right the way through. We lead by 1–7 to 1–6 at the break but in truth they could easily have been the team in front. I remember a Wieboldt piledriver crashing back off our crossbar so we were a little fortunate. We were a couple of points up with around five minutes to go when they were awarded a penalty. Thankfully, Conor Martin made a great save and even then that was not the end of it. The last three or four minutes were like an eternity. But we managed to hang on under severe Kerry pressure to win our first Minor title since 1957 by 2–11 to 2–9.

There was no one outstanding individual for us. Every man played his part in helping us to our historic moment. Then, after all the backslapping and the euphoria, again we made our way up into the Hogan Stand to shout on the Senior team. Unfortunately, for them, Cork got revenge for the defeats in the 1987 and 1988 finals at the hands of Meath. We were all brought right back down to earth with a huge thud.

One thing I will always remember from that day was, strangely enough, nothing to do with our magnificent success. When I was above in the stands afterwards, I vividly recall seeing Cork's Colm O'Neill striking out and hitting Mick Lyons. Because of Mick's tough guy image, we all expected him to immediately get revenge and strike back. But he just put his hand up to hold or feel his face and calmly walked away. I really admired that and I thought he showed great restraint. Many years later, I was to follow his example in an Aussie Rules match at Croke Park.

In mentioning our first All-Ireland Minor title in 33 years, I wonder how many of you can remember that great side from 1957? It was 16 years before I was born but I did manage to come across a newspaper article about that team in a scrapbook which my late grandmother, Rose Lawlor, kept and passed on to me. In goals was PJ Reilly who later went on to work in Dublin as a taxi-driver. The full-backs were Toss Gibney, Don Kelleher and the only player from that side who went on to Inter-County stardom, Bertie Cunningham.

Bertie won an All-Ireland Senior medal in 1967 and in that same year became Meath's first Footballer of the Year.

The half-backs were Jack Fagan, who later became property editor of *The Irish Times*, Tom Fitzsimons and Michael Clerkin.

In midfield were Jimmy Halpin and Seamus Clynch, who won six Keegan Cups (Meath Club Championships) in seven years between 1957 and 1963 with Navan O'Mahonys. The half-forward line was Paddy Hanley, Jackie Grey who went on to be a schoolteacher in Newry, and Brendan Cahill. Finally the full-forwards were Tom Monaghan, Mick Greville who worked in Lucan, Co Dublin as a butcher and the prolific goalscorer, Larry Drumm.

After our Minor triumph, we went to the Grand Hotel, Malahide for dinner. Also staying with us in the same hotel was the beaten Senior team. In our own state of excitement it was a very sobering sight to see their sad faces. It was definitely a case of celebrations and commiserations. But there were some very light-hearted moments, especially the comment from my team-mate Alan Nash to Mick Lyons: 'Ah sure, don't worry, Mick – you'll be some player when you get older!' David 'Jinksy' Beggy had a great sing-song going on the piano and I just remember thinking to myself how marvellous all of this was. Up until this point, we had never been with the Seniors and now there we were trying our best to cheer them all up.

Next day we hit the road for Meath. The celebrations went on for three or four days. The attitude was to get as much drink into us as possible and to visit as many pubs and clubs as we could! We strutted from every pub with our heads held high. We thought we were brilliant and then it ended. And when it died, I thought of the beaten Senior team and how lucky I was and that hopefully that luck would one day bring Sam Maguire back to Meath.

\* \* \* \* \* \*

## Reaching the Stars

After the Minor success in 1990, I definitely knew that I had what was required to go all the way. More to the point, I was really determined to go all the way. Everything seemed to be pointing and heading towards that ultimate goal; from enjoying the big match atmosphere as a kid, to winning a Minor All-Ireland medal to mixing with the Senior players and seeing at first hand the pain of defeat in the eyes of so many men I admired. So imagine my delight and utter disbelief when, just a few weeks after our big success, I was called into the Meath Senior panel for a National League game! Understandably, there were a few Senior players who needed a break and also a few injured cases after their All-Ireland defeat. Nevertheless, it was the big break I had been waiting for.

I made my Senior debut for Meath on 14 October 1990. We played Cork in Navan and it was a winning debut as we won by a point, 1–10 to 2–6. However, it did not last long for me. I was not named in the panel published in the match programme but I did come on as a substitute in the second half. When the players who were missing returned to the team, it meant that I was out and would have to wait another while for my chance at that level. It was disappointing but understandable.

However, one door closes and another opens. Soon after, I was told that I was going to be part of the Meath U-21 campaign. A couple of months later we were into 1991 and I was also made captain of the Minor team ready to defend its title. Over the following five or six months the record books will show that I had represented Meath at Senior, U-21 and Minor levels and that I led Navan Community College in their pursuit of glory. Looking back I do not know how I managed to fit it all in. But it was bound to take its toll and something just had to give.

The Minor side was still very strong and formidable. But this can make things even harder as other sides were now determined to knock you off your proud perch. Dublin in the first round was really the last thing we needed. If you are going to retain your crown, then you will have to beat teams of this calibre. But rather than playing them in the first round, and with respect to the other Leinster sides, Meath v Dublin is really a Leinster final deserving of a big day and big crowd at Croke Park.

To make things even harder, we had to face the Dubs in their backyard at Parnell Park. Sure enough, they had a real go at us and we struggled to keep in touch. In the end, I had to kick over a '50' to level the match and bring it back to a replay on our patch. When it came to the replay in Walterstown, Dublin had obviously regained some of the confidence from the first match and we simply never got going. Dublin put us out at the first hurdle. We were really brought back down to earth. There would be no more joyous days out for the Meath Minor team of 1991. We all had to pick up the pieces. For some that meant concentrating on their studies and for others it meant getting back into the routine of work. For me it meant more football – a lot more football, or so I thought. However, that defeat was just the beginning of my problems.

I was now part of the U-21 panel and I remember being immediately called up and travelling to Limerick to face the mighty Kerry. I do not think 'mighty' is too strong a word in terms of U-21 and the likes of Kerry and Dublin. You have heard it said that you never see a bad underage team in these and other strong counties. That is quite true as the young players on those teams will burst blood vessels in order to make it on to the Senior teams of the future.

One disaster followed another and we were taking an awful hammering from the Kingdom, when I was sent on for the last few minutes of what was a hopeless cause. A few minutes later, I remember jumping for a ball and ended up pulling a hamstring in the process. I was only on and then had to be taken off! A bad day ended with Kerry 'stuffing' us, and the Meath U-21s were out of the Championship. Thankfully, my injury was not too serious and, in any case, I now had plenty of time to let it heal.

Out of action on all fronts, I then concentrated on shouting on the Seniors and we all hoped that they could atone for their heartbreak of the previous September. What an amazing summer it turned out to be. It was without doubt one of the most memorable in Gaelic football history and I am glad I was able to witness it all unfold. There were so many trips up to Croke Park with replay after replay that you would be forgiven for losing count. I think it will be forever known as the 'Summer of Replays'.

The auld enemy Dublin were first up and it took an unbelievable, and unprecedented, four matches before it was finally settled! Those four matches with Dublin beat the previous Leinster record of three matches between Meath and Louth in 1949. Admittedly, we had some very lucky escapes along the way, but after three replays we finally got the better of a very good and gallant Dublin side. Wicklow were next up and they had some excellent players like midfielder Fergus Daly, and All Star Kevin O'Brien. Again we were a little fortunate to get a draw and yet another replay. After finally overcoming the brave Wicklow challenge, we beat Roscommon in the semi-final to face a showdown with Ulster Champions, Down, in the All-Ireland final.

Croke Park was enveloped in a sea of colour on that September day. The green and gold of Meath was set against the red and black of Down. It was a very tough match to predict especially with so much more at stake than the title itself. DJ Kane did not want to be the first Down captain to lose an All-Ireland and Meath were desperate to avoid a second successive defeat in the final.

Because of all that pressure and the fact that Down were very strong and very fast, especially with the very slippery James McCartan up front, I thought Meath started off all right, but then became very nervous. As a result, Down opened up a gap before half-time and they stretched it to a whopping 11 points with around 15 minutes to go. Meath supporters were silenced and it looked all over. After Meath had squandered some good goalscoring opportunities, it definitely was not to be their day. Then Liam Hayes gave Meath a bit of hope when he raced through and he slotted the ball to the back of the net. This inspired the players none more so than Colm O'Rourke, and the fans suddenly found their voices. Then point after point after point saw the gap further cut to just four while there were still a few minutes left. Down, in desperation, deliberately tried to wind down the clock by slowing things right down.

The Northerners looked a spent force as Meath were now finishing with a real flourish. Down manager, Pete McGrath, even bought more time by taking his time over sending on big Liam Austin for an injured player. Still Meath laid siege on the Down defences. The gap was down to just two points and now the Northern fans were silent with hands chewed to the bone. Meath were about to launch another last gasp attack from a sideline when the referee called time. All of our heroic efforts were to no avail as Down were victorious by two points. It may have been one of the all-time classic finals, but that was no consolation to Meath's disconsolate players. Two All-Ireland defeats in a row is the bitterest pill to swallow.

In September 1990, when I had seen the defeated Seniors in Malahide, I vowed to myself to hopefully one day help bring the All-Ireland back to the Royal County of my beloved Meath. In 1991 I think Meath won the hearts of the entire country with their courageous comeback against Down when the clock beat them. And I was even more determined than ever to win that ultimate prize. Once more, after the exhausting efforts of those Senior players, I was brought straight into the side for the National League campaign. Through the autumn and winter of 1991 and right into the spring of 1992, we actually acquitted ourselves very well. I was playing in my usual position in the back line and I was more than happy with my game. I was delighted to be playing in the Senior team and determined to hold onto my place.

We reached the League semi-final where we would meet another formidable Ulster side, Derry. As the referee got ready to throw up the ball, I was positioned at right half-back where I was marking a certain player by the name of Anthony Tohill. Thinking back now, that was a sort of coincidence as both of us on separate occasions in the following years would be invited across the water for trials with some major English soccer clubs, which will be told in a later chapter.

The game was not going our way at all and once again, disaster struck. Tohill and I were running for the ball when I fell awkwardly on my stomach. However, my stomach was not the problem, but my arm. As I fell, my elbow became wedged underneath me leaving me in terrible pain. Sean Boylan took me off and replaced me with Kevin Foley. It never rains but it pours and I suffered a triple whammy in that League semi-final with Derry. I was taken off injured although it was not a long lasting injury. We lost the match agonisingly by a point, 0–12 to 1–8 and my replacement, Kevin Foley, was to keep me out of the Senior side for the rest of 1992. It was all extremely disappointing especially sitting on the bench and not been able to do anything. But I suppose one man's bad luck is another man's gain and that is sport. And when you see players like Robbie O'Malley sitting on the bench beside you, you have really done well to get that far.

The years 1991 and 1992 were very disappointing for me and Meath after all the expectations we had following the Minor success of 1990. The Minors and U-21s had been dumped out of their respective championships at the first hurdle and then I picked up injuries with the U-21s and Seniors resulting in me losing my place. On the bright side, I had at least broken into the County side and with everything put behind me, and all injuries healed, I was hoping that 1993 would be a winning one.

No longer a Minor, and with no place in the Senior side, I began the campaign with the U-21s in the Leinster Championship. Our first test was away in Longford and we passed that with flying colours, winning by 2–10 to 1–1. Then we played Kilkenny in Navan and, in all fairness, the Cats do not really have a footballing tradition, but there were many raised eyebrows when they led at the break by 0–4 to 0–3. In the second half we came out and really showed our class. Kilkenny failed to score as we ran out comfortable winners at 1–14 to 0–4.

They were fairly easy games but we knew much tougher battles lay ahead. Wexford were our semi-final opponents in Leinster and they are a good, honest and workman-like county at all levels. Again we trailed at the break. Only Wexford would prove to be a very tough nut to crack as they led by three points, 2–3 to 0–6. We were very leaky in defence in that first half and we really tightened up after the interval. The crowd in Newbridge sensed a shock but we pulled through with a score of 1–13 to 2–7.

Who else but Dublin awaited our arrival in the Leinster U-21 final. For that final, we had 13 of the 15 players that won the Minor title. One of the new additions to the side was none other than Jimmy McGuinness. He was a very talented player who took time to come into his own. He was thought not to be up to the required standard in 1990 but he had improved greatly since. His biggest asset was leaping to field ball that had been kicked out by the goalkeeper or defenders. The final was played before the National League final replay between Donegal and Dublin. So the Dublin U-21 side had a fair amount of vocal support to call on that day. Typical of such encounters, it was very close throughout with no quarter given. We went in at half-time leading by a point and despite the crowd urging them on, we held on to win the Leinster title by 2–11 to 2–9.

It seemed like an eternity before we played again. In fact, it was almost three months before we lined out for the All-Ireland semi-final! In the meantime, I was called up for the Senior team for their Leinster campaign. I was thrilled and I guess it was on the strength of some of my U-21 performances. This time I was determined not to lose my place but once more disaster struck. We played Dublin in the Leinster semi-final and despite earning a Man of the Match award we lost by a solitary point. They got their winning score in injury time with virtually the last kick of the game to win by 1–10 to 0–12. Absolute agony. Another painful defeat and it seemed never-ending. My only hope, and the only hope for the county to salvage some pride, lay in the U-21 Championship.

Castleblaney was the venue and Derry would provide very strong opposition. They had four Senior players in their side and we faced a real uphill struggle, and in truth we looked doomed when Vinnie Ryan was sent off after half an hour. Things were looking bad, but in one of the best displays by a Meath team I played with up to this point, we battled back from three points behind to lead by two and Derry were rattled. It reminded me of the 1991 All-Ireland when Down had no answer to Meath's belated barrage.

Credit to Derry, they found new reserves of strength and character and a very late point helped them salvage a replay as the scores were tied at Derry 1–10 to our 0–13. After such an exciting encounter, the replay was a little one-sided. We lead by five points at the interval and although we won by two points, 0–11 to 1–6, the win was more comfortable than that scoreline might suggest. Huge relief as we had made the final. But that only brought even extra pressure as losing had become a bad habit we were trying hard to kick. Also, Meath had never ever won an All-Ireland U-21 and just like the Minors in 1990, we would meet the best of Kerry in the final.

Unlike our side which had 13 of the victorious Minors, I think Kerry only had four or five players in their side who had lined out in that 1990 final. Not that it matters one iota as Kerry have so much quality from which to choose. As we took our positions and the referee got ready to blow the whistle, I was marking Billy O'Shea. Soon after the first few minutes of play, I thought he was going to roast me right throughout that final. He was winning everything, he was faster to every ball and he was like a man on a mission. Almost as soon as the referee threw up the ball, Billy was so sharp. On one occasion he flew past me, got through on goal and let fly. The ball nearly smashed the crossbar and it was a huge let-off for us and I was mightily relieved. It was a very hot day on that afternoon in Portlaoise and Kerry were running our defence ragged in the early stages. I do not know how we managed to do it, but we battled back to lead by two points at half-time.

Cathal Sheridan had a great second half. He scored some great points from frees as well. But Kerry were not going down without a fight and they were hanging on to our coat-tails. I remember thinking that there was no way this was going to a replay as I was going on a holiday to Lanzarote the following week! So I went on a long solo run and I was brought down. The referee awarded us a free and I prayed Cathal would put a bit of daylight between Kerry and us. He duly obliged and despite a last gasp effort from Kerry, we hung on to win by 1–8 to 0–10.

The final whistle sparked off great celebrations. It was just fantastic to be part of a piece of history. We were the first Meath team to win the All-Ireland U-21 Football Championship. The partying went on well into the next week. After a wild night, the next day around 10 of us went to Hugh Carolan's house in Bettystown. It was a scorching day so we went to the beach where we played baseball and attempted to surf! Later that Monday evening, we all went to the Beechmount Hotel in Navan, a very popular spot at the time. In the night club, there was a fair bit of high jinks and a friend of mine Gerry Brady and another guy fell on top of me. The rest of the lads, all thinking they were fooling around, dived in on top of me and I ended up damaging knee ligaments!

There may have been barren years in 1991 and 1992, but 1993 was a great and historic year for Meath and me. I was climbing the stairway and after winning a Minor and then an U-21, I was hoping that the next step would be on the way up to lifting Sam.

# 2 Broken Bones, Brawls & Solicitors

After the glorious summer and the highs of 1993, I came back from Lanzarote and straight into training for the start of the 1993/1994 National League. We were drawn in a fairly tough division comprising Cork, Galway, Roscommon, Leitrim, Laois, Louth and Fermanagh. Most people feel that many of the counties do not take the League all that seriously. They believe that it is really a chance to rest players tired from the previous campaign, a chance also to try out new talent while getting other players fit and ready for the Championships. That is true to a point but if you start to win matches and reach the knockout stages, then you really start to take it seriously.

In our first match we beat a very weak Cork side fairly easily, 1–12 to 0–6. Then it was the turn of Leitrim away and we also won that by 1–10 to 0–8. Our third match at home did not go as planned. Roscommon beat us by a point, 2–7 to 1–9 and the dressing-room was very quiet afterwards. People expect you to win your home games and on that day we let them down. We performed badly and conceded soft scores. However, we made amends by having five points to spare over Louth in Dundalk, and so we were top of the group going into the winter break.

When the League resumed in February, we beat Fermanagh, 0–12 to 0–6 and Galway by 1–10 to 0–8. We were showing very good form. We had only lost one game and that was by a point. Things could not have been better as we looked forward to the Leinster. But we were given a boot up the backside by Laois. They beat us by 1–11 to 0–10 in a niggly match. But that was nothing since there was far worse to come when both counties would meet in the Leinster U-21 final a few months later.

After five wins and two losses, we made the quarter-finals and were rewarded with a tie against Down. It may have been the League but in any case, this match was on all Meath minds. Supporters and players had not forgotten the defeat to Down in that classic All-Ireland final. Now in a knockout stage of the League, we had the chance to exact some revenge. The quarter-final with Down was to prove every bit as gripping and exciting as the classic from 1991. I do not know why, but our matches with Northern sides always seem to be very close affairs. This match was no exception and I guess there was no surprise in that because there was much at stake for both sides. Not alone was there a semi-final berth for the winners, but there was a score to settle. Meath wanted nothing better than to get one back on their old rivals. Down knew it and would try their damnedest to repel the challenge.

As it turned out there was only a point between the sides at the finish. We hung on by our fingernails to record a 0–13 to 1–9 victory. If Down was a crucial game for Meath folk, then our semi-final was of even more importance. We were pitted against our fierce rivals and neighbours, Westmeath. What a match to play for such high stakes! There was simply no way we could afford to lose this match. You could compare it with a Merseyside Derby between Liverpool and Everton – or even Celtic v Rangers! With respect to Westmeath, we would be expected to win such an encounter and so there was no way we could walk down the streets of Navan, in any degree of comfort, were we to lose.

From what I can recall, it was not a great game by any means. I suppose you would have to expect that given what was at stake. There were obviously a lot of nerves on both sides. But we ran out winners by four points. That was no disgrace to Westmeath and they put up a very good showing. In fact, in the years following that game, Westmeath would improve so much that they would actually meet us on several occasions and start some of those games as the favourites in many people's eyes. That would have been unthinkable in the past. Back then, the bookies would have had Meath as 'unbackable' favourites.

Now yet another Northern team stood between us and lifting the National League title. But this was no ordinary Northern side. Armagh were red-hot favourites for the final and not because they were big, strong and robust. They were skilful and fast and at the time I remember people saying they only had to turn up to collect the trophy. That is no exaggeration and there were a few reasons for that, not least of all, Ger Houlahan.

Ger Houlahan was the name on almost everyone's lips. 'Houli' or 'Houdini' is what their supporters called him. But to the best of my knowledge, he never really had to get Armagh out of jail or help them escape from the jaws of defeat. He was a class player who did serious damage to teams from the moment the referee threw up the ball. So we could not afford to let Houlahan escape and run riot. Before we took to the field we were determined to shackle him good. Armagh did not have to rely on him alone. They had danger-men all over the pitch and I was marking one of them in the shape of Diarmuid Marsden. I was well aware of his reputation before the game. At that time he was their exciting and up-and-coming wing forward.

This was my first Senior final at Croke Park. After Minor and U-21 titles, I was determined to add another title to my name and make it a hat-trick of different medals. As we paraded on a glorious day, I remember seeing some banners and faces in the crowd that I knew. For my first Senior final it was a perfect setting. We seemed to be playing in a sea of orange and green and Armagh had an amazing amount of support. With all the support they had, and with all the pre-match hype surrounding them, I was really geared up and focused. But as the game got under way, I could not believe what was happening around me. It was so clear to my eyes that from a very early stage, there was only ever going to be one winner. It was as if all of my Meath team-mates were on the same wavelength as myself. We had a plan beforehand of keeping it tight and getting early ball into Tommy Dowd and Bernard Flynn. And in every area of the field we were quite solid and carrying out that plan so well that Armagh would have to do their level best to beat us.

Because there was only one point in it at the break, and we had our noses in front, it must have been very exciting to watch. The second half was a totally different story. After we scored the first goal of the game, Armagh seemed to lose their way. It seemed to knock them right back and they never recovered. We added to that goal and, although Houlahan crashed a ball against the woodwork in the closing minutes, we went on to win by an incredible nine points!

Meath had railroaded Armagh in every position and proved the so-called experts wrong. On a personal level, I was more than satisfied with my own performance having kept Marsden scoreless. The newspapers had the Man of the Match between Tommy Dowd and myself, but if ever there was a match when every single individual earned their corn, then this was it. Now that I had tasted Senior glory, I wanted to savour the ultimate prize. I remember getting the sense that this could be the start of another special era under Sean Boylan. We had a great panel of young players that had the experience of Minor, U-21 and now the League. There was still room for a lot more improvement.

It is easy to forget, in the middle of all the jubilation, the hard luck stories that happen to certain individuals. Earlier I mentioned about the lads who lose out to other players and therefore have to sit it out on the bench. Those lads are equally as good as those out on the pitch. But the selectors and management have to make a choice and sometimes it is so difficult that it may as well be the toss of a coin. But I would like to reflect on the bad luck that proved to be the beginning of the end for one such player in that final.

Tommy Hanley, another fine player from Athboy, was captain of the victorious U-21s in 1993 and was also on the Minor winning side in 1990. His display in that win over Armagh was simply outstanding and he was beginning to grab the attention of the media. The day after that win, all the newspapers gave him fine ratings, one of which was Vincent Hogan's in the *Irish Independent*: '[Tommy Hanley] had a great game. The fact that Barry O'Hagan was replaced speaks volumes. Used the ball well. Rating: 8'.

Tommy picked up a shoulder injury earlier in that National League campaign and in the final he aggravated it. It just shows the courage and the calibre of the guy that he played through the pain barrier. He had a near faultless performance but I fear it may have come at a cost. He picked up some sort of virus that not only forced him to miss training but weeks out of work as well. After the League win, Tommy surely must have been looking forward to a bright future and thoughts of possible All-Ireland final appearances. But the cruel hand of fate ensured that, like fellow Athboyman Scobey Martin, Tommy Hanley would never again experience big days out at Croke Park in the Meath jersey.

It must have been heartbreaking for him and I felt for him too. In Meath football terms, Tommy and myself grew up as part of a young family in the Minors. We were the best in the county and then became the best in the country at U-21 level. We were well on our way to a crack at the major honours in the Senior Championships after our League win, only for Tommy to be dealt a cruel blow. He and Scobey played a large part in the history of Meath football. From a town which has a great hurling tradition and which has produced very few county footballers, Athboy can be hugely proud of them and their achievements.

After the League win in 1994, training sessions in Navan were abuzz with the anticipation of what we might achieve in the forthcoming Leinster Championships. Of course, after being crowned the champions of Ireland in the League, our objectives were to win Leinster and then go on to win the All-Ireland. But first I was involved with the U-21s and little did I know what lay in store for me.

There were no real hiccups in our early round matches and we had a comfortable passage to the final of the U-21s where we played Laois. On both sides, there were quite a few players from the Senior sides. The most notable player from Laois was Hugh Emerson. But even before the start, there was something not quite right about this game. We met earlier in the year in a fairly niggly match and things were about to really get out of hand.

It was a tense, tight and tough encounter – too tough to say the least. I remember collecting a pass from Noel Collier midway through the second half. But as I did so, out of the corner of my eye I saw a Laois player coming towards me. I swivelled to avoid him and then two other Laois players came in but I managed to avoid them as well. However, another Laois player came at me from nowhere. I fisted the ball over his head but we collided head on. The Laois player in question was David Sweeney. He went down and stayed down while I got up and got on with the game. Later in the game, Sweeney was involved in another collision. This time it was with 'Boots' McGuinness and as a result, Sweeney went off injured. The match ended in a stalemate, but it later transpired that David Sweeney had suffered a broken jaw!

The replay was held in Newbridge and the match began as it had ended in the first clash. It was brutal stuff and it seemed as if every time we got the ball, there were Laois lads hammering into us. There is nothing Meath likes more than a good, tough physical battle. However, there was simply no way that any of us were going to back off. The trouble was neither would the Laois team and so something had to give.

I remember going to collect a ball in around the centre of the field. As I caught it I felt a sudden and sharp crack on my hand. A Laois player's elbow had caught me right between two knuckles on my hand. I knew immediately what had happened but I played on right to the very end. In the circumstances, I did not want to give them the satisfaction of seeing me go off. The crowd were all against us as well, so that made me even more determined to play on. My bravery or stupidity, whatever you may call it, did no good. Laois went on to win the game. Fair dues to them, they were the better team over the two games. I did not go to hospital with my hand until the following day. By then, my hand was up like a balloon and the doctors confirmed my worst fears. My hand was broken.

To add insult to injury, shortly after that, I received a solicitor's letter representing David Sweeney. The letter informed me that I had hit Sweeney. In addition, my team-mate, Jimmy McGuinness, received a similar letter. I felt a little aggrieved and angry to say the least. But I knew I was innocent of all charges. At no stage did I strike out at him, so I was never worried about solicitors or possible court proceedings. Jimmy McGuinness and I had to attend a Leinster Tribunal set up to investigate the incidents in that Laois game. There was a lot of furore in the press and also in both counties. To give you an insight into just how rough a game it was, the following account from Colm Keys appeared in *The Meath Chronicle:*

*The Leinster Council should order a full-scale inquiry into last Sunday's disgraceful Leinster U-21 final between Meath and Laois at Newbridge. They should look for answers to several incidents, on and off the ball, which brought great shame to the game and disgusted many in the large attendance who might never wish to see a game between these counties again.*

*They should ask why a Laois player wouldn't go off when reportedly ordered to by referee Pat O'Toole in extra-time. They should ask why there was so much off the ball intimidation with pushing, shoving and even spitting such a common feature. One Laois player was booked before the ball was thrown in! Should he have been allowed to continue?*

*They should read with great interest why Aidan Kealy retaliated against Damien Delaney and then find some solutions as to what was the general tone between the sides. Delaney seemed in some distress as he left the pitch on a stretcher. Perhaps the Leinster Council should also investigate the severity of his 'injury' and how long it took him to recover.*

*So many patrons, particularly those from Meath, were only too glad to hear the final whistle and get out of Newbridge in a hurry. And that had nothing to do with the defeat. The derogatory remarks of some Laois supporters went far beyond ordinary fanaticism. They had their roots in hatred which has never been heard in football grounds before.*

*In fairness to the Meath U-21 football team, they went out and tried to play football. But they lost and it's not hard to know why. With little protection and little sanity around them, they always looked on a loser. Laois were over possessed with victory. And the way they went about it, coupled with their supporters who openly encouraged such behaviour, they are welcome to it.*

'Boots' McGuinness and myself travelled to the Leinster Tribunal. How appropriate that it was held in Portlaoise. By now, we were probably feeling like hardened criminals up for trial. We were driven there by Meath County Board officials Fintan Ginnity and Liam Craven. They had the video of the game to present to the Tribunal Committee. David Sweeney was also there with Laois County Board officials and both cases were heard separately. Quite clearly, the video showed me fisting the ball over Sweeney's head and then he ran into me. I never had any doubt or even a moment's worry about this and when I saw it again on video, I felt vindicated. The Committee felt likewise so I was cleared and that was the end of the matter. Incidentally, Laois stalwart, Hugh Emerson, was also cleared of an incident in the semi-final win over Westmeath when a Westmeath player had his shorts pulled down during the game!

There was still, however, the matter of possible legal proceedings as a result of the solicitor's letter implicating 'Boots' McGuinness and me. So I got in touch with Micky Regan, a well-known solicitor and colourful character from Trim. After only a few minutes in his company, 'Boots' and myself knew we had no worries. Micky brought us up to his house and poured out a few brandies for us. We sat back, sipped our drinks and talked about football and everything else apart from the case in question. I think the only thing that Micky mentioned about it, which put us at ease immediately, was something to the effect that both of us could not possibly have struck the Laois player at the same time!

It was very annoying that a fellow player was trying to get me in trouble over something that was quite clearly an accident. In fairness to the Laois County Board, they did not really push the issue. It was all pursued by Sweeney and his family, in fact, and I could not understand why they went to such lengths as to get a solicitor involved. It was all a case of 'Verdict: Unfortunate Accident'. By chance, I met David Sweeney a few years after that. I was managing a well-known pub in Dublin's Parnell Street called Sam Maguire's. I knew a Garda who was a regular in the pub and as I went over to serve him one evening, he said to me: 'Graham, do you know this fella here?' Imagine my surprise when there standing beside him was David Sweeney. For a brief moment I thought he had contacted the Gardaí and pinned something else on me! We had to laugh and later he revealed to me that he never wanted things to go as far as they did. At the time he was under pressure from his club and his family to pursue it, according to himself.

With tribunals and a possible court case now out of the way, I had another big battle to contend with. I was in a race against time to get my broken hand healed before the Leinster Championships. There was no way I was going to make the Senior semi-final with Wexford, which was just over two weeks away. But if we got through that, I was really hoping to be fully fit for a possible Leinster final clash. X-rays revealed the hand was broken and it was bound with a big bandage. But I was training the following week doing everything apart from using my right hand. Three weeks later my hand was fully healed. Meath had beaten Wexford and so I would return to action in my very first Leinster final against Dublin.

The rapid recovery was all down to Meath manager, Sean Boylan. Sean runs a herbalist clinic in Dunboyne which is on the Meath–Dublin border. I attended his clinic every couple of days after I broke my hand and only for him, I would not have won my battle to play against the Dubs. As a treatment for my hand he made a poultice. I can only describe it as resembling a soggy and wet slice of Christmas pudding, containing some flour or bread. Anyway, he placed this over the damaged area of my hand, between the two knuckles, and every few days he would put a fresh covering on. In my opinion, and I am not giving Sean a plug, I feel that a medical doctor could not have healed my hand in quicker time. To this day it has never given me any problems or pain. The only tell-tale sign of anything amiss is a little bony lump which has never caused me any discomfort.

I was now fighting fit and raring to get back into action against Dublin. Matches against Dublin are always special. For all of us in Meath, it is really our All-Ireland final and that is how important that fixture is. The rest of the panel were as glad as I was that I had won my fitness battle. I think they saw me as a very important and strong member of the team. We were going to need all the help we could muster as Dublin were going to be very hard to beat. They had beaten us in the Leinster semi-final the previous year and naturally were very confident of beating us in front of their partisan crowd on the famous Hill 16.

As we raced out onto the field, I took my position in the half-back line and Dublin's Niall Guiden was the man I was marking. Before the game, Colm O'Rourke gave me a bit of advice. He told me to try and stop Guiden from scoring. According to Colm, if I could manage to achieve that, then the Leinster title would be Meath's. The first half was a real typical Meath–Dublin tussle. It was a frantic start with a lot of very nervous touches from each side. The defending champions got off to the slightly better start and they were two points up before John McDermott started to get to grips with matters in the centre of the field. With big John playing so well, we turned an early deficit into a 0–5 to 0–3 lead at the break.

Were it not for McDermott's excellent work and skills around midfield, we would have been behind at half-time. Unsurprisingly, I was a little ring rusty and Martin O'Connell struggled a little, especially with his clearances. Up front, Colm O'Rourke picked up an injury and maybe should have come off because he was not feeling so well in the dressing-room.

Dublin came out in the second half like men on a mission. They were determined to hang on to their title. Hence they made some substitutions which were tactically very good. Paul Clarke started to get the better of McDermott and that takes some doing. Vinnie Murphy in the Dublin attack was giving us all lots of problems and worries. As a result, Dublin were rampant. I think they scored five points without reply and turned a deficit into a 0–8 to 0–5 lead. I remember when I fisted our first point of the half that it must have taken us fully 20 minutes to get it. It also made amends for the point which my marker Niall Guiden scored for Dublin just before that.

Going into the last few minutes it was still anybody's match as Dublin lead by 0–8 to 0–6. But then came the turning point and a moment in football, especially in the chronicles of Dublin and Meath, which will be talked about for generations to come. Dublin were awarded a free from under the Hogan Stand. Charlie Redmond stepped up to take it and nobody could have forecast what was about to happen next. As the ball came in, our goalkeeper Michael McQuillan seemed to have the situation under control. But to our horror, the ball spilled out of his hands and underneath the bar into the back of the net! The ball may have been greasy but there were simply no excuses. Michael would be the first to stand up and say it was his fault, which he did in a silent dressing-room after the game. We lost but even then it was not without a typical last-gasp effort on our part.

After gifting Redmond that goal, we found ourselves even further behind when Dessie Farrell pointed to put six between the sides. It looked all over. Brendan Reilly got a point back for us and then after our substitute Jody Devine got through on the Dublin goal, I slammed the ball to the back of the Dublin net. Dublin were now edgy, not knowing what hit them so late on with just two points separating us now. Still there was time for yet more drama. Panic started to sweep through the Dubs as we went on the offensive again. Suddenly PJ Gillic burst through their defence and I raced through alongside him. He took his point when maybe he was better placed to pass it across to me. The chance of a goal and a famous Meath win evaporated.

Looking back now, it is easy to say that PJ should have passed, or at worst, gone for goal himself. But in truth, and on the big occasion with all eyes on you, you just have a split second to decide. Had he passed and I missed, people would then have blamed him for not pointing. And would you believe that Gillic had the chance to level with virtually the last kick of the game? But the chance went abegging. In the end it was not to be our day. Talk of freak goals and missed chances on our part is neither here nor there. The record books will show that Dublin won the title on a scoreline of 1–9 to 1–8. It was heartbreaking to lose especially to our biggest rivals. But what was even more hurtful, and I will deal with it in the following chapters, is that the freak goal should never have been, because I firmly lay the blame for that at the feet of Sean and our selectors.

Scant consolation for me was picking up the Man of the Match award for the second year in succession. So near and yet nothing for our great efforts. Had we won, then we would have been into an All-Ireland semi-final. Many of us thought that it was going to be our year. The year had begun on a high with the National League title and then it stuttered somewhat with the Sweeney affair and my broken hand. Then it came to an abrupt end with that defeat by Dublin. Once again it was going to be a long hot summer for Meath and the supporters.

# 3 For Club and County

Sean Boylan showed his ruthless streak in the build-up to the 1994 Leinster final with Dublin. At first he made a very brave decision to which I was in agreement. But in subsequent actions, he made a colossal mistake. To this day, I firmly believe that it cost us that Leinster title in 1994. Our goalkeeper during the successful League campaign of '93/'94 was Donal Smyth. In our League final victory over Armagh, he actually made a terrific save from a penalty awarded to Armagh late in the game. The ball was heading for the top corner when Donal dived and scrambled it away. It was on a par with one of the best penalty saves you are ever likely to witness anywhere.

Donal was a Garda and had the misfortune of getting head-butted in a pub by a drunk watching Ireland playing in the 1994 World Cup. A week later he lined up for Meath in the Leinster semi-final against Wexford. However, it was clear that all was not right with him. He felt very groggy during the match and a few days later it transpired that he had a displaced disc in his neck! In training one evening for the Leinster final, Sean took Donal aside and told him that he was dropping him. And he did not just mean dropping him for the Dublin game. He was spelling it out to Donal that it was the end of the line for him as a Senior member of the panel. We were all shocked and stunned. Donal had never done anything wrong and, if anything, he was doing everything right. He was our keeper and now had been shown the door.

Afterwards, Donal put on a brave face in front of us but surely he must have been gutted. The bottom must have fallen out of his world. That kind of decision was a rare one for Sean to make. Clearly, there must have been more to the matter. Obviously, Sean had a very good reason and who knows, perhaps for the sake of Donal's health, he was doing him a favour. If that was not the reason, and I had to hazard a guess, then maybe Sean did not like the fact that Donal hid his injury in the Wexford game. Every manager and coach expects 100 per cent honesty from his players and staff. Perhaps Sean felt that Donal had been selfish in hiding the extent of his injury. Who knows, but the fact is that we were now minus the services of our goalkeeper.

If Sean had his reasons for bringing the swift hand of execution down on Donal Smyth's Meath career, then his next decision was very hard to take. You stand or fall by decisions you make and in reality you never know if you are making the right one. Sean then made Micky McQuillan Meath's first-choice keeper to the astonishment of many of our players and supporters. I felt Sean was wrong and later events would back up not only my opinion but that of others. In hindsight, I wish Sean had consulted everyone and put it to a vote or at the very least talked about the situation. Michael McQuillan was an outstanding goalkeeper. But I emphasise the word *was*. Back in the Eighties, he was one of the best keepers in the country but we were now in the Nineties and Micky had retired!

Sean had brought back on board a player who had given his best to Meath in the past, but who over the best part of a year had hung up his boots. Now he was to be catapulted head first into the cauldron of a Leinster final with Dublin. It was simply unacceptable and I was not at all happy. I also believe that as a direct result of that selection, Sean and his selectors also dealt a cruel blow to two other players – McQuillan himself and Conor Martin. At the time I remember talking to Conor Martin who was very upset and even angry. He must have had his hopes up and had perfect reason to believe that he was going to be Meath's new first-choice keeper after Smyth was axed. For him it must have been a real kick in the teeth when they brought back someone who already had had his day and his share of glory.

When McQuillan let slip Charlie Redmond's free, and the ball fell into the back of the net, it just confirmed all of our worst fears. It was your worst nightmare come true. After all, how often do you see a goalie let a ball slip through his grasp in a big final? It certainly would not have happened to a young and fit keeper like Conor

Martin. In fact, Conor was such a good goalie that press reports were linking him to trials with English soccer clubs at that time.

We put up a tremendous effort in the last few minutes to try and claw our way back. Indeed, we almost burst blood vessels! The efforts and near misses by PJ Gillic and myself were borne out of sheer frustration and despair. At the end the deficit was a solitary point and that goal had clearly cost us the Leinster. We were not at all happy. In the dressing-room afterwards, you could have heard a pin drop. The silence said more about blame than the defeat. What happened next was even more unbelievable. It was grotesque and bizarre. Nobody said much until Sean came in and immediately stood up for Micky. According to Sean, McQuillan was not at fault for our defeat. Instead, he reckoned that we had kicked a good few wides!

That was a gross insult to all of our outfield players. Had that mistake not happened, we would have won the game? Sean's statement was a 'cop out' for himself, McQuillan and the whole messy decision. Why did he not hold his hand up and admit it instead of blaming us for 'all' the wides? Beyond all doubt, it was Micky's fault for that goal. There is also no question that it was Sean's fault for the entire episode and our defeat.

I admire Sean Boylan as much as anyone and I know he can take criticism. Admittedly, he has been a huge help to me in my career. He is a legend and books and all sorts of great things have been written well deservedly about him. But everyone makes mistakes and I want to put the record straight. One dark moment will never do anything to tarnish the record of a truly great manager. That incident has been eating at me for nine years and I now have put it to rest. The constant reminders of it would always annoy me and even hurt a little. For years people would come up to you in the pub or on the street and talk about it. Knowing Sean, however, I have no doubt that if he was ever asked that question, he would stand up and admit he got it wrong.

They say that 'the proof is in the pudding' and I will leave this subject once and for all by saying that after that Leinster final defeat, Conor Martin was installed as Meath's keeper. In fact, he was to make that position his own over the following years. Had he been put in when Smyth was dropped, we would have been Leinster champions. We were on a roll and full of confidence after the win over Armagh. Many felt that we could have beaten Dublin and gone all the way to winning the All-Ireland in 1994.

After all that, it was going to be a long summer for Meath players and fans. For me it meant that I could now focus my attention on just one competition. My club Seneschalstown had not won the Meath County Championship for 22 years. I had been playing fairly well for Meath and after a couple of weeks in London, which I will deal with later, I was bursting to do well for my club. We were drawn in a very tough group with Walterstown and the defending champions, Skryne. In particular, Skryne would be very difficult opponents. In 1992 we came very close to beating them in the final. Many people felt that we were the better side in that final and very unlucky not to have won it. Therefore, we were eager to prove our worth against them.

In the previous year, 1993, we were also somewhat unfortunate. We were actually undefeated but amazingly drew our three matches, and consequently failed to progress from the group. That is a very unusual occurrence in Gaelic Games, apart from the famous Dublin trilogy, and I wonder what the odds on drawing your first three matches are. Obviously, all of us in Seneschalstown were hopeful that 1994 would finally be our year. Before a ball was even kicked in the group, there was a great sense of optimism about our chances. My fellow county player, Colm Coyle, took over as player-manager and we had talented individuals like Padraig Coyle, Mattie McCabe, David Dillon and Kevin Macken on the team. There were also young players coming through the ranks, which is always a very good and important sign. Stephen Dillon, Alan Finnegan and Tony McDonnell were only teenagers but, nonetheless, were making their presence felt at the club.

We played Walterstown in our first match in Stamullen. Although Walterstown were struggling a little, it counted for nothing when faced with the challenge of playing us. We had not beaten 'the Blacks' since 1986 and naturally they wanted to keep that record going. Also, because of our drawn games the year before, we had not won a Championship game since our semi-final win over Dunderry in 1992. So whether a team was struggling or was in poor form over a long period, it meant nothing going into this game. Both sides had so much to prove. Because of that, the first 15 minutes were very nervy. In those early stages, we hit a lot of wides and found it hard to hit the target with our frees.

Midway through the first half things began to improve for us. We were trailing Walterstown by a point when we suddenly hit a purple patch. In that period we strung together a number of points without reply. Then on the stroke of half-time, the Walterstown keeper fumbled the ball and I was on hand to knock it in. We had notched up a goal and five points without reply and led at the break by 1–8 to 1–1.

The mumblings before the game of Walterstown struggling proved to be true. They were a very weakened side from the one that had performed so well the previous year. Their problems were made even worse only a few minutes into play, when Alan Browne had to go off. He was a big doubt before the game and lost his battle to carry on. So after his loss, Walterstown were a worried and lost side which probably went some way to explaining our purple patch. The second half started in much the same way. We stretched our lead to nine points and so barring miracles on their part, or a complete collapse on ours, we had the game well and truly won. Great credit to Walterstown who did rally before the final whistle. They scored another goal but we emerged the victors by 1–13 to 2–5.

Our next match against Skryne would be an entirely different affair. As defending champions they were favourites to win our group and also to win the title. But if we could beat them, and we knew we had a great chance after our unlucky loss to them in 1992, then we would be well on the way to making the semi-finals.

I actually missed the game with Skryne. Although I was very fortunate not to pick up any major injuries so far, that Championship would actually see me get my fair share. Broken bones can take weeks to heal but what every player dreads are muscle or bone injuries which can take months to heal or, even worse, keep recurring. In any event, I was not missed as we toppled Skryne to get revenge for the defeat in the 1992 final. As fate would have it, Skryne and ourselves topped the group which meant that we avoided each other in the semi-finals. But then we both won our respective semi-final matches, meaning we had to contest the final of the 1994 Meath County Championship.

So it seemed Seneschalstown were destined to get another crack at Skryne. As I already said, many observers felt that we were hard done by in the 1992 final. We wanted this win so badly. I returned to the team as did Liam Hayes – a former Meath star and author of *Out of our Skins* – after a two-year absence through injury. Now we had a level playing field. A repeat of the 1992 final and this time there would be no excuses. Both teams were at full strength and to the victors would go the title Kings of Meath. Hayes and myself were pitted against each other in midfield. In this position Skyrne had a huge advantage as Hayes' partner was none other than John McDermott.

Skryne were red-hot favourites. The tag applied to them because they were big men in size and very physical, not just in the centre of the field, but right throughout the team. That said, we had great spirit on our side and great resilience. What we lacked in height and stature we more than made up for in our mental approach and our willingness to run all day and to succeed. In that area we were as hard as nails. One man who typified this more than most was our inspirational skipper, Padraig Coyle. Because of him we got off to a flyer. The Skryne lads did not know what had hit them in those early stages. We were in their faces the whole time. Every ball was contested and midway through the half we led by 0–7 to 0–3. It was obvious that Hayes was struggling after his long absence.

However in the second half, Skryne started to get to grips with the situation. Maybe we also began to tire a little after all our efforts. In the end, it had to take a goal from our Captain Fantastic, Padraig Coyle, to settle the match. We had won the title by two points and victory was sweet. It was the first time we had won the Keegan Cup since 1972. It had taken us 22 years to win only our second Championship. We thoroughly deserved it and we were going to enjoy every moment of it. That triumph sparked off tremendous celebrations in Navan that evening. I was so proud and delighted for everyone involved. We had been through thick and thin together. We suffered the pain of unlucky defeat in 1992, we were undefeated in 1993 but ended up with nothing to show for it. But we kept plugging away and got our just rewards.

The question now on everyone's lips was how far could Seneschalstown go? How would we fare against the might of Leinster? Was it possible to believe we could win it? Sarsfields of

Kildare were to be our first-round opponents and we would only know after playing them, if we had the ability to trouble Leinster's finest.

The Kildare champions had much more experience in Leinster than us. They were an emerging side in the province with several well-known Inter-County players in their ranks. Perhaps the best known was Niall Buckley. He essentially was what made Sarsfields tick. If we had any chance at all of progressing, we had to keep him quiet. Before we knew it, we were two points down. But we gradually got back into the game and once more our captain Padraig Coyle was leading by example. In an incredible spell, we hit six points without reply and Padraig scored four of them. Sarsfields were stung back into action and they pulled a further two points back before the break. So at half-time we were in a great position, leading by 0–6 to 0–4.

Just into the second half I fell to the ground. My shoulder was in agony. In fact, I was in so much pain I told the medics attending me to cut my jersey off. I was carried off injured while Niall Buckley moved into midfield and took advantage of the situation, scoring twice to level the game. I thought we were doomed! Sarsfields would now use their experience well.

Earlier I referred to our resilience and tough-as-nails attitude. Now a couple of pointed frees from Mattie McCabe signalled we would not be pushed aside. After Buckley brilliantly slotted over two more points to level at 0–8 each, it was anybody's guess who would triumph. It was turning into a thrilling ding-dong battle. When I went off, momentarily we were at sixes and sevens and caught off guard. Kildare made a great switch in putting Buckley into the void left by me. He was a right menace and proving to be a real handful. So then our selectors played a masterstroke by moving Colm Coyle into midfield to counter Buckley.

Almost at once, Coyle sent his brother Padraig through but, with the goal at his mercy, he pointed. Padraig then put over a 'fifty' and when McCabe added another point soon after, we were three points clear. With only a little over five minutes to go, the heart had been ripped out of the Kildare men. In fact, they did not score again. We went on to win by five points and so record a famous win over Sarsfields by 0–13 to 0–8.

Amid all the joyous scenes following our great victory, I was really concerned about my shoulder. I feared that I would play no further part in the Leinster Club Championship. My shoulder was extremely stiff and sore. Later the diagnosis was that I had damaged rather than torn the shoulder ligaments. Though a relief, there was still a slim chance I would make the semi-final. But the chances were no more than fifty-fifty.

In late November, we faced the Laois champions, St Joseph's, in the Leinster semi-final. I would start the game but with my shoulder not as I would have liked it to be. Facing a Laois side that would obviously be physical and fight for every ball would not help matters at all. After all, my memories of playing against Laois players were painful! Looking back, perhaps I should not have played. But my club needed me and every little bit of help they could get. It was a case of all hands to the pump. In the event, I was really ineffective and more of a hindrance to our cause. So much so that in the second half, St Joseph's turned around a six-point deficit to earn a replay. We were lucky in the end. In hindsight, I should have opted out and given the shoulder more time to heal.

The replay with St Joseph's was played six days later in Newbridge. The stakes were high as the winner went forward to contest the Leinster Club final. My shoulder was much better and we were all eager to get the job done this time. There was no way that big lead should have slipped in the first meeting. So we were confident that we were the better team, having learnt our lessons from the first match. However, that confidence was blown out of the water in the first minute when they scored a goal. It caught us completely by surprise but equally sprang us into action. I started to make some good fast runs from midfield and young Alan Finnegan then started to shine. We scored five points without reply and went in at the break leading by 0–5 to 1–0. Finnegan scored two of those points, which was remarkable considering he was one of six players on our side aged 21 or under! In contrast, Mattie McCabe, in the twilight of his career, also chipped in with two points. We had responded very well and very positively to that opening blip. We bounced back so well in fact that we kept them scoreless for the rest of that opening period. They were not to score again for over half an hour.

St Joseph's reduced the arrears to a point early on in the second half. But again, Padraig Coyle was revelling in the heat of battle. Just after they scored, he ran onto a pass from Mal Hickey, sold their defence a dummy on his left, jinked to the right and slotted the ball under their keeper into the back of the net. We now led by four points at 1–5 to 1–1. After increasing our lead to six, a strange thing happened. In the first match we had thrown away just such a lead. And at this stage in the second half, St Joseph's battened down the hatches and started to stifle our challenge. We did not actually score for another 15 minutes. And although they did not do much damage, our defence had their work cut out to cope with them. They scored a point but also hit the crossbar and sent a few wide.

We weathered the storm and after popping over some late points, it was all over for St Joseph's. We won the game by eight points, 1–11 to 1–3, and had reached our first ever Leinster Club final. As you can imagine we were all over the moon. We were on a rollercoaster ride and the beauty of it all not knowing where it would lead us. But the next match was, at the outset, our ultimate goal: to reach the Leinster final and give ourselves the chance to prove ourselves as the best club in Leinster!

The first half of that semi-final saw me produce the best form I had displayed in some time with my club. But the injury picked up was still niggling away at me. When St Joseph's tightened up on us in the second half, they became very physical and so I got another bad bang on the shoulder. Even in the celebrations I could not let my hair down as I was in some pain. I was very worried that I would not make the final and was desperate to help my club win a Leinster title. It was all a little unreal, the feeling we were sharing. Seneschalstown had won their first Keegan Cup for 22 years and now we were one match away from becoming Leinster champions. Meath may be seen as one of the big powers at Inter-County level but our clubs have always struggled. I am lost for a reason as to why that is so. But the fact remains that only three Meath sides have won the Leinster Club Championship. Summerhill have won it, Walterstown were twice winners and Dunshaughlin won it in 2003. Now we had a chance to join an elite group, where other great Meath clubs like Navan O'Mahonys and Skryne had failed.

If we were going to lift the title, then we would have to move heaven and earth given that Kilmacud Crokes were our opponents in the final. But I suppose that whoever we met in the final, it was always going to be a hard task. There are simply no easy games anymore at any level and especially in finals. Not surprisingly then, we were very much the outsiders going into the final. This great Dublin side are steeped in club success. They have a marvellous record in Leinster and above all they had vast experience. Quite simply, Kilmacud Crokes are one of the best clubs Leinster has ever produced. They were, and still are, up there with the elite. Down through the years, you remember hearing the great club names of Leinster; famous names like St Vincent's, Ballymun Kickhams and Eire Óg. We were in the big league now and had a mountain to overcome.

On their way to the final, Crokes had destroyed Ferbane of Offaly and Baltinglass of Wicklow. They had a team of tall, fast and superbly fit athletes who could be very physical as well. Take for instance their midfielder, Mick Leahy. He stood 6 ft 6 in tall and not surprisingly was a former basketball player. I would have a hard job trying to field ball against someone of that stature. The players were strong in every corner of the pitch and, of course, their experience was the big plus. More so, they were used to playing together at this very high level. Other players we had to watch were Mick Dillon, Leahy's midfield partner. He was a great playmaker and really inspired the team. But their most potent weapon was their forward line. Maurice Leahy was very good at full-forward while Peter Ward was quite nippy and a good carrier of the ball. Perhaps their most famous names were Pauric Dalton and Niall Clancy. Indeed, Clancy had played for Dublin against Meath in a Leinster final.

Their defence was a very solid unit which gave no quarter and was superbly marshalled by Mick Pender. Many people were regarding this as another big Dublin–Meath final. They were looking to the likes of myself, Colm Coyle and Mattie McCabe to perhaps cause an upset. We had the experience to cope with them but it all depended on how we inspired and motivated the young lads in our side. If they rose to the challenge then we had a great chance. So often though, the majority of inexperienced players 'freeze'. On the other hand, the Dubliners had no such problems, which is why they were the warm favourites.

Our preparations were not ideal. Mattie McCabe had limped off injured in the semi-final and my shoulder injury was still giving me problems. All the odds were weighted heavily against us. Was this to be our last stand? Not if the youngsters could rise to the occasion and especially if the Coyle brothers could give us just one more blinding and inspirational display. There were a few other things in our favour. We were on a roll and never knew when we were beaten. We were also underdogs so we had nothing to lose. On the other hand, Crokes were seemingly home and hosed, which in itself put a little pressure on them. There was also a feeling among quite a few people that Kilmacud were one of the first sides in the country to 'buy' a team. By that I mean that they were a rich club who had plenty of money in the kitty. They could afford to use the transfer system to their advantage and go out and get the best players from around Ireland. So from that point we had all the neutrals on our side.

A very similar scenario faced Summerhill in 1977 when they faced mighty St Vincent's. As far as I know, this was the last Dublin–Meath Leinster final before ours. That Vincent's team had household names like Brian Mullins, Bobby Doyle, Jimmy Keaveney and Tony Hanahoe. But it did not stop the Meath side from thrashing them by a really amazing score of 5–4 to 0–6! We were hoping that was a good sign for us.

Taking to the field in Newbridge, we entered to a massive explosion of noise. The place was jam-packed and there seemed little space in the crowd estimated at 8,000. Kilmacud were sharp out of the blocks. They probably wanted to show us just what we were up against. In no time they had put two points on the board as we tried to settle. Colm Coyle set up Padraig for our first point but Crokes upped to a higher gear and scored two more to put three points between us. Veteran McCabe pulled another back for us but again the Dublin side surged further ahead. At that stage we found the going very tough. Trailing by 0–6 to 0–2, the gulf in class was showing, making us realise the level and standard we were playing at. We had to show some fighting spirit and keep with them, seeing that the game was slipping away from us.

It was Mattie who answered our desperate call as he knocked over another point for us. I was struggling in the game and one of the few things I did was to set up Padraig Coyle for his second point. But that was between two more points for the Dubs and they had the last laugh before going in at the interval leading by 0–8 to 0–4.

Things went from bad to worse when the match resumed. Crokes sent over three unanswered points and suddenly a big gap had developed. We were in deep trouble and when Padraig pointed a free, we were really only hanging on by our fingernails to a class outfit. It was perhaps a bridge too far for us as they now led by 0–11 to 0–5. Part of our problem was that my shoulder was restricting me. I was really jumping with just one arm. Add to that the 'basketballer' I was marking and I really was all at sea. We had to change tactics and get the ball to bypass the midfield and up into our forwards as quickly as possible.

McCabe, probably sensing that days out like this were numbered in his long career, was having a stormer! He pulled another point back and then suddenly we were thrown a lifeline. Crokes' normally reliable defence made a rare mistake. They made a hash of clearing a ball and Tony McDonnell took advantage to score a goal. We were right back in it and now trailed by just two points, 0–11 to 1–6. There was still around 10 minutes to go and then the unbelievable happened. From looking as if we were out of the game, we were level after two quick points from McCabe and Coyle. They had now scored four points each. The Dublin lads were rattled. You could see the disbelief and worried looks on all their faces. It is a funny game, all right. All of their classy work had been undone because of one mistake. Now it was us who had the upper hand.

Then for the remaining minutes a strange lull took over. It was as if both teams were in No-Man's-Land. They were visibly shocked at what had happened and I suppose that affected us. We were now afraid to go through with our effort and tightened things up. Also, we had come from a position of no hope but now that we were level, we did not want to give anything silly away. It turned out to be the wrong thing to do. We let them off the hook instead of nailing them. Seeing and sensing that we were not going through with our effort, they found another spurt near the end and scored what turned out to be the winning point. We were utterly devastated. It may have been thrilling to watch for the packed crowd but it all ended in tears and heartbreak for us.

I cannot understand why we took our foot off the gas. We had the momentum and it was so disappointing that we did not go through with it. Even before they scored the winner, we had a few chances to get our noses in front for the first time. The best chance involved our two best players on the day, McCabe and Padraig Coyle, but they got in each other's way and the chance was gone. Some will argue that Mattie was pulled down and we should have got a free. That said, it was just not our day despite having come so close to winning.

After the downpour of defeat, a ray of sunshine shone in my direction. A few days later I received notification that I had been nominated for an All Star award. I was surprised as I had not set the world alight that year. But I suppose I was chosen on the strength of our National League win over Armagh. When choosing All Stars back then, a few lads from the League winners were always picked. Also my Man of the Match display in the Leinster final probably helped my cause. I am not entirely sure how the All Stars are selected. I do know, however, that each year every county player gets a letter in the post in which he is asked to select who, in his opinion, was the best player in each of the 15 positions. You are also asked to state your personal choice for Player of the Year. When all the letters return from the counties, the voting begins and the winner of an All Star is the player who received the most votes for his particular position. In addition, there are votes cast by a committee made up mostly of sports writers.

I attended the awards at the Burlington Hotel just a week before Christmas. I was sitting at the back of the stage and when I heard my name called out, I could not believe it. It was a nice surprise and my first All Star. Truly, it is a great honour to be chosen by your fellow players from all over the country. So when you realise that fact, it becomes very special indeed. Even better news was the fact that Tommy Dowd won an All Star that evening as well. It was a case for double celebrations for Meath and, coming so close to the Christmas festivities, it was a great way to end the year. The disaster against Dublin and the agonising loss to Kilmacud Crokes were history. We could only look forward to improvement in 1995.

Looking back on the year 1994, I suppose it was not a bad haul. A League winner's medal, a Leinster Club medal and an All Star were not to be sniffed at. Certainly, there are many players who would give their right arm for just one of them. But I was still longing for that ultimate prize, the Sam Maguire. To win that, Meath would have to finally get their hands on that elusive Leinster title.

# 4 The Arsenal Trial

A surprise guest turned up at Croke Park on the day of the 1994 Leinster final between Meath and Dublin. It was none other than Sir Alex Ferguson, the manager of Manchester United. After the final, Sir Alex was interviewed on RTÉ and among other questions, he was asked about what players he thought had performed well. Now I have not seen the interview, but I am reliably informed that he replied: 'I really liked the No. 5 for Meath.' I can tell you it was a pleasant surprise and very flattering to hear that someone as famous as Sir Alex had also been impressed with my performance. But you have to be joking if you think I ever thought something might come of it. When friends told me about it afterwards, I just took it all in and never gave it a second thought. After all, because I had performed well, hundreds of thousands of people all over Ireland would also have nominated me as their Man of the Match.

However, that remark coming from the manager of one of the most famous soccer clubs in the world was indeed an honour. Indeed managers from premier league clubs are no strangers to Croke Park either. Remember what happened when another Manchester United manager turned up in the early Eighties to see Dublin playing. On that occasion, Dave Sexton was so impressed with Dublin's Kevin Moran that he brought him over to Old Trafford for a trial. As a result Kevin Moran went on to become one of United's greatest ever defenders – and also the most infamous when he became the first player ever to be sent off in an FA Cup final.

Never in my wildest dreams, as a result of Ferguson's comment, did I ever expect to be called over to the 'Theatre of Dreams' for a trial. I had other things on my mind. I was a little dejected after our loss to Dublin and just wanted to drown my sorrows. However, the very next morning, I received a phone call that left me in a state of shock and disbelief. Lying in bed, I literally believed I was dreaming. It was normal procedure for many Meath players, who had earlier played in a big match, to visit the Beechmount Hotel in Navan later in the evening. On this occasion we were all drowning our sorrows and had quite a bit to drink. In fact, I drank so much and was having such a good night that I booked a room in the hotel for the night! Next morning, I almost jumped out of the bed when the phone next to me rang. For a brief second I did not know where I was or who was calling. Imagine how shocked I was to learn that it was my father on the other end of the line. Especially as I was in bed in a hotel in Navan with someone! In my ear I had my father, but I was just glad the woman beside me never uttered a word! Then came shock number two, which went something like this:

'Dad, what are you up to?' I enquired.

'What are you doing in the Beechmount?' he demanded.

'Ah, I had a bit of a late night, so I decided to stay… What's up with you?' I asked.

'Look, I'll be over to collect you in half an hour. There's a scout from Arsenal going to be here at the house at around 12.30!' he answered.

'Will you stop! So you saw Alex Ferguson mention me as well – very funny,' I said.

'I'm telling you, I'm serious! I'll be over to pick you up, so be ready,' he replied before hanging up the phone.

Still in disbelief, I lay back in the bed for a few minutes. Gradually, I realised that he was serious and I became more curious. My head was not the best and neither did I look the best. But I got myself cleaned up and said goodbye to my lady friend. Dad arrived on time and we drove back to the family home in Kentstown.

When the Arsenal scout duly arrived, he introduced himself as Bill Darby, Arsenal's chief scout in Ireland, who was based in Dublin. By this time I was not feeling at all well. I had a really bad head, but thankfully Dad did most of the talking and questioning. Bill explained that Arsenal had been interested and looking at me for some time. They liked the way I made runs and generally attacked from the back. In fact, that was precisely what they were looking for! They had been searching high and wide for a replacement for England and Arsenal full-back, Lee Dixon!

Alex Ferguson, Arsenal, Lee Dixon – I was still trying to take it all in and with a bad hangover to boot. I felt a little doubtful about it all. I mean, it was not as if I was some big soccer star in Ireland. I was not even a top GAA player. Instead I was a beaten Leinster finalist; nonetheless, here was one of British soccer's finest clubs eyeing me up as a possible replacement for a great full-back in Lee Dixon! At the end of our meeting, Bill got up to leave and said he would be back in touch with me later in the week. Everything had to be reported back to the powers-that-be in Highbury, the home of Arsenal. Finally, Bill informed me that they would invite me over for a week's trial, which meant organising flights and accommodation.

Being honest, I never got above myself or excited about it. The media really went to town on the story and had a field day. But I was realistic to know that Gaelic football and soccer require two entirely different skills. After all, I was brought up from a very young age learning and fine-tuning the skills of football. My other favourite sports after that, as mentioned earlier, were athletics and basketball. I did play soccer occasionally but in truth it was not one of my favourite games. Running with the ball in your hand or soloing, hand-passing, fielding, weaving and dodging, shooting from the hand and lobbing high are all skills that I have learned from childhood. It is a very different ball game from soccer where you have to control the ball almost entirely with your feet. Even 'chesting' and 'heading' the ball are so different to what I am used to doing. I was beginning to wonder how I would adjust.

That said, I did have some soccer experience, though limited. I played with Kentstown Rovers in the Meath & District League. That level of soccer is light years away from League of Ireland, which in turn is well behind what is required for the Premiership in England. In reality most Gaelic footballers play in these Sunday morning soccer matches in order to keep in shape through the winter break.

It would be wrong for me to say that my heart was therefore not in it. Nothing could be further from the truth. As I told the media, it would be everyone's dream to play in English football and I would certainly jump at the opportunity. I had certain advantages like my fitness and my physique but my soccer skills and control were big disadvantages as mentioned. You also have to look at all the youngsters who have their hearts and dreams broken each year when they are turned away by the big clubs. Many of them have been playing soccer since the age of eight and under.

True to his word, Bill rang back by the end of the week. He gave me the details and times of my flight. I was to make my way to Dublin Airport on the Friday and catch a flight to London. When I arrived at Heathrow Airport in London, there would be an Arsenal official waiting there to pick me up. Everything went according to plan. The representative was also called Graham and we left Heathrow and made for Arsenal's training ground. I arrived there just in time to see some very familiar faces finishing a training session. Trooping off the pitch, I recognised great players like Tony Adams, Paul Merson, Steve Bould – and Lee Dixon!

From there, Graham brought me to where I was staying. It turned out to be in digs with a nice Italian couple. They were living in Tottenham not far from Arsenal's home at Highbury, North London. Soccer fans will know that Tottenham, or Spurs as they are more commonly known, and Arsenal are fierce local rivals. Graham, after introducing us, left but would be back next day to pick me up. The following morning, after a nice and healthy breakfast, Graham duly arrived. He brought me to Highbury to see Arsenal play in the Makita Tournament. This was a sort of mini pre-season tournament involving some of Europe's top teams. It was great experiencing Highbury and the tremendous atmosphere. In fact, it was the first ever soccer match I had attended in England and, though it was only a friendly, I really enjoyed it.

Despite the subject of soccer not being a 'big thing' in the Geraghty household, it did not stop me from becoming a Liverpool supporter in the strangest of circumstances. When I was very young, I can recall sitting watching a soccer match on the television with my father. Liverpool were playing Man United and because my father was shouting on United, I decided to plump for Liverpool instead! Ever since, I have been a Liverpool supporter, though I must admit, I am far from being a die-hard Red.

Following the game, Graham brought me back to where I was staying and I remember the lovely smell of Mediterranean cooking as I entered the house. I was so hungry and never ate so much pasta in all my entire life as I did that day! The next day, Sunday, I was brought to the final of the Makita Tournament. Unfortunately, it was not a great game and Arsenal won it beating the Italian side, Napoli, by 1–0. As Graham drove me back to my digs, he instructed me to have my bags packed for the next morning as I was moving to a new area. Finally, I was to start training.

On Monday morning, Graham picked me up and brought me over to my new digs in Wood Green. This time the house I was staying in was owned by a man named, Bill Graves. Bill was a lovely man – a real gentleman – who was in charge of the Arsenal Celebrity soccer teams. These teams were usually made up of famous people who lined out in the Arsenal shirt for charity purposes. There were a few other lads in the house and we all got on fairly well. The house situated in the Wood Green area was ideal because we were only 15 minutes or so from the training ground. As we left the house to go training, it was then that the nerves hit me. When I looked around me and saw the famous faces, I could not help but feel nervous and apprehensive. Surrounding me were little groups and clusters of players. I was actually in a small group that consisted of young players, some of whom are household names in English soccer circles today. Players like Martin Keown, Ian Selley and Ray Parlour were in the same age bracket as myself but already they were becoming well known and establishing themselves on the fringes of the first team.

I could not help therefore feeling just a little intimidated, kicking a ball around with these fellas. It was natural for me to feel a little inferior and that I might do something silly. After all, here I was, a young Gaelic footballer from Kentstown in Navan, mingling with guys who were later to go on and become huge stars. Martin Keown, who has many close relatives in Ireland, has now taken over from Tony Adams as their first-choice centre-back. He and Ray Parlour helped Arsenal to the Premiership in 2002 and both have been capped by England.

Training involved light warm-ups and one-touch games. The various little groups consisted of five-a-sides, playing the ball around fairly lightly because to do it more physically and vigorously would only risk unnecessary injury. This sort of training is similar in a way to our own Gaelic football training. At this stage of the season's training, all the pre-season and stamina training has been completed leaving just light sessions. Sprints were also a big part of our training schedule. Maybe because I have been running since I was very young, I particularly liked the sprinting. Here, at least, I felt that I could give my all and hold my own against anyone. Even back home in Páirc Tailteann or Dalgan Park, I always looked forward to the sprints. It has always been a strong point of my game. On the field of play, I have loved nothing more than to burst forth and run with the ball.

My fitness did not go unnoticed. Paul Merson, the former Arsenal star who won 21 caps for England and who played a big part in helping Portsmouth win the First Division and so gain promotion to the Premiership in 2003, actually mentioned me in his well-publicised and bestselling autobiography *Hero and Villain*. He must have made a mental note of me as a young Irish lad over for that trial, because he referred to me as the fittest player he had ever seen.

If Alex Ferguson said something complimentary about me, then these were mighty words indeed. But it was very nice of Paul to say that and I cannot speak for him to know what he saw in me. Perhaps it was that I could keep up my sprinting over and over again without wavering or tiring. For example, if I ran 100 metres in 11 seconds, then I could keep repeating it with very little variation in the time. In training we were not sprinting anywhere near those distances. It was really short and sharp bursts over quite short distances. Many of the guys I saw over there are great over say, 10 or 20 metres, but they tend to blow up after that. They cannot keep it up for longer, which is where my speed and stamina came into play. After a while, some of the guys became very tired, whereas I still kept going and I suppose that is what Paul Merson meant.

That sort of training routine happened every day during my trial. Finally on the following Saturday my first big test came. I played for the Arsenal reserve team in a testimonial match against Dover Athletic, who were then in the Vauxhall League. Arsenal legend, George Armstrong was the reserve team manager (not to be confused with former Northern Ireland stalwart Gerry Armstrong), and was a great help to me. He made me feel relaxed and told me to just go out and enjoy myself.

In that game, they played me on the right side of midfield. It took me a little time to settle down, which was to be expected. There I was, playing for Arsenal reserves, and I had never played anywhere near this level before. In fact, I had played very little soccer before! Anytime I received the ball, I found myself laying the ball off to a colleague as quickly as I could. I was 'copping out' which is not expected of a player playing in the wide right position. In the second half, I came more into the game and started to do the things expected of me. I got in some good crosses, I defended fairly well and then my big moment came. I remember the ball came to me but with some Dover players bearing down quickly on me, I had to react swiftly. I decided to have a pop at goal and so I let fly. I struck it very sweetly and to my surprise it headed for the top corner of the net. For a split second I thought it was in and then it turned and hit the junction of post and crossbar and rebounded to safety.

That was my one and only big chance in my first trial match. If it had gone in, it would have been a really sensational start for me. For that one second I could see the headlines in all the newspapers back home: 'GERAGHTY SCORES FOR ARSENAL IN FIRST MATCH!' It was not to be. We won that match 3–1 with a crowd of over 1500 present. Regarding my own performance, I felt I played all right. After a slow start I rose to the occasion and gradually felt my way into the game. I was very pleased with my second-half performance and in particular the chance that came my way. George Armstrong must have seen something as well. After the game he took me aside and said he wanted to see a little more of me. So my trial was extended for a further two weeks.

On the coach going to that game, a player Paul Davis sat in beside me. He was also playing in that match and later went on to have a brief spell with the first team when he helped 'the Gunners' to win the old First Division Championship – now the Premiership. He was a very nice guy and asked how I was and was generally trying to be helpful towards me. Another player who was perhaps the biggest help was former Irish international Eddie McGoldrick. I hurt my ankle in the win over Dover, and while I was having treatment in the physiotherapist's room one day, Eddie was on the treatment table next to me. As I was talking to the physiotherapist, Eddie recognised my accent and shouted over to me: 'Who is this Irish guy? I hear you play Gaelic, so how's it going over there?'

That remark really made me feel a little at home. Later as we chatted and walked down the corridor together, a very funny thing happened. In fact it had me in stitches laughing as I thought it was so funny. We had walked past a room, where someone said something to Eddie, who just shouted back: 'Fuck off, you black bastard!' I kept walking but as I looked back, around 10 black heads popped out from the room and one of them said: 'Oi, what did you just say?' Eddie looked back and shouted at the top of his voice: 'Fuck off, ALL you black bastards!' It is strange how things turn out. At the time, I thought that remark was so funny. I cannot say that the whole situation was so humorous that I decided to keep that line to use one day for an opportune moment of my own. Maybe it is just a figure of speech we use very crudely and ignorantly. A few years later, I was to pay for using a similar remark, but that is for a later chapter.

Eddie and Paul Davis were a huge support to me. I was sad to read recently about the big bust-up between Paul Davis and Irish legend, Liam Brady. Davis alleged that Brady turned him down for the post of an Arsenal underage team manager on the grounds of 'racism' – something Brady strenuously denies. In fact, because of their support and friendliness, many of the other players also warmed to me. It made me feel a whole lot better because it was a very competitive atmosphere over there. Lads were all very serious and they all had their minds set on winning a place at Highbury. No matter what happened to me at that trial in London, I was definitely one of the lucky ones. The amount of players going over for trials was staggering. The majority of them were just over for a trial for one day. One particular occasion I recall was when two guys from Barbados arrived over. They were just there for the day and then flew back home again.

The following week brought the usual training. We started around 10.30 am and finished at 1.30 pm. Then came my second test on the Saturday when we played Barnet. This time along with the prying eyes of George Armstrong was the Arsenal manager, none other than George Graham himself. Graham, a Scotsman, guided Arsenal to a brace of title wins in 1989 and 1991 that included the memorable 2–0 win at my beloved Liverpool, which actually gave Arsenal the title ahead of the Reds. He later went on to manage Leeds United, with former Arsenal and Ireland defender David O'Leary as his assistant.

When I saw George Graham there, I knew that it was his eyes which were going to be the ultimate judge of my worth. This was confirmed, in my own mind, when I started the game in the right-back position. From the moment Bill Darby told me they were looking at me as a possible replacement for Lee Dixon to when I was told to start in Dixon's right-back position, I knew that this was the crucial game for me. It was make or break time. If I impressed the bosses, then the least I could have expected would have been a longer extension. If I failed, there would be no further stay in London. We played Barnet out on the training ground and the less said about it the better. When it really mattered, I did not play at all well and I just did not feel comfortable in that right-back slot.

A few days later, I was taken aside and told I was not going to make it as an Arsenal player. Instead someone else was going to be taken on. It had been between me and this other player, but they felt he had more experience than me. Hand on heart, I really knew the decision before they informed me. I just did not have all the weapons in my armoury. Looking back now, and with all things considered, I think I gave a good account of myself and at least I was in no way disgraced. I possessed good pace, I was not bad at passing and heading and I had that half-chance to score against Dover. But the two things that really counted against me were experience and my ball control.

A friend of mine, Mal Hickey, also said this to me. But that was no surprise and I always felt that I was going to struggle with this aspect of the game. At the pace they play soccer now, ball control is probably the single most important thing for any young lad starting out. It is as basic as a fish taking to water but it is the most important ingredient that goes into the making of a top soccer player. I was a Gaelic footballer and, with the odd exception, you cannot teach an old dog new tricks.

I remember seeing the guy that they took on instead of me, but I have no idea of his name or whether he became successful. But there were other players there and two of them were so good that I knew they would make it. Lee Hughes was a very exciting young player. But with the big squad at Highbury, his opportunities were limited and so he had to move on. He is now with West Bromwich Albion who were in the Premiership before being relegated in 2003.

The other player was Paul Dickov. When he burst on the scene, I suppose many people thought he would take after that lanky but prolific Arsenal goalscorer, Alan Smith. However, he also became lost in the big squad and later moved to Manchester City. He is now doing very well for himself at Leicester City. He played a big part in scoring his share of goals and helping them win promotion to the Premiership.

Another very peculiar thing which I noticed during my time over there was the habit which a player named Stefan Schwartz had. I remember he was a big-money signing from SL Benfica and much was expected of him. When I was in the dressing-room one day, I noticed him standing over the sink and pouring water directly from the tap into his football boots, which he then put on! I never saw anything like it before and I have never seen the like of it since. It seemed very odd, especially with footballers prone to arthritis later in life.

Initially, when I was invited over, I wanted to make the most of such an exciting opportunity. But I now know how hard it is for all the young lads who go over. I was only there for a few weeks and I was homesick. In the end, when I was given the bad news, I felt a great sense of relief that it was all over. In fact, I could not wait to get out of London and home to Ireland. The minute I got the news, I made arrangements for my return journey. Not wanting any fuss made or any media lying in wait for me, I never rang to tell my family or friends. I arrived home and I remember just going to a friend's wedding. But even then, I could not escape questions as everyone was asking about the trial. By the following morning, it seemed like I had talked the night away. Later, I found out the reason for the sudden interest in me.

While I was away in London, my family kept all the newspaper clippings of the trial. I could not believe the level of interest and the things that were written about me. Sure I answered queries from the Irish media while I was over there, but I did not think it would snowball into almost every newspaper covering it. You could be forgiven for thinking that I was a super skilful soccer player with some of the things written. Indeed, some papers were saying that I was on the verge of signing a megabucks deal with Arsenal! In reality, I was just given a slim chance of a shot at the small target. I was not that far off the mark but 'not far off' is not nearly good enough.

Arising from that trial in England, a few opportunities popped up for me with League of Ireland clubs. A short time after arriving home, Bohemian's manager, Turlough O'Connor, asked me to play for them. After a few reserve games, I packed it in. Then the same thing happened with Drogheda United. Similarly, one of their directors, Eamonn Duignan, got in touch with me. So myself and another Meath player, Jimmy McGuinness, went to see him and we agreed to give it a go. We started in the reserves and both of us played well. Then I picked up an ankle injury and just got fed up with the whole soccer situation. The final straw came when some fellow rang me from Limerick. According to him, another London club, Leyton Orient from the lower divisions, were interested in bringing me over. So much so that Pepe Jeans would in fact sponsor me. Having told him I would think about it, he promised to ring me back. I never heard from him again and so ended all my links with English and Irish soccer clubs.

In hindsight, the trial was invaluable and my thanks goes to Bill Darby and everyone else connected with Arsenal FC for giving me such a great opportunity, and especially for all their kindness and hospitality. I know that I was very lucky and that many young lads would jump at such a chance. It was a great experience for me as well as an honour to pull on the famous red and white jersey of Arsenal. A jersey which was famously worn by famous Irish players like Brady, Stapleton, O'Leary and Quinn. Arsenal are a fantastic club. They are steeped in tradition and I know they have a huge Irish following, both in North London and here in Ireland. They won the title in England in 2002 and they and Manchester United are currently the two big powers in English soccer. I feel very privileged to have passed through the corridors and halls of Highbury and I will not forget my time there.

To be honest, though, my heart never was and never will be in soccer. I tired of it all very quickly and, with all due respect to the League of Ireland clubs, after playing alongside some great players at Arsenal, coming home to play in the reserves here was a backward step. Gaelic football was and always will be the only game for me, and I could not wait to get back playing again.

# 5 Meath, Mayo & Madmen

The 1995 campaign did not start at all well. We surrendered our League crown very tamely. Nevertheless, we were all focused on that elusive Leinster title. The spirit was fairly good in the camp, especially since the goalkeeping position had been sorted out. Conor Martin was now installed as Meath's net-minder and everything was in place. Things got even better when we trounced the opposition in the early rounds of the Leinster Championship. We beat Offaly by 10 points, Longford by 17 points and Wicklow by 14 points. That was fairly impressive stuff and it more than showed that we meant business.

It was no surprise that the auld enemy were waiting for us in the Leinster final. But we could not care less. Our confidence was sky high as this was what we had been setting our sights on. We were so desperate to put right the mistake which cost us dear the previous year. Dublin knew they would have a real battle on their hands and must have been impressed with the way we started in those early rounds.

Matches between Meath and Dublin are always tense and close encounters. The first half in this one proved no different and at half-time we led by just a point. Then came a downpour of heavy rain. That was an unexpected turn of events and with it the match totally changed. Who could ever have predicted that after the great form we showed, in our first three matches and even in that first half, that the Dubs would trounce us? They ran out 10-point winners by 1–18 to 1–8 and we were absolutely devastated. I thought that it was very cruel on our overall performance. We simply did not deserve to lose that match so heavily and the score was very misleading.

We had matched Dublin right through the game and it was only in the last 10 minutes that things began to run in their favour. It was

The fair-haired boy of sport – Graham (left) with sisters Karen and Sandra.

First Communion, 1979.

Gaedheal-Chumann Lúth-Chleas Na nÓg

*THIS IS TO CERTIFY THAT*

Graham Geraghty  Seneschalstown  A.C.

*SET A NEW RECORD IN*

Boys Under 8  50m  (7.16s) ................. Event

At 1981 ........................ Track & Field Championships

Miceál Mc Cormac

Cathaoirleach

Margaret Ranbe

Runal

Representing Seneschalstown Athletic Club in 1981, Graham sets a new
record in the Boys U–8 50 metres Track & Field Championships at the
Mardyke, Cork, and retains it to this day.

Winner takes all – Graham following the Rás na hÉireann U-9 Cross-Country Championships, 1982.

1983 U-10 All-Ireland NACA Cross-Country Champions, representing Seneschalstown Athletic Club (left to right) Raymond Butler, Graham Geraghty, David Dillon, David Carter, Alan Oakes and Kevin Clarke.

Serving the community – boy scouts Graham and Kevin Clarke.

Meath supporters (left to right), father Ger, Sandra, Graham, grandmother Rose Lawlor, Karen and Lisa (back row) in a picture taken by Graham's mother, Jean.

Winning household – Graham, Sandra and Karen Geraghty.

Graham in possession – Kentstown Rovers v Kilmessan in November 1989.

All–Ireland Minor Champions, 1990 – Meath reclaims the title after 33 years.

The first Meath team to win the All-Ireland U-21s Football Championship, 1993 (below) with Graham in action (left).

our worst performance against them and our heaviest loss to them since 1980. It is a very rare occurrence to play well and then to get 'stuffed'. However, it never rains but it pours. Paul Clarke, who fisted Dublin's killer goal in that game, also delivered a knockout blow to me. To add injury to insult, I remember he swung at me from behind and caught me full force in the mouth. I ended up with some teeth chipped and that just summed up that entire day. That disaster actually signalled the end for some of Meath's outstanding footballers of the past. There was a right mass exodus from the camp following that defeat. Colm O'Rourke, Brian Stafford, Terry Ferguson and PJ Gillic all hung up their boots. However, Gillic did make a brief comeback a few years later.

Personally, I had other plans and there was no way I was going to hang around all summer. I got a phone call from America asking if I would like to go over and play with a Meath junior team. Gerry 'Nipper' Heavey and Mick Fitzsimons from Skryne were also on the side. All flights, accommodation, work and some appearance money would be arranged. The way I was feeling after that embarrassing defeat to Dublin, it was an offer too good to resist. So two weeks after the Leinster final, I flew to New York. Travelling with me were fellow players Tommy Hanley, Jody Devine and Terry O'Connor. All four of us stayed in Nipper's apartment in the Bronx. A short time later, Tony Byrne from Dunboyne travelled from Boston to join up with us.

Generally people know the Bronx as a really rough area of New York. As it happened, there was a lot of unrest in that area during our time there. Contrary to what you hear and believe, it was not the black community who were the cause of all the crime. In reality, the Irish were more to blame. Many people travelling over from Ireland for the first time were mugged at the hands of second-generation Irish. The reason they were robbing and assaulting their own was because they felt the influx of Irish workers was counting against them. Their jobs were being taken from them, effectively meaning there were less opportunities for them.

While staying in New York, we were always told never to venture out on our own. It was far too risky and dangerous. So if we went out, we always took taxis or if we were eating or drinking, we would have it delivered. Of course, it was not always like that while we were there, but you did have to be constantly alert and aware. Most of us were working in construction. I was restoring old houses but you could not really call it work. It seemed like we were forever going to work for just a few hours. Then we would all down tools and head off somewhere for the afternoon and evening. When we were supposed to be at work, a lot of us were out playing golf! I think we must have played golf almost every second day for five weeks! After we finished on the 18th hole, we would go to the 19th for rounds of a very different kind. We drank in well-known pubs like 'Fiona's', 'The Aquaduct' and 'The South Bend'. Usually, Fiona's on a Friday was packed. That was the day we all collected our wages and went to the pub to cash cheques. On Tuesdays and Thursdays after work, we went to New York's famous Gaelic Grounds to train with the Meath juniors. It was marvellous to meet and talk with lads from all over Ireland. Later in the bars, we would chat well into the early hours about football and memories of great games we had played in. It was all great craic and of course there were plenty of women around as well!

Eventually all our hard work and training paid off! We reached the final of the competition and were to face Cavan. Just a few days before that final, I went on a real 'bender' with a few lads and very nearly missed the match. I was drinking in The South Bend with Ciaran Duff and another guy named Barry who ran a bar on New York's Third Avenue. Many people will recall Duff as a former Dublin great and it just goes to show that we really can be friends off the pitch. We were drinking right through the night and into the early morning. In most areas of New York, the bars stay open 24 hours. All of a sudden, Duff said to us: 'Why don't we go outside and have a race to see who is the fittest?' Without hesitating, the three of us got up from our bar stools and headed outside for a race. Across the road from the bar there was a green belt called Van Courtland Park. At that hour of the morning, people used the park to go jogging or to take a short-cut to work. Can you imagine the looks we received from passers-by? Three loud and drunken Paddies crouched down as if on starting blocks! We were wondering how the race would start and then Duff had a bright idea: 'I'm the oldest, so I'll say, "On your marks, get set... GO!"' Ciaran was sandwiched between Barry and myself and just as he said the word 'GO', he flung his fists up between us where the sun doesn't shine! Needless to say, he raced off to win as we were left sprawled on the pavement! I had a final to play against Cavan but with all the fun, I totally lost track of time. Little did I know that Nipper had sent out an SOS for me. Nobody knew where I was and several people were out searching for me. When I eventually arrived back at Nipper's apartment, he nearly killed me! After all, he had brought me to America for a specific purpose. Meath juniors beat Cavan so all was forgiven. More days of drinking and fun followed before it was time to say goodbye.

When I arrived home to Navan, the memories of that hot summer in New York quickly faded. Soon after, I faced into an autumn and winter of gloom and discontent in Meath. In my 12 years playing with the Meath Senior team, 1995 was without doubt the most disappointing. There was no question about it but there would have to be huge improvements in 1996.

Before our opening match against Carlow in the 1996 Leinster Championship, my girlfriend (and later wife) Amanda Egan told me that she felt they were going to beat us. At the time, she was only echoing a lot of what Meath people were saying. It was commonly said that after all our disappointments in Leinster we were going nowhere. We were now a fairly young and inexperienced side and Carlow were likely to expose us. They would dump us out in the first round. In response, I distinctly remember telling her that we were going to go the whole way and win the All-Ireland! It was just a very strong feeling I had at that time and it would all start off with victory against Carlow. They had the Eire Óg factor going for them, but having a great club side can also work against the county.

Defeat did not even bear thinking about. It would have been a disaster too far and too great to even begin thinking about the consequences. With due respect to Carlow, I felt that if we lost to them, then all of us might as well have packed it in. I also felt that it was very unfair for people to be writing us off so quickly. They had very short memories as far as I was concerned. Had they forgotten that the only team that stood in our way of a Leinster title was Dublin? Two of our three previous meetings could so easily have swung our way.

Our National League campaign did not go too badly. However, the jury was still out after some of our performances. We qualified for the quarter-finals at the end of March and faced Mayo in Hyde

Park, Roscommon. The less said about that game the better. We were appalling (even though I scored three points), and Mayo went through to the semi-final, having beaten us by 2–10 to 1–10. After the retirements of Colm O'Rourke and Brian Stafford, we were only finding our way as a fairly new and young side. So the League was a time for re-grouping and pulling ourselves together. In light of that, it was unfair to write us off after the terrible performance against Mayo and the previous years against Dublin. Meath folk were also beginning to feel that the Dubs had an Indian sign on us. I knew that we were far better than what was reported and was just hoping for a change in our luck.

Against Carlow, we never had any anxious moments. Everyone played very well and the result was never ever in doubt. The scoreline of 0–24 to 0–6, similar to our early victories the year before, showed that we meant business. It certainly proved a lot of doubters wrong – including Amanda! It only reaffirmed my opinion that we were going to take some stopping. I scored a few points in that match and I was very happy with my fitness and performance level.

All of us felt that Laois in the next round would prove to be a much tougher nut to crack. They relished the challenge with us – especially the physical aspect. If there was going to be a 'banana skin', then it would be Laois. We expected a bruising encounter with them and duly got it. However, because we expected it, we had our homework done. The result was never really in doubt and again we cruised to a fairly easy win by 2–14 to 1–9. Our performances were impressive and I was thrilled with all aspects of our play. We were showing All-Ireland quality and like the year before, it was a case of bring them all on. It was always on the cards that we would play Dublin in the Leinster final. When they beat Louth in somewhat of a struggle, it was Dublin and Meath in a Leinster final for the third year in a row. In terms of my own displays, I could not have been happier. After Carlow, I scored a goal and two points against Laois earning me the Man of the Match award. I felt that I was approaching the same sort of form that I produced in 1994. If I could manage to reproduce my performance in the final with Dublin that year, and with the way we were playing now, there was no doubt that we would finally win the Leinster title.

On Sunday, 28 July, I was hit by a red bolt from the blue on the very morning of that 1996 Leinster final. It was one of the biggest shocks I have ever had to deal with in life. Around ten o'clock that morning, I got a phone call from my sister who told me that my best friend, Leslie Crinion, had been killed in a car crash the previous night. I was numb with shock, and did not know what to do. There I was preparing for a huge and very important game and then was given such tragic news. Leslie was as close as family. We did practically everything together. He was my best friend at school, we grew up together and were almost inseparable.

With all those thoughts in my head, I hardly know how I got through that match. I knew I had to focus on the job at hand but as hard as I tried, all I could think about was my lost friend who would no doubt have been watching me play in that final, if he had been alive. Even when I tried to block it out, something would happen to trigger the thoughts again. Before the match, the selectors, supporters and even the players seemed to be talking about Leslie's death. It became even harder when a few players came up to me, and not knowing how close he was to me, asked: 'Did you hear Leslie Crinion was killed in a car crash last night?' The hardest part was lining up and trying to stand still for the National Anthem. I will never forget how hard that was. As I stood there in Croke Park, with my hands behind my back, little did the crowd and television audience know how I felt. I was fighting very hard to choke back the tears.

As far as Dublin–Meath Leinster finals go, this one promised so much but delivered little. It was one of the least exciting matches between us. Although the gap between us at the end may have suggested that it was a cliffhanger, it was anything but. The game was scrappy and the low scoring said it all. However, that mattered little to us, seeing that we were relieved to win the Leinster title at long last. The 0–10 to 0–8 victory also ended our bad run against Dublin, leaving us overjoyed to have reached the All-Ireland semi-final. Under the circumstances, you will not be surprised to learn that I did not play well. All my intentions were to try my hardest for the memory of Leslie Crinion. But there are 29 other guys out there with plenty of intentions as well. Therefore, it was not easy.

Victory in that Leinster final was very important to all of us in Meath. We could finally hold our heads high. We had achieved something at last. We were Champions of Leinster and now just one match away from our ultimate dream. If we could get past Ulster Champions Tyrone, then we would have a date with Sam Maguire. The celebrations in the County Club in Dunshaughlin and then in Navan were not as expected. There was great joy at finally beating Dublin and winning a title, but for me and others, there was also a funeral to attend. We may have won but we also lost an important Meath supporter, and a guy who was a great friend and help to me.

After beating Dublin, the relief was palpable. It was as if we had been freed from years of imprisonment in shackles. The hope now was that we would run riot and express ourselves freely once again. I had predicted at the outset that this would be Meath's year. All of us now felt we could do it. Dublin held a psychological edge over us in previous years. A team can be in fine physical shape but it must also be sound mentally. Just look at the evidence presented before both Leinster finals with the Dubs in 1995 and 1996. We won all our matches easily the previous year before falling very badly to Dublin at the last hurdle. Then in 1996 we hit 24 points against Carlow, 2–14 against Laois, yet we only managed 10 points in that final with Dublin. That was a poor tally which most teams would score in a first half.

Tyrone were next up and we were ready to release our best football again. Even after the first couple of minutes of that All-Ireland semi-final with Tyrone, I knew it was going to be our day. On a personal note, I was very sharp. I was getting ball from almost everywhere and making good runs. After I managed to notch up a few points, I started to feel very comfortable. I got into a groove and when you reach this vein of form, it transmits itself to the rest of the side. Confidence began to ooze from us. In contrast, Tyrone found themselves in almost total disarray. I knew when they began making switches and putting different fellas over to mark me that they were in deep trouble. They simply had no answer to our play. Although I notched up 1–4 for the team, the most important thing was that we had scored 2–15 to their 0–12 and we were into the All-Ireland final. To beat Tyrone by nine points was a stunning result.

Meath were now into their first final since the loss to Down in 1991. It was my first All-Ireland and it seemed like it would never come. After the pain and embarrassment of the previous four years, you keep telling yourself that the breaks will come but you do begin to wonder. All our hard work and persistence had finally paid off. Mayo under their fine manager, John Maughan, were all that stood between us and lifting the Sam Maguire Cup. We really knew it was going to be a hell of a hard match to win. Maughan is a real fitness fanatic and you could see in him and his players their fine physiques and supreme levels of fitness. One thing was certain, there was no way we were going to win this match pulling up.

On the Saturday evening before the big game at around six o'clock, we trained in Dalgan Park, just outside Navan. It was only a light training session and normally before big matches, we could expect to have a sizeable crowd watching us. But because it was an unusually late hour for us to be having a runaround, not many people knew we were going to be there. I think Sean Boylan wanted it that way to ease any pressure. After training, you may be surprised to know that we went to Bellinter for Saturday evening Mass. This was a regular thing before big games on a Sunday. I suppose some players and selectors, as well as Sean himself, did not wish to miss Mass on Sunday so we all had the alternative of the Saturday night. We also did not wish to miss out on God's blessing as we needed every bit of help against Mayo! Mass was followed by a light meal in Bellinter House where Sean said a few words; nothing of particular note or importance other than to get to sleep as early as we could. I think I got to bed around 10.30 pm, and slept very well. Before any match, I have always slept soundly, so I guess I have been lucky as a good sleep is always very important.

On the morning of the All-Ireland final, Jimmy McGuinness and myself left from my house in Kentstown. All the neighbours in our housing estate were out taking photographs and generally wishing us luck. The hairs rose on the back of my neck just seeing them all. There was a great atmosphere as well as huge excitement. The estate also looked lovely with all the bunting and decorations. We left Kentstown and drove to Dunshaughlin where we met up with the rest of the team at the County Club. Again, this was always the same routine when playing in Croke Park. Another was our gentle kickabout in the hotel's car park. There we kicked balls around in our shoes and clothes with the All-Ireland only a few short hours' away. I remember car owners making their way to and from their vehicles rather sheepishly in case they or their cars were damaged!

An hour before the big game, a few of us went into the stands to see the All-Ireland Minor final. This reminded me of previous years when as Minors and U-21s we would go up into the stands to watch the Seniors play. After a while, we came back into the dressing-room to get togged out. There was the usual laughter and small talk but also a sense of quiet and nervous tension. Outside the dressing-rooms, there was a warm-up area. There we could run and stretch and do some exercises. If lads needed strapping or a rub, then Ann Burton, the physio, or Mocky Regan, the masseuse, were on hand to provide it. As the time neared for taking to the field, Sean Boylan called us in and gathered us all together. He asked us to get down on the floor and we all lay flat on our backs. Next he told us to put our hands flat on our stomachs and to take deep breaths in and out. This was not at all unusual as Sean got us to do it fairly often. It helped to relax the team and get rid of any stress or tension.

A few minutes later, we all stood up. Sean then gave us his last instructions before we ran out onto Croke Park. His last words to us were very plain and simple: 'Go hard for the ball, let the ball do the work, get the ball into the forwards and just be competitive.' That was a real Sean Boylan saying. He constantly drummed that line into us about 'going hard for the ball'. I think people have always labelled us very unfairly as a 'dirty' team. In effect, we have only ever put Sean's words into practice. In reality, I feel we are just very competitive. To us the white ball is the same as a red rag to a bull. We play hard but fair. I love the big match atmosphere and the battle ahead. I try to take it all in. Most lads are the same but a few are quite different. For instance, Darren Fay has always kept to himself. He was always as quiet as a mouse and would never utter so much as a word to anyone. That was his way and it worked for him.

Running out onto the pitch was incredible. The explosion of noise was deafening. After a kickabout, we then marched around behind the Artane Boys Band. I looked into every section of the crowd as we paraded around but did not recognise a single person. Then we stood in line as the President of Ireland, Mary Robinson, greeted both teams. I remember giving her a really firm handshake and she just wished me and the rest of the Meath team the best of luck. Though I did not know it at the time, she hails from Ballina. So obviously she was hoping for a Mayo victory!

Every man then took his position and the Meath team lined out as follows: Conor Martin was in goals, the full-backs were Mark O'Reilly, Darren Fay and Martin O'Connell. The half-backs were Colm Coyle, Enda McManus and Paddy Reynolds while the midfield duo were Jimmy McGuinness and John McDermott. The half-forward line was myself, Trevor Giles and Tommy Dowd and the full-forwards were Evan Kelly, Brendan Reilly and Barry Callaghan.

When the formal introductions and National Anthem were over, it was toss-up time. Pat McEnaney was the referee and he is certainly one of the very best around. We won the toss and our captain, Tommy Dowd, elected to play against the wind. That is something of another Meath tradition. If we win the toss, we usually always play into the wind. I think the reason being that it usually takes teams, on average, about 10 minutes to settle down. If we do not settle and find ourselves behind, then at least we know what is required in the second period and we have the aid of the wind.

My marker was Pat Holmes. Like many Mayo players, he was a big man. Typical of John Maughan, his team was fit and fast. He must have had his players running up mountains in training because Holmes was a lot faster than I thought. Inside the first minute though, I got away from him but he managed to get back and block my shot which I thought was going over. After that, I found it hard to get past Holmes. It took all of seven minutes for the first point and it was Mayo's nippy forward, James Horan, who scored. For those first few minutes it is typically helter-skelter. Players are all out of position because of nerves and tension. A minute after that point, the referee took me aside and told me to calm down. I got a little excited and almost brought Colm McMenamin down. He caused us a fair amount of concern in those early moments. Mayo were getting a foothold on the game and when they added a second point a couple of minutes later, I was feeling very frustrated. Sean always wanted ball played into the forwards as quickly as possible. I think I only touched the ball once in the first 10 minutes!

Soon after, my chance came. I ran onto a pass from Trevor Giles but lost control. However, I managed to regain the ball and turned the Mayo defender left and then right before scoring off the inside of the post. I had another quick chance but my long-range effort went wide. We were just a point behind. The game was very scrappy and then my period of frustration returned. I was not getting any ball and did not like it one bit. Our forward, Barry Callaghan, was then booked but I felt McMenamin should have been booked. I was not at all happy about the way things were going and when I tripped James Nallon, I was then booked! James Horan was causing us a lot of bother and when he scored a terrific point, we trailed by 0–4 to 0–2. With only 10 minutes to the break, we were in disarray. Credit must be given to Mayo for making the running and putting us on the rack.

To make matters worse, we gave away a silly free which they easily converted. At this early stage we were worried. We could not get to grips with Mayo who were getting stronger by the minute. Then I conceded a soft free, and in my anger I almost scored a wonder goal. I ran on to a loose ball from the midfield area. I then dribbled it around several players and all the way up to the Mayo goal. I struck it but it was too close to their keeper who saved with his legs. It was a wonder I did not get called for another cross-channel trial after that! Had I scored, they would have talked about it for years! But I do not think the powers-that-be in the GAA would have been happy. A soccer-style goal does not go down too well with Gaelic football purists.

At this point, we were playing catch-up with Mayo, so we could have done with a goal. Just before the break, however, Trevor Giles scored a much-needed point for us. We trailed Mayo by 0–7 to 0–4 but a few things gave us concern. We were not in the game at all and only scored at huge intervals. Our first point took all of 10 minutes to get and our last point took 13 minutes! On the whole, I think it was a poor first half. Both teams had scrappy spells and Mayo must have been disappointed not to have made the most of several other good chances. Sean was not concerned despite what we may have felt. He told us to stick to the game-plan. Furthermore, he reminded us that we had the wind in the second half. Our marking was also very slack. They seemed to have three or four lads going for every ball.

On resumption of the game, I was fouled by Holmes and then Trevor popped over the free to reduce our arrears. I then had a great chance to point which would have reduced it to one. Everyone thought the ball was going out over the sideline but I managed to sprint and keep it in. As I had caught them all unawares, I had plenty of time to make a better angle for myself but I hurried the shot and so I fluffed it wide. I was very disappointed with that miss. It took nearly 10 minutes for the next score and when it came, it was a comedy of errors. Our defence was sloppy and failed to clear an easy ball. Mayo scored a goal and I was disgusted with Paddy Reynolds. Whatever he was thinking, I just do not know. He should have made a no-nonsense clearance but he fumbled it and allowed them to pounce. We were now in seriously deep trouble and it was not looking good. Trailing by 1–8 to 0–5, Sean acted swiftly. He brought in Colm Brady which had an immediate impact. Colm is another player who was unlucky with Meath. He suffered lots of injuries in his career which forced him out of many big games. We knuckled down and fought back well and actually reduced the arrears to three points. Things were hotting up and John McDermott was warned by the referee for an attack on Dempsey. But he did not do anything wrong as Dempsey from Mayo was like an old woman. For a man of 6 ft 4 in and well built, he went down far too easily.

Time was running out fast for us. With little under 10 minutes to go, Sean brought in Jody Devine for 'Boots' McGuinness. We now had to throw everything at Mayo. Trevor's kicking had to be spot on and thankfully it was. He further reduced our deficit and with Colm Brady's vision and the running of Tommy Dowd, we got to within a point. Suddenly it was Mayo on the back foot. Their tanks seemed to be emptying fast. With only a couple of minutes to go, we sensed that we might just be able to snatch a draw. Then the big chance came and it fell to me. It was a great chance from about 40 metres out and straight in front of the posts. I hit it sweetly but at the last second, it swung wide. It was sheer agony. I walked away with my head down. I could only think of what might have been and the talk of me missing a great chance to level. The referee looked at his watch and time was almost up. The ball came to Colm Coyle who was a good distance out. He sent in a high hopeful ball towards me and Dowd. We ran towards it just ahead of some chasing Mayo defenders. To our amazement, the ball beat us all and bounced over the bar!

Seconds later and McEnaney blew for time. It was all over and the match finished tied at 1–9 to our 0–12. That must surely have been the freakiest point ever to end an All-Ireland final. We got out of jail. In all honesty, we had no right to draw as Mayo really deserved to win. They had been six points ahead, but again you must give Meath credit for their fighting spirit. We got a lucky point and lived to fight another day and a replay. In my opinion, it was a very poor final even allowing for all the drama at the end. We did not play well and there were no scores for long periods of play. Mayo's top scorers during the year, Nestor and Casey, had poor games too. I was also very disappointed with my performance, believing that Pat Holmes had the better of me. He was in the game much more than I was. In fact, I was just running around trying to get involved.

There was no question but that we were the happier team at the end. Nevertheless, we only had a second bite at the cherry and we knew we would have to play far better to have any chance of winning. We knew Maughan and his men would learn from their mistakes, so we were still very much up against it.

\*\*\*\*\*\*

## Play It Again for Sam

In preparation for this book I watched the video of our final with Mayo and the replay. Admittedly, it was the first time I had watched it in years. I am not the kind of person who looks back over past performances. In fact, I do not like looking at myself on television at all, especially when it involves interviews. However, there were a few interesting comments made on RTÉ's *The Sunday Game* before both matches. I thought that Martin Carney made a very good point when he talked about the nine substitutes. Naming nine substitutes when only a maximum of six are permitted to play is grossly unfair on the three who will not start. The GAA should change this rule. Colm O'Rourke was also glad to see Meath in a changed strip of yellow jerseys and green shorts for the replay. He thought that the green shirts of both sides clashed in the first game. In response, Marty Morrissey revealed that the GAA had instructed Mayo to change their shirts but the Connaught side refused to do so. The GAA were then saved any embarrassment by Meath agreeing to change theirs! This was all news to me, as back then I never knew anything about it. Meath officials obviously kept it quiet!

For the replay, there were two major changes involving both teams. David Nestor, who had been one of Mayo's best players all year but had had a poor first match, was dropped. Meath's Colm Brady, who was introduced as a substitute to great affect in the original game, kept his place. Evan Kelly therefore was the unlucky one to lose out. Again it was a very scrappy opening few minutes and once more it took a long time for the first score to be registered. That came after 10 minutes following a huge bust-up. I suppose this replayed final will be forever known as 'The Row'. If you mention the 1996 final to people in Meath, in most cases they will smile and say, 'The Row!'

When I look back, it was amazing to see loads of players having a right go at each other in front of the President and thousands watching on television. I suppose that in the heat of the moment, and with so much at stake, there is no time to think. In fairness, it was all 'handbags' and I have seen an awful lot worse than that. It all started when a Mayo ball came in and our keeper, Conor Martin, grabbed it. But he got an elbow in the face and then all hell broke loose. There were fellows flying in from all directions. I did not see much of what was going on because I was fighting my own battle with a Mayo player! I was behind the goal-line at the side of the upright. Mayo's Ray Dempsey was squaring up to me. He is a big man, and it was funny because I remember he was about to land a big one on me when *Wham!*, he disappeared as Colm Coyle came in quickly and floored him! I suppose it was a case of one clubman sticking up for another as Colm is a team-mate of mine at Seneschalstown. Unfortunately for Colm, he was not thinking about the umpires who were standing by the posts. So when it died down, the referee Pat McEnaney went to consult with them. As a result, Colm and Mayo's Liam McHale were both sent off. I suppose the referee had to set an example but he got the wrong man in sending off Colm. Judging from the video, there was a lot worse going on elsewhere. There were lads pulling, swinging and kicking at each other.

Later when talking to McEnaney and another official, I learned that they were going to send off McHale and Meath's John McDermott. I know Colm swung a punch at Dempsey but it was wrong to send him off alone. I feel that because Colm went Dempsey and Finnerty should also have walked. By his own admission, John McDermott was also lucky to stay on and likewise he should have been sent off. After a delay of over three minutes, the game restarted and I was immediately booked for a late challenge. I deserved it because I was all pumped up after seeing Colm Coyle red-carded. Mayo then put over the first point and in the next seven minutes they were four points up to our no score. Once again, James Horan played brilliantly and scored several points in the process. On the strength of that he received an All Star award later in the year.

The replay was turning out to be almost exactly the same as the first game. Mayo were making all the running. They were causing us havoc and we found ourselves well behind. Like the drawn game, I was feeling like a fish out of water. I found myself getting very little ball and was forever running back to help out our defence. Defence is where I first started out playing, but as a half-forward I was supposed to be receiving ball. It was very frustrating that I was going in search of the ball rather than having it played in to me. Luckily, Tommy Dowd came to our rescue. He scored a great point which, like my effort in the first match, went over off the inside of the post. That left us three points behind but then disaster struck. Mayo went down the other end and scored a goal through PJ Loftus. It was a poor goal for us to concede and it was again down to sloppy defending. You have to give credit to Loftus for a superb, no-nonsense finish.

Just like the first match, we were once again at panic stations. We were six points behind and facing into yet another uphill struggle. Mayo were once more proving to be very difficult to get to grips with. In particular, Colm McMenamin was in unstoppable form. He was their playmaker and we simply had to put a stop to him. Trevor Giles was then thrust into the spotlight. One of our men ran through their defence and was bearing down on goal, when he was brought down. The referee pointed to the penalty spot and waved away all the Mayo protests. But I remember screaming at him because the ball had already crossed the line. So the advantage should have been played in our favour and the goal allowed to stand.

It was nearing the break and what a pressure kick for Trevor. If he scored he would reduce our arrears to three. If he missed then we were facing an even bigger task than that which confronted us in the drawn match. I know it is Trevor's job to take penalties but it is an unenviable task. In the event, we need not have worried. Trevor scored one of the best penalties ever seen in an All-Ireland final. He hit it into 'position A' right between the right-hand post and back stansion. It was a superb kick and even the Mayo keeper acknowledged it. As he gathered the ball from the net, the keeper could be seen throwing up his arms as if acknowledging that there was nothing he could have done to save it. Not even Shay Given could have saved it. Relief once more that we had clawed our way back! There was a lot of injury time added on because of the schmozzle at the start. That gave Mayo the chance to extend their lead following a needless free which we gave away. We trailed 1–6 to 1–2 at half-time. The question now was could we raise ourselves again for one more supreme effort which would overhaul an almost never-ending Mayo lead?

No doubt the vast majority of spectators missed an incident in that first half. I first heard about it after the match when a few of our players and supporters were discussing it. If you do happen to have the tape of that final, then fast-forward to the 32nd minute of the first half. It is a fairly funny incident but I would say that at the time, it was far from comical for Meath's John McDermott. In a 'hop-ball' situation, the referee was about to throw the ball up between a Meath and Mayo player. Mayo's David Brady and Meath's McDermott are side by side. As the referee was just about to throw it up, you can clearly see Brady slide his hand under John's 'arse' and start to pat him! He was obviously trying to wind him up for some reason. Perhaps he felt like many others that John should have been sent off along with McHale. There he was, trying to get John to swing a punch at him. He was provoking him in order to try and get him sent off. All I can say is, fair play to John for keeping his head and not reacting.

During the half-time talk, we were told the same as always. We were to go for every ball, we were not to panic and again we had the advantage of the wind. The breeze was so strong in that second period that it aided our cause enormously. Their keeper was struggling to reach the Mayo midfield and as a result, we got off to a flyer which was just what we needed. Colm Brady had moved into the centre to partner with 'Boots' going into the half-forward berth. So we had the benefit of three big men and it began to work in our favour. We scored three quick points and so we now only trailed by the minimum.

On a personal note, I am unable to look back on the two matches with any degree of comfort or even fondness. They were not great games by any means. In the second half, so frustrated at not seeing enough of the ball, I boiled over. By looking at what I did – the body language, so to speak – it tells you how I was feeling. During a break in play, I knocked the ball out of a Mayo player's hands and was very lucky the referee did not call me over. Something else that really frustrates me is when players deliberately slow the game down or when they refuse to give back the ball after the referee has awarded you a set-piece. Again they are winding the opposition up or wasting valuable time which is often not added on at the end of the game. These are other things the match officials and indeed the rule-makers in the GAA should do something about.

Martin Sheridan pointed a good free and so Mayo went two clear, 1–7 to 1–5. Ten minutes into the second half, they brought on Fallon. It was a good move by the Mayo selectors. He is another big man and obviously they were trying to come to terms with our midfield, who were now getting on top. Seeing as we got off to a great start on resuming, I felt they should have introduced him earlier, perhaps at the break. Even at that fairly early stage in the second-half, I sensed they were beginning to show signs of cracking. They were taking a lot out of the ball with all their hand-passing movements. This along with their spoiling tactics was designed to slow the clock right down. They could not wait for the final whistle to come.

For so long Mayo were the better side and had us running around at sixes and sevens. But now with 20 or so minutes to go, we had a real match on the cards. Tommy Dowd and Giles were keeping Mayo on their toes. At this period in the second half, the 1996 final really started in earnest and it was only then that we saw a good game of football. We hit three points and they also scored three so still the gap remained at two. Then came the turning point and at long last I got involved in the game. I won a free close to their goal and I knew that Tommy Dowd was ahead of me. I took it quickly and it found its way into his path. Tommy then showed great determination to get the ball into the net at all costs. For the first time in both matches we were ahead by a point, 2–8 to 1–10.

It was not the greatest goal you will ever see at Croke Park, but Mayo were shell-shocked. Nonetheless, they hit back almost at once and it was level. With under 10 minutes to go, it was anybody's All-Ireland. Then Mayo seemed to crack again and raise the white flag. Instead of going all out for it, they slowed the game down and started to waste time. Their players were feigning injury and, as a result of all that needless negativity, we sensed victory was there for the taking. It is very hard to understand the reason why Mayo were resorting to this baffling behaviour. I mean to say it was not as if there was a minute to go and they were looking for the clock to save them. I sensed this from Mayo in the early part of the second half when we scored quick points. Then they resorted to it again for almost all of the last 10 minutes of the game.

I will never forget what happened next. Trevor Giles, who had a great game, was the man who made it happen. He won a tackle to dispossess a Mayo player and his pass found its way to Brendan Reilly. From a very narrow angle, Brendan scored a really magnificent point. We now went back in front by a single point, 2–9 to 1–11. The last couple of minutes were intense. Mayo now had to come out of their shell and summon all of their energies for one last burst. But the next chance was to come our way. Meath were awarded a free, albeit from a good distance out. If Trevor popped this one over then it would be the insurance point and Mayo would need a goal to win.

Trevor missed the chance but still there was time for more drama. Mayo were now looking like condemned men but in a last-gasp attack laid siege on our goal. 'Boots' stupidly lost possession to John Casey who had a great chance of equalising for Mayo. He had an easy point at his mercy but he elected to pass the ball across and the chance was lost. Seconds later, Pat McEnaney blew the very final whistle. We were jubilant while Mayo slumped back shattered. I had won an All-Ireland and it was an unbelievable feeling. We had looked dead and buried in both games, but somehow managed to dig in and then claw our way out.

The celebrations began on the pitch and I had to laugh at Brian Smyth running as fast as he could to give Tommy Dowd his false teeth! As a youngster, Tommy lost his front teeth, which would have looked far from nice on television. After all, as our captain he would not have wanted to give the victory speech with a wide, toothless mouth.

It was an unreal feeling and then all the crowd spilled onto the pitch. You could have been killed in the crush that followed! I know that the GAA powers have largely put a stop to these scenes. It is all part of the All-Ireland tradition but I suppose safety is of paramount importance today. I can understand why the fans run on and they deserve to be part of the glory. The dressing-room was an even worse place to be. You could hardly move in there. It was packed with family, friends and supporters. We were on a real high and I did not want it to end. It was without doubt the highlight of my career and one of the greatest days of my life.

Celebrations continued well into the night. We adjourned to the Davenport Hotel for the winner's banquet. All of Meath must have been in there! In fact, the next day we were due at a function in Kilmainham but it was moved to Croke Park's Cusack Stand because of the sheer volume of support. I will always remember looking out over Croke Park as we watched Tommy Dowd lift the Sam Maguire. You could not see a blade of grass for all our supporters out on the pitch. The feeling of great pride overwhelmed me as I saw all the banners and smiles on the happy faces. Incidently, a very funny thing happened on the way into Croke Park for the function in the Cusack Stand. I was standing beside Tommy who had the cup in his hands. Imagine our shock and surprise when the security guards, having failed to recognise him, would not let us in because we were ticketless! Thankfully, it was all sorted out eventually.

After a meal at Croke Park, we began our journey home through Meath. First stop was Kepak, the headquarters of our sponsors in Clonee, outside Dublin. Kepak are a meat processing company and at the plant they had a real live bull painted in the Meath colours! The Sam Maguire Cup was then placed triumphantly on his back and people took photographs of the occasion.

We continued on into Dunboyne, Dunshaughlin, Dunderry, Trim and ended up in Navan. I was amazed at the crowds there after such a long day. It was well after midnight and we were all probably feeling the effects of the day. Many of them had been waiting there since ten o'clock and our spirits were lifted at that lovely sight. In Meath we have always had such great and loyal fans.

Since 1994 and the great League win over Armagh, I had experienced nothing but heartbreak. The most painful were the defeats by Dublin in the Leinster in 1993, 1994 and 1995. Now there I was with the ultimate prize and the one I had dreamed about since I was a kid. I now had the complete set of All-Irelands at Minor, U-21 and Senior as well as Leinster, National League and Club titles.

Sparing a thought for Mayo, I have said already that I find it hard to understand their play and their tactics in the second period of that replay. I can only think that it was lack of experience of the big match atmosphere. There is no question in my mind, and many Meath fans will openly admit it, they were the better side in both matches. When I was managing the Sam Maguire pub in Dublin, many Mayo people would come in and have a drink from time to time. They ribbed me about how 'lucky' we were in 1996 and I think they were always shocked to hear me agreeing with them! All sport is littered with hard luck stories. They may have been the better side and played the better football, but Meath have always played for the full 70 minutes. In the end, that is what won us the title. Mayo built up big leads in both games, but failed to hold their handsome advantage. If they had played for the full time, they would have won the All-Ireland in 1996.

Later in the year, Trevor Giles was named Footballer of the Year and that crowned a great year for Meath and also for Trevor. He was a colossus in both matches and we will always remember his great penalty that brought us back from the brink of defeat. Winning an All-Ireland Senior medal is what every footballer strives for. Some really outstanding players never even get the chance to play in a major final, never mind holding the Sam Maguire. The broken-hearted Meath players in Malahide back in 1991 were now distant memories. And now that I had tasted the sweetest success of all, I felt that there were more All-Irelands to be won.

# 6 Up, Up the Aisle

The gloss was taken off our great All-Ireland win for me when I received a threatening letter shortly afterwards. The letter arrived at the family home in Kentstown about two weeks after our title win. I knew instantly it didn't contain money as it was not a brown envelope! On a more serious note, it did contain a nasty message but, after digesting it, we just laughed it off and threw it in the bin. It sounded more like a bit of begrudgery than anything to notify the Gardaí about. On a white envelope postmarked in Drogheda, the letter was addressed to Graham Geraghty, Meath Footballer, Navan. Enclosed on a small piece of paper were the words: HANG YOUR ALL-IRELAND MEDAL OVER YOUR FIRST BORN'S NECK AND TELL THEM HOW THE WEST WAS WON. THE MEATH TEAM ARE THUGS.

You always read about people getting 'hate mail' but this was the first time I had encountered it. Never having received any mail of a bad nature, I did not really stop to consider who might have sent it. The handwriting was definitely that of an adult, possibly a man's as it was rough looking. However, just because we had beaten Mayo, it did not necessarily mean it came from a Mayo supporter. It could have come from anywhere.

Nonetheless, 1996 was the year I could proudly hang an All-Ireland medal around my neck. It is a great feeling knowing that you have achieved your boyhood dream. Many great footballers never even get the chance to play in an All-Ireland final. Now that I had helped Meath to the title, however, I was hungry for more. That said, there was another priority which I felt deserved greater attention. As previously mentioned, I benefited greatly from growing up in a house full of women. In fact I found that I could relate very well with the opposite sex. Of course, it does help enormously when you are a footballer with Meath! There are always women around especially after the big matches – though I must stress we are neither big nor rich enough yet to label these women as 'groupies'!

In the early part of my footballing career, there was never any serious relationship. Besides, I had more than enough to contend with. I had my big ambitions with Meath which involved a lot of hard training and dedication. There was also the matter of building a career for myself. This proved to be very difficult and confusing. After very brief spells as a salesman, during which I tried my hand at selling insurance and even mineral water, I decided it was not for me. Eventually, I got into the pub trade and felt really at home. At first I managed a few small pubs in Meath and Dublin before settling at Doran's Bar in Athboy in April 2002. Doran's is owned by wealthy businessman, Mr Patrick Kerrigan. He is also involved in Cortown GFC and his son Colm is a member of the Meath Minor team.

It is peculiar how so many footballers become managers or publicans in the licensed trade. If people think it is because the job is easy or a so-called 'cushy number', then they are hugely mistaken. Doran's is a very modern pub and a venue for bands who travel from all over the country. All that has to be arranged and catered for along with the day-to-day running of staff. And when you add in football training, it is no easy life.

Consequently, women were very much down the list in terms of my main ambitions. That is not to say that I ignored them. On the contrary, like many red-blooded males, it was very much the opposite. I partied and had a very good time when the occasion arose, but I never had any firm plans to settle down.

All of that changed suddenly when I met Amanda Egan from Athboy in 1995. At the time she was a part-time model with the well-known Assets Modelling Agency in Dublin. I remember meeting her the first time in Robbie O'Malley's pub in Navan. Needless to say, it was a very popular pub with Meath footballers and fans.

A year after we first met, I decided to take her out for a first anniversary dinner. I booked a table for two at Kilcarn House which is a well-known restaurant just outside Navan. I had only one thing on my mind. I felt that the time was right and that Amanda was the one for me. During the dinner, I proposed. She accepted much to my absolute joy. However, on a night of great joy for Amanda and myself, unknown to me a terrible and tragic accident had occurred. My best friend, Leslie Crinion, was killed in a traffic accident at a notorious black spot in Slane, as previously mentioned. It was all such a strange set of circumstances with me due to line out in the Leinster final the next day.

The following year, on 27 September 1997 and just over two years after we first met, I married Amanda. It was a lovely ceremony held in St James' Church, Athboy. The only thing missing from the day was Leslie. He would have been my best man had he lived to see the day. Kevin Clarke, affectionately known as 'Clarkey', did the honours for me instead. Like Leslie, Kevin was the brother I never had and did a great job as my best man. The entire Meath football panel were also present in a guest list of over 400. At the reception afterwards, there were three times that number! Following the wedding, Amanda and myself went on our honeymoon to Africa. We went to Kenya which is such a beautiful country and full of lovely, friendly people. As you can imagine, the weather was very hot which was just what we needed at that time of the year. Altogether, we spent three weeks there, mostly in the beautiful city of Mombasa.

I was very happy that everything had gone well with the wedding. Although, there was one funny incident that happened beforehand. When we sat down to plan the wedding a year before, we booked it for Sunday, 27th September. At the time, that date was a week after the All-Ireland final. Sometime after that, the GAA fixtures were changed for some reason. The new date of the final only happened to fall on our planned wedding day. I was really glad we did not make it to the final. It would have been a hell of a difficult decision!

\* \* \* \* \* \*

Earlier in that summer of 1997, we started out on the road to defending our Leinster and All-Ireland titles. We had a very tough opening match against Dublin. This is never a nice situation for two big counties – one giant was going to fall at the first hurdle. Nevertheless, we were very determined it was not going to be us. Dublin had caused us so much heartache and hassle in the previous years. Then we made our big breakthrough against them in 1996 which more than made up for our previous bad loss to them. That was very important for us and mentally we now had an advantage over them. They were no longer our bogey team in Leinster and it was crucial for us to prove ourselves against them once more.

As it turned out, we were on fire that day in mid-June. The Dubs did not know what had hit them. We were scoring points from all over the field. Even then, we only had a lead of a couple of points at the break. In the dressing-room we talked of how we expected them to come at us in droves after the interval. They were like a pack of rats cornered in their own yard and would not go down without a fight. Our expectations proved correct. The Dubs came out full of energy and drive. The match, which we had started so brightly, was now a ding-dong battle. I remember we were leading by three points when they were awarded a penalty in the last minute. A goal for them would mean a replay and we would have been deflated.

When they were given the penalty, I also recall a sort of lull. It seemed like a big pause in play as none of the Dublin players was sure what to do next. It seemed as if no player wanted to step up and take the responsibility. Dublin have had a troubled history in the art of penalty-taking. Over the years, they have missed some very crucial kicks, and players like Charlie Redmond and Keith Barr immediately spring to mind. Eventually, Paul Bealin stepped up to take the all-important kick. I think he was chosen because he was fairly handy at soccer. It seemed like an eternity between the decision and the taking of the penalty. In front of an expectant Croke Park, Bealin had the chance to give Dublin a second bite at us. Bealin ran up, shot and hit it very well. It was destined for the bottom corner of the net but at the last second it struck the crossbar. He sank straight down to his knees with his head held in his hands. It was agony for him and for Dublin but a huge let-off for us. We won the game by 1–13 to 1–10. There was a massive sense of relief afterwards. In truth, we deserved to win that game. I do not know what it is with Dublin and penalties. All I can say is that because of their history, there will now always be a little bit more pressure on future Dublin spot-kicks. They will always have to contend with the ghosts of Redmond, Barr, Bealin and Co.

It was a very sweet feeling for all of us. We had beaten Dublin twice in successive years. I felt that after our Leinster and All-Ireland wins, we never truly got the recognition we deserved. It was always a case of 'Mayo should have won' or 'Mayo let huge lead slip' or even 'McHale was a big loss'. Maybe because we were not given much credit for our win over Mayo, the glory of that win seemed to die as quickly as it arrived. There was no real praise from the general media for our battling back from the brink of defeat. It was all about Mayo. Now I felt we had finally silenced everybody. Our double over Dublin was a case of saying that we were the big force in Leinster. Furthermore, we were here to stay.

Next up in Leinster was a clash with the Lilywhites of Kildare. They were an emerging county under the great Kerry legend, Mick O'Dwyer. Kildare were also a young side obviously looking forward to the challenge. They could measure their potential against the All-Ireland Champions. A match such as this is always dangerous because of those very reasons. They had everything to gain and very little to lose. I remember it as a very scrappy match. Kildare are a running team, which was never really to our liking. It has always been difficult for us to get used to Kildare's running and hand-passing style of play. We like to get at the ball unlike Kildare who have it over your head and from one end of the pitch to the other. At times in that match, we had players way out of position. Such is the nature of the style of play involved, we also were at sixes and sevens. In the end we managed to come out of a tricky situation with a draw. It was a close run thing but we avoided the slip. The replay gave us time to deal with the tactics required to beat them and we were confident of having the right approach for the replay.

In that first game, Martin Lynch had given them a dream start. He scored a goal in the very first minute so I suppose we did well to come back from that. Facing an uphill struggle, we clawed our way back and grabbed a last minute equaliser. Even then it was not over. Kildare had a chance in the dying seconds to win it but the scores remained tied at 0–12 to 1–9. That Kildare chance came from a '45'. A little like Paul Bealin in the previous game, Kildare relied on

Niall Buckley. As he stepped up to take it, I did not expect him to miss. Perhaps realising the enormity of his kick, Niall also felt the pressure. His kick dropped short, was cleared and we lived to fight another day.

In our first two matches in Leinster, I had fairly quiet games. Two weeks later in the replay with Kildare, I was in the thick of it all. They were now cocky and had an air of confidence about them. They knew after the first match that they had the beating of us. They were strutting their stuff and it all proved too much. It was also yet another frustrating match for me. Kildare were proving to be a very tough nut to crack and I could not get to grips with their constant running. I remember coming along the end-line and fisting the ball back to one of my team-mates. Out of nowhere, Davy Dalton came in on me and elbowed me in the side of the head. As a result, we did not even get so much as a free.

After that, I became more and more frustrated. All I was doing was running around and not much else. I was desperately trying to get into the game. As if things were not already bad, they got a lot worse. I recall getting the ball and Glenn Ryan tugging at my jersey. In fact a video of the game shows my shirt fully stretched from him tugging at it. Then he got hold of the ball so I deliberately tripped him, believing that he had retrieved it wrongly. I had been fouled twice in the game and on both occasions justice was not done. Suddenly the referee brandished the red card and sent me off. He saw it as malice on my part. I simply could not believe it. With all the treatment I was getting, I was the one who was off. I thought it was grossly unfair. In the dug-out, all the lads were full of sympathy. They tried to make me feel better but it did not work. We were struggling out there and now reduced to 14 men.

Sean Boylan then played a really brilliant trump card. He brought on Jody Devine and the move worked a treat. Jody immediately kicked into gear. He hit three points in quick succession to level the game. With time nearly up, he kicked us ahead but just as we thought we had snatched it, Paul McCormack levelled for Kildare. Jody actually had a chance to win that game. At the Canal End, he let fly but it was just a matter of inches wide. The game finished in another draw, 2–20 to their 3–17 – an unbelievable score and a very high scoring game. I cannot say that we deserved another crack at Kildare. They were the better team once more but again you have to allow for our never-say-die spirit. It was also an inspired substitution by Sean, and Jody Devine really deserved the headlines he got in the newspapers the following day.

The third match, and second replay with Kildare, was full of incident. After Kildare's Davy Dalton was sent off early on, we raced into a six-point lead. Then Mark O'Reilly struck Kildare's Brian Murphy and both players were sent off. Despite having 13 men, they fought back and reduced the deficit to four points as we went in leading by 0–9 to 0–5 at half-time. In effect, the turning point came early in the second half when they were awarded a penalty. The ball was struck powerfully but went over the bar, giving them only a point out of it. Their heads went down a little after that. Despite the fact that we also finished with 13 men, as Fay was sent off for striking Martin Lynch, we finally ended their brave challenge on a scoreline of 1–12 to 1–10.

Something I will never forget from that match with Kildare was the shock most of us felt at the omission of Jody Devine. After bringing back Micky McQuillan instead of Conor Martin in 1994, Sean Boylan's decision here was even more puzzling. Had we lost to Kildare, I think Sean would have had a lot to answer for. Even after his master stroke in bringing on Jody in the second game, leaving him out of the third match was a stunner. Nobody knows why Jody Devine was dropped again. Only Sean and his selectors can answer that. However, I do know that many of the players were really disgusted with the way he was treated. Almost single-handedly, Jody had hauled us out of a deep hole in the first replay. Surely he had done enough to keep his place. He should have been rewarded because, without him, we would not have beaten Kildare. To make matters even worse, and perhaps more insulting to Jody, was the fact that we used three subs that day and he was still left sitting in the dug-out. After that game I saw Jody and he was very down. In fact, he was so angry he wanted to hang up his boots there and then. I felt that the name of Jody Devine after his magnificent display in the replay should have been the first on the team-sheet.

In the middle of August, we faced Offaly in the Leinster final. However, after the Kildare saga, we were left a very weakened side. Darren Fay, Mark O'Reilly and myself were all suspended for the final. Even worse for Fay and O'Reilly was their month's ban from the GAA's Disciplinary Committee for 'striking'. Another huge loss was Martin O'Connell. In the win over Kildare, Martin was moved into the full-back position and did a really good job in trying to shore up the defence. With our entire full-back line missing, we faced a huge task. We fielded a weary and very weakened side and Offaly would surely try and work on that weakness.

Kevin Cahill was drafted into our side. He was put into the centre-half position where he had never played before. Enda McManus was also brought in. This was far from an ideal preparation for a Leinster final. It was all a bit of a nightmare. Now on top of our weariness and weakened team, we were unsettled and inexperienced. I can vividly remember one example which really illustrated our problems. Offaly's Roy Malone collected a ball on the sideline and must have ran fully 50 yards with it before slotting it to the net. The defence was frail and he had waltzed through virtually unchallenged to score a goal.

All things considered, I thought we actually played quite well in that final. Brendan Reilly from Carnaross had a great game for us. He scored seven points but it was Offaly's three goals in a golden spell which ended our challenge, 3–17 to 1–15. Fair dues to Offaly who were crowned Leinster Champions. I doubt they would have hit three goals if we had our full-back line of Fay, O'Reilly and O'Connell playing. It was a very disappointing end to our hopes of retaining our titles. However, the pain was eased somewhat by realising that we were dealt a cruel hand at a crucial stage.

\*\*\*\*\*\*

In December 1997, the best thing possible happened. My wife Amanda became pregnant with our first child. Already I knew that 1998 was going to be a brilliant year. If all went according to plan, I was to become a father for the first time. The baby was due to be born in September so all going well, I was hoping that it would be a case of double joy and celebrations.

In 1998, Brendan Reilly, who played so well in the defeat against Offaly, was made captain, taking over the reigns from Tommy Dowd. The first round draw pitted us against Offaly and so a chance to get revenge. Darren Fay and Mark O'Reilly were back on the team and everything was gelling nicely into place. We were almost at full strength and could not wait for the Offaly game.

Revenge is sweet and we simply played Offaly off the park. I played well in that game as did all of us. Getting your own back is always a great feeling and it certainly is a big part of Gaelic Games. The most pleasing aspect of our performance in destroying Offaly was, somewhat ironically, our defence. They only scored one point against our full-back line which proved our previous arguments and excuses. Darren Fay was superb. We also scored three goals and I was delighted to have played a part in helping set them up. Aside from gaining revenge, the 12-point win proved we were where we wanted to be. I have always said that if we had always had our full 15, then we would have won more titles. In previous years against Offaly and Dublin, we were really blighted by bad luck.

At the end of June 1998, we played the Wee County of Louth and not for the first time, this match ended in high controversy. We survived by the skin of our teeth to edge out Louth by a point, 0–15 to 1–11. However, many others will say that we survived thanks to the generosity of the referee, Brian White. In the opening seconds, Louth got off to a flyer. They sent over the opening point and after that, we were struggling to keep up with them. They were playing way above themselves and what we expected of them. When we finally woke up and realised we were in a match, we had a bit of a mountain to climb. One of Louth's best players of the modern era, Stefan White, scored a great goal. That score helped them to a four-point lead over us at the break. Louth did not rest there. The second-half had barely begun, when they sent over another point. We now found ourselves with a huge task and trailed by five points.

When the history of Gaelic football is written one day, it will no doubt show that Meath were the 'Comeback Kings'. I have lost count, as I am sure many supporters have, of the amount of times we came from behind to win or draw. Like Jody Devine against Kildare in 1997, it was Tommy Dowd who came to our rescue. He sent over a hat-trick of points which brought us back into the game. This obviously had an effect on the Louth team and a few minutes after Tommy's third point, Louth were left totally stumped by a controversial incident. The ball came to me and from a fair distance out, I decided to have a go. I remember the ball was extremely high in the air and it was very close to the post as it flew over.

Nevertheless, I was confident I had scored and then an umpire waved it wide. I was furious and raced to the referee to complain. Thankfully he over-ruled the umpire. In fairness, the referee like myself was in a direct line with the post. An umpire can be at a disadvantage as he has to look directly up and sometimes can be left confused. The ball was also unusually high that day and when it is way higher than the post, and especially when it is close to the post, it can be so hard to judge whether it is a point or a wide.

The referee is always up with the play and has a much better view of the shot. In the past there have been many incidents like this and there are likely to be many more in future. It is especially hard to call close shaves of this nature, especially in hurling, and this is another area that the Games Administrations should scrutinise. It is also not fair on the counties involved as they are always left wondering.

Louth lost all of their momentum after that. Obviously it was on their minds and they found it hard to get on with the game and to concentrate. Tommy Dowd took full advantage and from having a handsome lead, they were three behind. To their great credit, they lifted themselves for one final effort. They got to within a point when the referee called time. As you would expect, Louth were in a rage at the final whistle.

The decision to overrule the umpire did not go down at all well. If you take away that decision, then it would have been a draw at the very least. There was talk of a re-match but that soon petered out. We were lucky to win. I thought we grossly underestimated Louth. We should not have done so. All matches at this level are tough and in some, the rivalry is fierce.

There was a huge time span before we lined up with Kildare in the Leinster final. After taking three matches to beat them the year before, we knew this was going to be tough. Kildare would also be hell-bent on revenge. They knew they had the beating of us and perhaps felt a little aggrieved and unlucky to have been beaten by us. I have already said that I dislike their style of play. It can make for good television and is pleasing to the eye, but when you are playing against it, the constant running and chasing can take its toll. Furthermore, it can be very energy-sapping and I know that it took a lot out of us the previous year. But we were very confident and after a barren and fruitless 1997, we were determined to show our true worth and our form of 1996.

Our new captain was Brendan Reilly but almost immediately things started to go wrong for him. He came off injured against Offaly and his injury resurfaced against Louth when he played on through the pain barrier. In the Leinster final, he was sent off midway through the second half and that proved to be the turning point. Until that moment, we were sticking with Kildare and matching them point for point in a close match. Down to 14 men, Kildare's style of play reaped rewards. They really exposed us and used their extra man to great advantage. To make matters worse, we then lost Trevor Giles who went off injured 10 minutes from the end.

The Lilywhites went on to win the Leinster title beating us by five points. For the second successive year we had to endure the heartbreak of losing a Leinster final. It really hurt especially knowing that we had lost four out of the last five finals. After this defeat it was going to be very hard to pick ourselves up. When Dublin beat us in 1994 and 1995, we bounced back in 1996. We all felt that was going to be the springboard for us. Even allowing for injuries and all the bad luck, it was so hard to take losing to Offaly and Kildare after finally getting the better of Dublin.

From a neutral's point of view, I suppose everyone was delighted to see those two counties win a Leinster. I take my hat off to them as well and it was lovely to see Micko finally bring success to Kildare. Despite the knockers, they persisted with their style and it paid off. Micko must have been so proud of his side and of the fact that he had brought Kildare their first title since the early Fifties.

The dream continued for Kildare when they beat Kerry by a point to reach their first All-Ireland final for over 60 years. At least we had some comfort in knowing that the team that had beaten us in Leinster went on to beat mighty Kerry and reach the final. All the focus was now on Mick O'Dwyer. Could the legend deliver the Sam Maguire to Kildare just as he had done on countless number of occasions as a player and manager with Kerry? I was at Croke Park for that 1998 All-Ireland final between Kildare and Galway. All year Kildare's attacking and running style had reaped rewards and in the first half of the final, they had a handsome lead. For years many people doubted the new set up with Micko but now the impossible dream was about to unfold. Galway had other ideas and must have had their ears bashed by manager John O'Mahony at the interval. They came out in the second half and absolutely blitzed Kildare. It was the real classic case of 'a game of two halves'. At the end, the men from west of the Shannon had triumphed and Kildare's dreams were in tatters.

A few weeks before that final, my year ended in the very best possible way. On 10th September, my wife Amanda gave birth to our first child at Our Lady of Lourdes Hospital in Drogheda. Our child was a beautiful baby girl and, at Amanda's suggestion, we named her Sophia. Without any doubt it was one of the happiest and proudest days of my life. It was such an unbelievable high that it is so hard to put the feeling into words. The disappointing season we had really was so insignificant in comparison to that magical moment. You can win all the medals and honours you like, but there is nothing like having your own flesh and blood.

# 7 Down, Down Under

During the final trial of matches to select the Ireland team for the 1998 International Rules at Croke Park, Colm O'Rourke took me to one side. He was brutally honest when he looked me in the eye and said: 'Graham, look, you're going to have to play very well today to make the panel.' Despite the fact that it was early October and it was coming to the end of a disappointing year for me, I was determined to make it on to the team. It's fair to say that every player's dream is to put on the national colours and represent your country regardless of the sport you play.

In the event, I did not play well and failed to make the team. There were no excuses. Other players had longer and more tiring campaigns than I had and made it nonetheless. I was also given an extra incentive by Colm with his ultimatum but still I did not perform. Coming on the back of a couple of disappointing seasons with Meath, it was yet another blow. I did learn a lot from the trials, however, and seeing the enthusiasm of the rest of the lads really made me more determined to succeed.

The following year, I was rewarded for my endeavours. I was given a place in the Ireland team to play in Australia. I was thrilled and could not wait to pull on the green jersey. But my great joy soon turned into a horror story. On a chilly autumn morning in 1999, spirits were high as we boarded the plane at Dublin Airport en route to Australia. By the time we had arrived, I knew the meaning of 'Down Under'. Australia really is at the far side of the world and it took us a whopping 27 hours of travelling before we finally arrived!

The First Test was to be played on a Friday but in the meantime we had a warm-up match scheduled for the preceding Tuesday.

That match would enable us to get used to this new and different ball game and we could also run off the jet lag. The friendly was also to be played in the same venue as the First Test, i.e. the world famous Melbourne Cricket Ground. It was also vitally important to get the feel of that stadium. Our opponents on the Tuesday were known as 'The Students'. In fact, they were part of a special Australian U-18 academy that helps nurture future talent. Most of the side we were due to play had played in Ireland the previous Easter. They had been part of an Australian U-17 side that toured Ireland and dished out a heavy hammering to an Irish Minor side in the process.

The Melbourne Cricket Ground under floodlights is a sight to behold. It is truly massive, making you feel so small within its confines. Taking to the field that night, many of us sported black lines directly beneath our eyes. The lines came from a kind of oil or paint designed to protect the eyes from the very strong glare of the floodlights. It works by deflecting the powerful light away from the eyes and is used most commonly in American football.

In the match itself, the young Australian side made a very impressive start. The game was played over 23-minute periods and once we got the hang of things in that first period, we really started to enjoy ourselves. We lead by 20–7 and I recall setting up a goal, worth six points, for Dermot Earley. In the second period, Peter Canavan came on and really made his presence felt. He hit two great overs worth three points each and then capped it off with a goal. Entering the final period, and leading by 44–15, we never looked back and got even stronger. I set up Dessie Dolan for our third and final goal as we ended up easy winners. Colm O'Rourke was very happy and the visiting Australian coach, Dermot Brereton, went away with plenty of food for thought. Although we were expected to win, I do not think they expected us to do it as convincingly as the 66–17 scoreline showed.

There were some outstanding performances in that friendly. Anthony Tohill, Ciaran Whelan, Darren Fay, Dessie Dolan and Dermot Earley were all excellent. But the real star on view was Peter Canavan. I did my bit as well, scoring 10 points. I set up two goals and I also hit the post. Sadly for me, and for the Irish camp, the 'story' of that match was about to unfold. It was to be the story of the entire Rules series that year and the beginning of a traumatic nightmare for me. In the course of that friendly, I felt that some of the Australian tackling was brutal. The physical nature of the game in Australia is only too well known to me. It is, however, not part of our game here and seeing that there are compromises in the rules of both codes, there should have been something done about it.

Throughout the game, I noticed one guy in particular, who seemed to be flooring every Irish guy he could get his hands on. For students, they were all big guys and this fellow was no exception. From my recollection of events, Ciaran McManus had the ball and was then absolutely flattened by an Aussie who just ran into him. I was really annoyed by this and in a split second of real anger said to him: 'You fuck off, you black cunt.' Similar remarks are said in every GAA, soccer and rugby match at all levels in Ireland, so I thought nothing of it at the time. We all just dusted ourselves down, calmed down and got on with the game. But for the intrusion of the media afterwards, I would probably have forgotten what I said to that player.

As the hooter signified the end of the game, Colm O'Rourke told me that the referee had overheard my remark. Moreover, the referee had informed the Australian manager, Jim Stynes. The wisest course of action, according to Colm, was for me to apologise to the Australian player. So I duly followed his instruction. Damian Cupido was the name of the Australian player I had verbally abused. He was 17 and actually born in South Africa. I told him that I was sorry for the remark, to which he replied: 'Don't worry about it, mate.' In fairness to him and to Jim Stynes and the Australian camp, that was the end of the matter as far as they were concerned. In fact, in one newspaper, Cupido was reported as saying: 'They didn't really hurt me. They were only words and I am the kind of fella who gets on with things.' He also admitted his part in the physical challenge on Ciaran McManus, by saying: 'I hit him really hard and that is when his team-mate walked past and said that [the remark].'

Unlike their Australian counterparts, the matter was far from over where the Irish were concerned. Subsequently, I felt that the Irish media and the GAA officials handled the situation very badly. Colm O'Rourke, who had been given a two-year contract by the GAA to take charge of the team in 1998 and 1999, was very angry with officials. After that, morale in the Irish camp was low, which obviously deeply affected Colm. He was as shattered and disappointed by the whole affair as I was. However, things were to get a lot worse.

The next day, Wednesday, the Irish tour manager, Albert Fallon, approached me. He told me that the media had got wind of the story and were going to break it. His words came with a warning that it was no ordinary story but front-page news. To prepare Amanda and my parents, he advised me to ring home to let them know the truth of what was to unfold. Even then, I thought Albert was exaggerating. With the Aussies forgetting about it, I did not think for one moment that the Irish media would take such an interest. If anything, I felt that it would all die down. How wrong I was. The gravity of the situation finally dawned on me when I was summoned to a meeting with the GAA.

It was on a Thursday that I faced a group of GAA officials in a room at the five-star Carlton Crest Hotel in Melbourne. Also present with me were Colm and my Meath team-mate and Irish captain John McDermott, both of whom really pushed for me. Colm said that I should not be punished. As far as he was concerned, he had a big match to get on with and that the entire matter should be put to bed. John McDermott also spoke very highly of me. I felt like a man on trial for a serious crime. Nothing John and Colm said could have saved me, however. The GAA officials did not even look me in the eye and I knew that they had already made up their minds before we even went into that room. So I do not know why we spent three hours in there. It was just a question of what sort of punishment befitted my 'crime'.

By now I knew the situation was very serious. In fact, I was becoming so worried about the punishment, I could not sleep for two nights. I was tossing and turning and was stressed out about the whole affair. Words spat out in the heat of the moment were now coming back to haunt me. My biggest fear was to be sent home in disgrace. If that happened, then I did not know how I could handle it. To have been sent home alone on a long journey, while all my team-mates were still in Australia, was a chilling thought. When the decision finally came, you could say that I was very relieved not to have been sent home. I was banned for the First Test which was played the next day. Even so, I was still gutted. I had come halfway around the world to play for my country and could not wait to get started, especially since I had played well in that friendly. It was very disheartening to have to sit it out.

The GAA officials actually went to great lengths to explain fully their decision to me. In fairness, and when you consider I could have been sent home or even banned from both Tests, they had chosen the softer option. Some of their reasoning stood up and because of that, I will never blame them fully for the entire episode. In essence, they said that the Australian authorities were not really going to stand up and punish a foreign player. In other words, I was not one of their own and they felt it was not their job to act against me.

Earlier in the year, the Australian Football League (AFL) had fined one of their players AUS$10,000 for a similar offence. They termed it 'racial vilification' and were taking a very tough stance on issues such as racism. Therefore, the GAA felt that they had to act accordingly. They had to hand me some form of punishment that would seem appropriate. I attribute full blame for what happened subsequently to the members of the Irish media who were present.

Following the decision, press statements were then prepared by the GAA and myself, which were then released to the media. My statement read as follows:

*During the course of the friendly against the Australian Institute of Sport AFL Academy team on Tuesday night, I made a comment against my immediate opponent in the heat of the game. Immediately after the game it was brought to my attention that my remark would have caused serious offence to my opponent and I immediately went to the player involved and to the Australian authorities and conveyed my sincere apologies and regret at the remark.*

*I understood from the reaction of the player and the AFL officials, that the matter was closed and I want to reiterate my sincere apology for my remark and my condemnation and abhorrence of any remarks of a racial nature. I also want to apologise again to both Associations for the consequences of my remarks.*

The GAA officials who interviewed me were the then president Joe McDonagh; president-elect, Sean McCague; director general, Liam Mulvihill as well as Ulster chairman, Danny Murphy and Leinster chairman, Seamus Aldridge. They also issued a fairly long statement, the essence of which was:

> *It was accepted that Graham Geraghty was most contrite and sincere in his apology. It was also noted that he was repentant in the immediate aftermath of the incident.*

[The statement went on to say]

> *However, it was felt that the GAA should take a sanction against the player and it was therefore agreed by the management representatives that the team management be directed not to select the player for the First Test on Friday night. The GAA wishes to place on record its condemnation of any racist remark by players and officials and our regrets and apologies have been conveyed to Damian Cupido, his family and the AFL for the remarks made in this instance.*

In the aftermath Colm O'Rourke apologised to the Irish media for deliberately misleading them. In answering a question after the friendly, Colm originally responded by saying that I had apologised for a 'rough tackle' on Damian Cupido. He admitted to misleading the media at the time because he did not think it was a 'big deal'. It was only later, he said, that he realised racism remarks are taken very seriously in Australia. Because he misled them, Colm also became a target of the media. In fact they also wanted him sent home along with me. Up until that point in my career, I never realised how mischievous and intrusive the Irish media can be.

At that time I was running a small pub called 'The Swan Inn', located in the small townland of Coolronan in Co Meath. While I was away in Australia, my wife Amanda was looking after it. Night and day she was bombarded with phone calls from the press. They even travelled to Coolronan to talk to locals in the hope of getting the feelings of local people. However, they were to go away very disappointed as everyone spoke highly of me. When locals did give a comment, they declined to be named. For their support at that very difficult time, I owe a debt of gratitude to the people of Coolronan,

Athboy, Navan and all over Meath. Indeed, Meath people have always been very good to me. No so the media. As well as causing a lot of harm to me, my family and friends, they caused huge disruption to the Ireland team in Australia.

Irish journalists were staying in the same hotel as the team in Melbourne. However, after the bad news which they spread about Colm and myself, all the players ignored them. The rest of the players were disgusted at their behaviour. In the end, they decided to boycott the Irish media and refused to give them any interviews. I am not saying that I did not want them to report the facts and to report what had happened. They had the right to report what occurred, but it was the headlines, the quotes and the mood or tone of what was written that separated the good journalists from the bad ones. In fact, there were some good, honest and hardworking scribes out there with us. Jim O'Sullivan of *The Examiner* actually came up to me and apologised for what was going on. He said that he had to cover the story but had nothing to do with the 'witch-hunt' against me. From the same newspaper, Brendan Mooney wrote a piece about me under the headline 'TROUBLED PLAYER FEARLESS AND FAIR'. Amid all the diatribe written about me it was nice to read words from someone who was trying to bring a little balance to my cause. To quote a few of Brendan's lines: 'his dynamic personality and his passion for the game of football hold him perpetually on the fringe. But his discipline has never been a problem'. In that same article, he quoted Brendan Cummins, Meath County Board PRO, as saying: 'Dissent would be more his problem and he has been known to question a decision or two. But you could never term him a physical player by any account'. The tabloid newspapers were the real culprits but there are also bad apples in the basket and *The Examiner* does not escape. Eamonn Sweeney wrote a piece under the headline, 'GERAGHTY SHOULD BE SENT HOME ON THE VERY FIRST PLANE'. That headline, coupled with what he wrote, smacked of sensationalism and was nothing short of attention-seeking.

Talking about sensational headlines that were hurtful to me and my family, it cannot get any bigger than the front page. On Friday, 8 October 1999, *The Irish Star* printed a happy photo of me and my young daughter Sophia on the front page under a headline: 'FROM HERO TO ZERO'. Under that banner headline, they printed a sub-headline which, even worse, read: 'GAA PLAYER CALLED AUSSIE A BLACK C**T'. There were pages and pages of negative material written in so many publications that you would have thought they had better and more important issues to write about.

Australian newspapers did not seem to be bothered with it at all. I remember trawling through them when I was out there and the only thing I saw was a tiny paragraph in one sports page. For a country renowned for taking such a tough stance on racism, I think that they at least got their priorities right. The Irish media should be ashamed of themselves over it all. I think it was one of their blackest days in Irish sports journalism. They went out there and deliberately got it wrong. Despite the fact that they knew everything was settled between myself, Damian Cupido, Jim Stynes and the AFL, they decided to pursue the story and loved every minute of their cheap and so-called scoop.

At the end of the day, I hold my hand up and admit that I was wrong. I made a racist remark. I apologised and was given a very fair punishment. Others may think differently, but sending me home would have been unjust. I feel that it is important at this stage to raise another point. When the Irish team travelled to Australia, never once were we warned about making racist or other remarks. It is vitally important that from now on that Irish teams going over to Australia need to be briefed on all these issues. The GAA, and indeed other sports bodies, would be very irresponsible not to take steps to try and ensure such an incident never happens again.

In finishing this subject, a rather humorous but serious piece appeared on a Gaelic Games internet site, 'An Fear Rua' (*www.anfearrua.com*) at the time, under the title: 'GEH' HUP YA BHOY YA GRAHAM!' I think you may enjoy reading this particular piece:

> *The lads – and indeed lassies – beyond in places like Fergie Maguire's pub in Kilmessan, in the County Meath, must have been a bit taken aback at the idea of Graham Geraghty being banned in Australia for calling Rules footballer Damian Cupido a black c**t.... after all, they've been calling each other that...or even worse, around Meath for many years...*

> *Indeed, many's the time on GAA business in the Royal County – for example, presenting trophies to camogie teams and the like –*

*An Fear Rua remarked to himself on the vile language that seems to be commonplace in the licensed premises of that county. He can recall another occasion in a Meath pub when literally every second word out of the mouth of one patron with his arms plonked on the counter was 'f\*\*\*\*n this' and 'f\*\*\*\*n that'. The same individual seemed to think that these verbal emissions were enormously hilarious, as he spluttered into his pint glass, and his behaviour brought no more than smiles of benevolent indulgence from the other customers. In any other part of the country the bar person would have warned him as to his behaviour and in a decent pub like the legendary Tom Maher's Moondarrig House below in Waterford City, he'd have been instantaneously barred for life.*

*All of the above is certainly not by way of making a case for the defence of Graham Geraghty... The fact that Graham may have grown up in a county where the words 'c\*\*t', 'f\*\*k', 's\*\*t' and 'b\*\*\*\*\*\*s' account for approximately 50 per cent of normal male converse is no justification for his actions in Australia.*

*An Fear Rua has no hesitation in going further. The fact that Graham is one of the nicest fellas you could meet in the thirty two counties of Ireland only serves to make his actions all the more shocking.... it is perhaps a great pity, as well as being something of a paradox, that one of the most decent stars of the modern gaelic football era has had to be the one to be sacrificed in order to make a simple point: there is no place whatsoever, good bad or indifferent – as An Fear Rua's old pal Albert Reynolds used to say – for even the slightest hint of racism in the GAA.*

*...We live, unfortunately, in a world of Sudans, Rwandas, East Timors and former Yugoslavias where murderous, virulent racism has been taken to extremes that might give pause to even some of the darker elements of Hitler's SS. It behoves all of us, in whatever small way we can, to combat this ugly phenomenon whenever it rears its ugly countenance. The action taken by the GAA in Australia is a small, but important, statement of leadership by 'd'Association'.*

*It is no more than An Fear Rua would have expected from a decent Galwayman like Joe McDonagh, who has shown on more*

*than one occasion during his term of office that his political
instincts are good, and that he recognises the fantastic leadership
role of the GAA in Irish society. As [they] might say up in the
pubs of Kilmessan or Oldcastle: 'Good man yerself Joe ...Even if
yer only a f\*\*\*\*\*g Galway b\*\*\*\*\*\*s!'.*

\*\*\*\*\*\*

I had to sit out the First Test because of the ban. However, there
was some satisfaction at seeing us record a marvellous 70–62 win.
Still, there is no substitute for playing and it was a pity I missed out
on what turned out to be an historic match. The crowd, in excess of
64,000, was a record attendance for a Series game at the time.

When the Second Test came around in Adelaide the following
week, I finally got the chance to pull on the green jersey. Australia
were trailing by eight points after the first game, so we knew they
were going to throw everything at us. Before we ran out on the
field, some guy gave us the black paint to put under our eyes. It was
important to put it on as the stadium was very small and compact
and the floodlights were very low. In spite of all the off-field events,
I felt such a buzz running out onto the pitch. It is a great feeling of
pride to have worn your country's colours. I did not feel that all
eyes were on me after all that had happened. In other words, I did
not feel like a lone figure. The opposite was in fact true. There were
so many tricolours in the crowd, you would be forgiven for thinking
that you were playing back home. Because of that, I could hear
much sympathetic support for me. I did not have to wait too long
before finding out about how physical the game is Down Under. I
think I was 'roughed up' with my very first touch of the ball. That is
the way the game was played. One minute you were in possession of
the ball and the next moment you were picking yourself up after
been floored! The challenges came in thick and fast and from all
angles.

Going into the last quarter, I remember that there was very little
in it. So, because of our slight lead from the first game, we always
had that little degree of comfort with the clock running down. I
know that anything can happen in sport, especially if they grabbed a
goal but sometimes you just get that feeling that it is your day.

Australia also seemed to be having one of those nights when nothing seemed to be going right for them. They were spurning a lot of fairly easy chances. The game finished in a draw, 52–52. Because of our slender lead going into the game, we had won the Rules on an aggregate of 122–114. So in the end my first taste of Aussie Rules was not a winning one. But neither was it a losing one and it helped to win us the Series.

My overall performance was fairly good. I made my own contribution of five points and so, in some small way, made up for my misdemeanour. My football did the talking and as a result, I helped the team and it therefore had been the right decision not to send me home. Even though we were all over the moon at the final hooter, I felt a little subdued. I could not let my hair down like the rest of the lads. Everything was far outweighed by the racist comment. Nothing I can say or do will ever change what happened. It will stick in people's minds for a long, long time.

Next day, we left our hotel and packed our bags for Sydney. From the time we had arrived, we had virtually no time to relax. Now we were off on what was, in effect, a five-day holiday before flying home to Ireland. The newspapers carried several photographs of joyous Ireland players, and I spotted one of Colm O'Rourke and myself in a smiling embrace – if a picture could paint a thousand words!

In Sydney, we finally relaxed and relieved all the hidden stress and tension as well as nursing all the open wounds and bruises from battle. What better place to do that than on Sydney's famous Bondi Beach. We could also visit the Opera House and the Harbour Bridge, better known as 'The Coat-hanger'. Instead though, we did what the Aussies think they do best – drink! Then after five glorious days of getting tanned, bronzed and inebriated, it was time to fly home to face into the bleak Irish winter.

# 8 The Second Coming

When we set out on our quest for glory at the start of the 1999 season, nothing much was said. Sean and the selectors could not really say to us to just keep it up – if that was the case then, after our fruitless years in 1997 and 1998, we would have won nothing. Though I suspect that Sean knew if we kept on playing the way we had been, then eventually things would come right for us. Although we were beaten in the two previous Leinster finals, we had not really done a lot wrong. In the 1997 final, Offaly got the scores that mattered at a crucial stage. Up until their golden spell when they scored some killer goals, I felt we had been the better team. Those scores came as a hammer blow since by that stage of the game, it was far too late for one of our famous rallies.

Kildare were really after our scalps when we had beaten them following two replays in 1997. So in 1998, we knew they were going to have a real go at us. In fairness, we played well and did have our fair share of chances. But it was just not going to be our day and in any case, nothing was going to stand in Kildare's way that afternoon. They were really keyed up and credit to them, they got their just reward. One thing that did change prior to that 1999 campaign was the captaincy. Sean took me aside one evening during training and told me that he was making me captain for the year. It did not really come as a surprise to me. Sean had a habit of rotating the captains and I was now taking over the role from Brendan Reilly.

In early June, and without either team having played a previous match, we were pitted against Wicklow in the Leinster quarter-finals. Although the statistics showed that Wicklow had only ever beaten us once in over 50 years in Leinster, make no mistake about it, this was a tough match. Records are there to be broken and besides, in this modern era, any team can win on the day. As each year goes by, Wicklow will want desperately to lay that ghost to rest. They have had some terrific and very talented players down through the years – the likes of Kevin O'Brien, who won an All Star, and Fergus Daly. They were both part of a very good Wicklow side in the early 1990s. They were so good that they should have beaten Meath in 1991 but then Meath struggled to get the better of them in the replay.

There were quite a few changes for that first match with Wicklow. We suffered a major setback when John McDermott suffered a bout of flu and his place was taken by Jimmy McGuinness. Alongside 'Boots' in midfield, was teenager Nigel Crawford. Nigel was making his first ever appearance for the Meath Seniors and what a baptism for him. We had a makeshift midfield taking on a big and experienced Wicklow midfield of Darren Coffey and Fergus Daly. It was also my first Leinster match as captain and with it, a new starting position. I was now put into the forward line after playing well in that position in a challenge against Cork in Thurles. I had always been an attacking back and now Sean wanted an extra edge and zip added to the attack. To complete the changes, Trevor Giles was back playing in his first game after damaging knee ligaments in the Leinster final with Kildare.

I distinctly remember Trevor having an excellent first game back, and when Tommy Dowd scored a goal, things were looking good. Then we had Hank Traynor sent off for a second bookable offence. Wicklow had battled well to go in trailing at the break by 1–5 to 0–4 and must surely have fancied their chances with us down to 14 men. There was another change made by Sean at half-time. Jimmy McGuinness, who had been called in to replace McDermott, was himself replaced by Enda McManus. Things were far from ideal for us.

Wicklow started the second period with great hope and that was boosted even further when they sent over a point to narrow the gap to three points. But that is where Wicklow's challenge ended. I think they only scored one more point as we took control. When I scored our second goal it capped a very good first performance by me in the attack. I scored a total of 1–4 and was named Man of the Match. I may have scored well, but I thought Trevor Giles and Tommy Dowd were the real stars of that game. It was also an impressive result for a fairly makeshift side as we won by 2–10 to 0–6. In truth, that match really showed that some of Wicklow's star players were now over the hill. I was marking Hugh Kenny and he was perhaps one of the best full-backs, if not the best in the country, when he was at his peak. I have already mentioned O'Brien and Daly but they were really only a shadow of the very fine players they once were. Nonetheless, it was a very good start for us and especially the new lads that Sean had brought in. Nigel Crawford played well and Sean also introduced Paul Shankey and Richie Kealy as substitutes. I thought they blended in very well with the established players. This all helped to provide a healthy competition for places in the side. But there was also a great spirit and harmony in the camp.

On 4th July we faced Offaly. We were ready to explode and there would be plenty of fireworks in this encounter. After the defeat by them in the 1997 Leinster final, we crushed them the following year. But we wanted to prove again that we had mastered them. The easy manner in which we had brushed them aside the previous year was sweet revenge for that painful defeat in the 1997 final. But it was not enough. I have always felt that they only won the Leinster that year because of the golden spell of goals they scored. However, the main reason they beat us was because we had four players out including our entire full-back line. They would never have scored three goals if we had our full team that day. Take any side's entire full-back line out, and they face an uphill struggle.

We had a point to prove against Offaly the following year and we proved it emphatically. Now we wanted to put a nail into their coffin once and for all. I also felt that they had a cocky and arrogant streak about them which only served to make me and my team-mates even more determined. But all said, Offaly were a very good side. They beat Kildare by four points in their quarter-final so our match with them would be tough.

From what I recall, the first half was very exciting. There were some fantastic scores from play and it was end-to-end stuff with some fantastic running football. Offaly wanted it every bit as much as we did and that made for a great game. At the break, nothing separated the sides and the scores were level at 0–7 each. Ciaran McManus was causing us plenty concern in that first half. He could so easily have given them the lead going in at the interval. He had a great opportunity of scoring a goal but blazed it over for a point. Offaly had rattled us a little. We did not expect them to put up such a bold display even allowing for their great win over Kildare. Sean was also very worried that we were not taking up our markers.

Sean had even more cause for concern after the break. I remember we were hitting a lot of wayward wides. Offaly took advantage and edged in front before we battled back to level. It was turning into a real thriller. Then came the defining moment of the game. It was definitely the turning point that swung the game. I remember we won a lose ball around the centre of the field which was sent in high towards me. I managed to catch it and ran towards their goal. Out of the corner of my eye I caught a glimpse of my team-mate Ollie Murphy running beside me. I passed it to him and he scored a goal. You could see the Offaly heads going down following that. They scored very little after that and we went on to win by 1–13 to 0–9. But hats off to them. I think this match showed that Offaly were now a big fish in Leinster and a team that were, not only to be feared and respected, but also a team that were here to stay. I certainly admired their performance that day. They proved that they were worthy champions over us in 1997 and had done themselves, their management and their supporters very proud.

More than anything else in that win over Offaly, it was our half-back line of Paddy Reynolds, Enda McManus and Hank Traynor whose performances helped us to that 1999 Leinster final. With an already strong full-back line, this was very heartening. Another man who performed very well that day, was our goalie Cormac Sullivan. The goalkeeping position had been a problematic one for us over the years. Just when we thought we had sorted it out when Conor Martin took over, he then lost all interest. I suppose after winning an All-Ireland medal in 1996, Conor felt that it could not get any bigger than that. I suppose you could not blame him. That was his decision and you have to respect it. He also found many other things getting in the way. Working in the financial sector, his workload was huge. As a result, Cormac came into the panel in 1998. He was not really tested against Wicklow but in the Offaly game he really came of age. He made a couple of brilliant saves in that game. One very good save was made in the first half, and then in the second half another outstanding one at the hands of Offaly star, Vinnie Claffey.

Another momentous occasion happened in that match. My old friend Tommy Lyons announced his retirement. I suppose he felt he had taken Offaly as far as he could and wanted to give someone else a chance at the wheel. Tommy did a magnificent job, bringing football to a whole new phase in the county. He introduced neutron diets and a whole new fitness and training regime. It all bore fruit and thanks to him, Offaly can look back with pride on their 1997 success.

Yet again we were to face Dublin in a Leinster final. But it could so easily have been Laois. The Laois lads, largely due to their excellent forwards Hugh Emerson and Damien Delaney, were very unlucky not to have beaten the Dubs. A week earlier, they were leading Dublin by four points with just over a minute to go. Dublin then snatched an all-or-nothing goal and with the last kick of the game in injury time, they levelled with a controversial point. Many felt that the Dublin hero that day, Ian Robertson, had in fact picked the ball off the ground before pointing. As is so often the case, the underdogs only get one bite at the cherry and Dublin won the replay by two points. They had an eight-point lead over Laois midway through the second half. Laois also had Delaney sent off. Fair dues to Laois who came mighty close to reaching a Leinster final. It is a real 'sickener' to lose a game when you are leading by so much with time almost up. But that is the nature of this game. A goal can make all the difference and that is precisely what happened.

On 1st August we faced Dublin. In recent years we had their measure and were very confident of victory again. They also had a hard task overcoming Laois while we had a relatively smooth passage. But Dublin now had a new weapon in the shape of their full-forward Ian Robertson. Our very reliable defence would now be tested and we would have to keep a real sharp eye on him. Our team showed two changes from the side that beat Offaly. Tommy Dowd was out, as he had an operation on a troublesome back in a Dublin hospital the day before. His place in the corner was taken by Donal Curtis who in turn had his place taken by Nigel Nestor.

The thought of defeat, after losing in the two previous finals of 1997 and 1998, did not even bear thinking about. We had a job to do and we were very focused. We had beaten the Dubs in 1996 and 1997 but if we lost to them now it would be a setback of huge proportions. It would have been a catastrophe quite similar to the situation which faced the Kilkenny hurlers in 2000.

I was off the blocks quite quickly and I remember scoring a point which put us 0–2 to 0–1 ahead. I mentioned Cormac Sullivan earlier and, were it not for him, we could quite possibly have been facing a big struggle from early on. Cormac made an outstanding save from Jason Sherlock. In fact, Dublin had the slight advantage over us in that first half. However, they failed to convert that advantage into scores. They had a lot of possession but failed to make anything of it. We had the ever-reliable Trevor Giles to thank for giving us a half-time lead of 0–6 to 0–4. It was a rather strange first half for another reason. Two very important players from both sides had to go off injured within the space of a few minutes. Dublin's captain Dessie Farrell had to go off at a very early stage and was a huge blow to them, especially their attack. A few minutes later we lost our half-back Enda McManus who had to hobble off. His place was then taken by Richie Kealy.

Both sides traded points after the interval and then Trevor put us 0–9 to 0–6 ahead with a beautifully taken point. He had another monumental game that day and capped it by creating a goal for Ollie Murphy. That goal, after Dublin had rallied to within a point, proved a killer for the Dubs. Leading by 1–9 to 0–8, Ollie sent over another few points which gave us a commanding lead with around 10 minutes to go. But Dublin showed that their fight back against Laois was no fluke when they rallied their troops for one final effort. In those final 10 minutes, they hit four points and suddenly we had our nerves jangling. Thankfully, we did not panic and if anything, our determination not to lose another Leinster just spurred us on. We added a few further scores and when I added a point we ran out winners by 1–14 to 0–12.

I can tell you that we were so relieved at the final whistle. We had avoided the dreaded three-in-a-row. People talk about Ollie Murphy as the star that day but, for me, if ever there was a case of a true team effort, then this was it. We all knuckled down and fought as if our lives depended on it. Ollie contributed 1–5 but Trevor was again a colossus and our back-line was brilliant, especially when the Dubs started a bit of a rally.

Looking back now, there are two things I remember from that 1999 final. I think it was one of Trevor Giles' finest performances. Ollie may have received all the praise but the work Trevor put in was amazing. He scored five points but also set up other scores including Ollie's all-important goal. I also remember the Dublin corner-back, Peadar Andrews. He was absolutely roasted all day by Ollie Murphy. Even though I scored a brace of points myself, I had a very quiet game. So much so that I could see the torrid time poor Peadar was having. He was like a fish out of water, which must have been very embarrassing for him. In hindsight, they should have switched Paddy Christie onto Ollie. Undoubtedly, Tommy Carr made a huge mistake there. But I suppose that when you are sitting on the sideline it is hard to come to a decision. If they had switched Christie, then who knows, that may have opened up a whole can of other more devastating problems. Besides, Ollie was playing so well that he would probably have run rings around any defender that day.

Winning our first Leinster title since 1996 was a great feeling. I remember feeling very proud to be captain that day. There was a huge amount of pressure on us going into that game and in victory, it had all been swept away. We did not have to worry about it ever again. Now we could look forward to an All-Ireland semi-final.

Ulster's Armagh were our semi-final opponents. That immediately brought back sweet memories. We had beaten them in the 1994 National League final and that was my first Senior medal. I was hoping that would be a good omen. Armagh had opened up against Donegal in the quarter-final in Ulster. That match finished in a draw, although Oisin McConville scored seven points. Armagh then won the replay very comfortably but McConville was involved in a very controversial incident. The referee, Michael Curley, sent off McConville after a Donegal player clashed with him. But the Armagh County Board later appealed and in an unusual case, the GAA issued a statement which struck out McConville's red card. A very strange match also saw Curley book a Donegal player at the start of the second half for an offence which took place at the end of the first half! The GAA also threw out that booking. Unprecedented and bizarre to say the least.

Armagh then beat Derry in injury time in the semi-final. Diarmuid Marsden, another big danger, hit the winning point and

Oisin McConville scored 1–2 that day. On the same day we played Dublin in Leinster, Armagh faced Down for the Ulster title. They trounced the Mournemen by 11 points and scored three goals in the process. McConville scored a whopping 2–7 in that final! Marsden chipped in with 1–2 so we knew we had a huge job on our hands. The Northerners had the 'M&M's' to fill the boots of that great player I faced in '94 – Ger Houlahan. But aside from Marsden and McConville they had strength right through the side. In defence they had Kieran McGeeney, Ger Reid and the McNulty brothers, Justin and Enda. Their captain Jarlath Burns and Paul McGrane marshalled the midfield and also up front they had dangerous forwards in Paddy McKeever, John McEntee and Cathal O'Rourke. This was a real fifty-fifty match with both sides seemingly very evenly matched.

The Armagh steamroller started almost immediately as they came at us in droves. They took the opening point but then we hit back to lead by 0–3 to 0–1. Then just as we thought we were quelling them, Marsden struck. A good move saw the Armagh marksman finish to the net and then to our shock, they scored another goal a few minutes later. We did not know what hit us. From leading by two points, we now found ourselves trailing by 2–1 to 0–4. Even worse was to follow. We lost Ollie Murphy which was a huge blow to our hopes of reaching the All-Ireland final. He had to be stretchered off and his place was taken by Ray Magee. But then the Meath fighting character seemed to take over us all. Trailing by a few points and minus one of our most potent weapons in Murphy, we responded like men possessed.

I think all of our forward line, apart from Ollie, had got on the scoresheet by the break. One man I will single out is Ray Magee. Not a household name in Meath, you would have thought he was a Meath regular by the way he played that day. He really answered the Meath call. Ray played very well when he came on and even scored a very important point in the second half. As I said, he has never been well known but he is known to all of us! A great footballer with great potential, he was one of those players who shoots points over from all angles in training but never seems to carry it onto the field of play. In fairness, he did not get too many chances in the Senior's up until that Armagh match. When he did, he took his chance and really shone. Indeed, Ray Magee is one of the best left-footed players that I have ever seen.

This was another game of two halves. Ahead by 2–4 to 0–8 at the interval, a rampant Armagh in that first half suddenly seemed to deflate in the second half. It seemed as if they could not hit the target at all. They shot wide after wide and their misery was made even worse when their full-back Ger Reid was sent off for a foul on me. It was his second booking. I was getting a lot of ball but he was pulling and dragging me. The referee Paddy Russell booked him and then warned him. I was so surprised when, only a minute or so after he had been warned, he did it again and the referee had no option but to send him to the line. This made us very happy as we knew that it was a big setback for an already concerned Armagh. On top of their anxiety about the wides they were hitting, they now had the added problem of making switches to counter Reid's dismissal. It did not work. Armagh went on to score only a solitary point in the entire second half and that came in the first 10 minutes.

Faced with elimination, Armagh was like a wounded animal but I can remember that we almost lost the game as well. Later on, Marsden went through and had the goal at his mercy but spurned the chance. I think one more damning statistic for Armagh that day, apart from the sending off and all the wides, was the fact that Oisin McConville failed to score. That really says it all.

We jumped for joy as the final whistle sounded. We had beaten mighty Armagh by 0–15 to 2–5 and were into another All-Ireland final. I was thrilled to bits and very proud to be captaining Meath in what would be my second appearance in the final. Cork were to be our opponents on the last Sunday in September. They had beaten Mayo by 2–12 to 0–12 in the other semi-final. I think Mayo must surely go down as the unluckiest side of the Nineties. They actually led Cork by five points midway through the second half only to let slip yet another big lead.

\* \* \* \* \* \*

A couple of weeks before the big day, we all gathered for training as usual. Then, a very surprising and peculiar thing happened. Sean Boylan called me over and asked:

'What are you at on Saturday?'

'Nothing much,' I replied.

'Good 'cause we'll be going to Holyhead in Wales for the day. Keep it quiet and don't say anything to the others just yet,' he said.

To be honest, I was flabbergasted. I wondered why we were going over to Holyhead. After training, Sean then told the rest of the team. He then asked if anyone could not make it. There was silence and when he announced that everyone was to meet at Kepak in Clonee at 5.15 am on the Saturday, everyone just looked at one another! A few lads actually laughed but Sean said he was serious.

On the Friday night before our departure, I set my alarm clock for 4.30 am. To my horror, I never heard the alarm go off and woke at 5.15! Immediately, I rang James Reilly and told him to tell the others I would be a little late. I ran out the door and into the car around 5.25 am. When I reached the ferry at Dún Laoghaire, it was 6 am. It had taken me just over half an hour to get there from my home in Meath. If there had been any Gardaí on the road that morning, I would surely have been arrested!

Getting on the boat, I sat with Evan Kelly and a few of the lads. The next thing we knew, two women sat down next to us and ordered champagne! They told us they had been nite-clubbing in Dún Laoghaire and could not get served any more drink. So instead they decided to board the ferry in order to get more drink! One of the women told us her name was Amanda Brunker. She was a former 'Miss Ireland' and is now a columnist with the *Sunday World*.

When we reached Holyhead, we all went to change in a nearby hotel. A coach then brought us to a very basic soccer pitch a couple of miles outside the town. I remember that it was bitterly cold from the wind sweeping in from the Irish Sea. Even though it was unbelievably cold, half of us were still asleep! After about an hour of light training, we went back to the hotel for breakfast. When breakfast was finished, Sean put on a video. At this stage, we were wrecked. Many of the lads were nodding off in their chairs. Trevor Giles and myself fell asleep with our heads on each other's shoulders! Sean did not mind at all. In fact, the whole purpose of the trip was to do something different. It was just to bring everyone together for a day trip away from the usual training. In other words, it broke the monotony of our routines in Dalgan Park or Páirc Tailteann. As we boarded the return ferry for Dublin later that afternoon, who did we bump into but the two women who had sat with us on the journey over. By this time, they had really sobered up and were looking very sorry for themselves!

******

With all the training complete, the day that mattered soon arrived. Meath and Sean Boylan have actually enjoyed great success over Cork. They beat the Leesiders in the finals of 1988 and 1989 but then lost to them in 1990. But apart from the cherished All-Ireland title, there were a number of other things at stake. To us players it does not mean anything really but to the statisticians it means a lot. Meath and Cork had lifted the Sam Maguire six times each so both counties were now bidding for number seven. Both counties were also looking to win the last All-Ireland of the millennium. Cork were also looking to win 'the double' having won the hurling title a few weeks earlier. Coupled to that, Seán Óg Ó hAilpín was hoping to become only the second player in GAA history to win All-Ireland medals in both codes in the same year. The only man to have achieved this feat is Teddy McCarthy. He helped Cork to win the All-Ireland football and hurling titles in 1990.

In the final, I was actually marking Seán Óg. Beforehand many people were saying that this was the crucial head to head on the pitch. Seán Óg, who was actually born in Fiji, was a rock solid full-back who gave nothing away. I had played all right during the Championship without setting it alight. Marking Seán Óg, I would really have to play well and was hoping to rise to the occasion. But it is a team game and we would all have to play well, in all corners of the pitch, to get the better of the wily Cork men.

On a rainy day, we got off to a flyer, thanks to points from Evan Kelly and Trevor Giles. But midway through the first half, Cork were level at 0–2 each. Donal Curtis then gave us the lead again but I was struggling. I was finding it very difficult to get my hands on the ball. Coming in very high and on a wet pitch, the ball was greasy which was difficult to catch and especially difficult to control. On top of all that, Seán Óg more than had the measure of me. Then, 10 minutes from the break, a high ball actually worked to our advantage. Trevor sent in a high, hopeful ball and I managed to knock it into the path of Ollie Murphy. He finished it to the net and that put us in the driving seat. We now led by 1–3 to 0–2 before Cork went down the other end and pulled one back. Two more points from Cork but then a brace from Meath's Evan Kelly left us leading by 1–5 to 0–5 at half-time.

At the interval, Sean told us that three points was no cushion. It was plain to see he was very worried about Cork and he impressed on us to keep it up or else Cork would punish us. In his estimation, the second half would only be the start as Cork had proved all year that they were a much better team after the break. Sure to form, Sean's words rang true. Within the first five minutes of that second half, Cork incredibly went into the lead. Philip Clifford, who scored two points in that first half, pulled another back and then disaster struck. Our defence fell to sleep and allowed Cork to punish us for our sloppiness.

Cork's Joe Kavanagh picked up the ball and went on a long run. He soloed and then weaved his way through our entire defence. He then played a 'one-two' and finished the ball to the back of our net. It was a brilliant goal and put them in front for the first time in the match, 1–6 to 1–5. It was a big blow to us and we now had a real fight on our hands. Cork were proving to be an entirely different team after the break and we really had to roll up our sleeves. But everyone knows that a scrap and a fight really suits Meath teams. We did not really panic. There was a long way to go and we had often come back from a lot further behind. There was only a point in it and we knew we had the right men in the side to more than get us out of trouble.

Things could have been so different if we had taken a great chance presented to us at the very start of the half. Seán Óg, who really had the better of me in the first period, tugged at my shirt as I went for a ball and it put me off balance. Out of nowhere, the referee Michael Curley handed us a penalty! Trevor stepped up to take it. All of Meath must have expected him to score as I certainly did. If he did, then we would have been six points clear and Cork would have needed a miracle. Trevor went to place the ball into the corner but there was no pace in the shot and their keeper, Kevin

O'Dwyer, made an easy save. That miss gave Cork great heart and in the next few minutes they punished us for that missed chance.

If our penalty miss gave them heart, then their goal really spurred us on. I got a knock from Seán Óg in that first half and my calf muscle was so sore that I had to get it rubbed at the break. The pain of seeing their goal, allied to my painful leg, only made me more determined. I started to get into the game more and began to get to grips with Seán Óg. He had been forced into an early mistake in fouling me for our penalty. Then a few minutes after their goal, I levelled. The referee allowed play to continue after Ollie Lynch fouled Murphy and I pointed. From a neutral's view, the second half must have been very exciting. A penalty miss, a great Cork goal and after I levelled, Trevor put us back in the lead. I then scored my second point only for Cork to reply, and when they scored another point, the teams were level again at 1–8 each. It was tit for tat and anybody's guess who was going to win.

Trevor Giles then put us in front from a '45', and when he pointed a free shortly after that, there was a gap of two between the teams. Not content with his dead ball skills, Trevor then sent a lovely long curling pass to me and I sent it over the bar. My third point of the game and suddenly there were three points between us. There was only four or five minutes left to play. Such a short space of time but it really felt like an eternity. We need not have worried as there were no more scores and no more drama. Meath won their seventh All-Ireland on a score of 1–11 to 1–8.

All hell broke loose! We screamed and roared and jumped for joy. Everywhere I turned there were congratulatory hugs and slaps. There were smiles everywhere while on the ground, distraught, were the red and white figures of the Cork players. As captain, I was a very proud man lifting the Sam Maguire Cup. Even then, the enormity of what I had achieved did not sink in. I had won my second All-Ireland medal and it was two from two. A very good and enviable record but still it had not really registered. Then we went on a lap of honour with the cup, accepting all the applause from ecstatic Meath supporters in every corner of Croke Park. There were wild scenes everywhere and then a moment of calm as my daughter Sophia was handed to me. In that moment, and because she was a year old just a few days earlier, this was the greatest present I could give her. So I placed her in the cup and raised it above my head. I could not believe when I saw that photograph on the front page of every paper the next day – my baby, my wife and myself. It was just such a fantastic day. And when I think of victory, I think also of my parents. The real reason why I am playing football is all down to them. Everything has been made possible because of them. That is when the moment finally hit me. When I saw them, and the pride and joy in their faces under the Hogan Stand, I burst into tears of happiness. I realised then how lucky and privileged I was to be surrounded by family, friends, supporters and a fantastic group of players.

It was also a special day in that it was exactly 50 years since Meath had lifted their very first All-Ireland back in 1949. This was our seventh which I think put us fourth in the all-time winners' list, behind the likes of Kerry and Dublin. Some of that 1949 side were actually present in Croke Park that day and it must have been a very emotional moment for them too. I also think that it was the day I really came of age as a player and being captain may have had something to do with it. The captain is supposed to lead by example and has a lot of responsibilities to himself as well as the team. Before I was given that role, I used to moan and groan and bicker to the referees quite frequently down through the years.

There were a few examples of my new approach in the final itself. Bruised and battered by Seán Óg in the first half, I just knuckled down after that and took what was dished out to me rather than complain. Also, when Ollie Murphy was fouled and the referee played on, perhaps before I would have roared at the referee looking for the free instead of playing on. However, I feel there was one aspect of the game that really told the story. I think I only had three chances in that second half and pointed from them all. In contrast, Cork hit many wides. There were certain undertones that Cork were the better side in that final. I disagree and apart from the old adage that 'the score does not lie', the statistics also show interesting facts. We had 12 scores to Cork's nine. But if Cork hit 15 wides, of which seven were in the second period, we hit 12 wides and also had seven in the second half.

Meath's Mark O'Reilly was named Man of the Match and he thoroughly deserved it. I only really got going in the last half hour after a fairly poor first half. But in truth it was a whole team effort. I thought we were very strong all over the pitch – even allowing for our defensive mistake. Paddy Reynolds and Darren Fay were very good back there and Evan Kelly also played very well. But for me, Trevor Giles was excellent. He really was perhaps our best player all year.

Remembering the losers, Philip Clifford was one of Cork's best players but I felt they *all* played well. Certainly, Seán Óg Ó hAilpín was terrific and really left his mark on me! I was also struck by his great sportsmanship afterwards. In every single interview he gave, he was very honest and forthright. He had some nice things to say about me and Meath. However, in admitting his own heartbreak, he said he was more heartbroken for the rest of the guys on the team because at least he had a winner's medal in hurling. It is also worth remembering a certain Tommy Dowd. To the delight of all Meath people, Tommy, who had surgery on his back a few weeks earlier, was brought on late in the game for Evan Kelly. It was a lovely touch from Sean and his selectors who had not forgotten how much Tommy gave Meath in his career and earlier in the year.

Celebrations were the order of the night as we partied away in our Dublin hotel. Next day we headed on the road home to Meath and as usual Kepak in Clonee was the first stop. On this occasion there was no live bull painted in our colours! The team coach then travelled on to Dunboyne, Dunderry, Garlow Cross, Ross Cross and into my townland of Kentstown. There must have been three to four thousand people who had gathered in Kentstown and I was overwhelmed at the sight. I clearly remember that when I took to the stage the cheering and clapping and whistling was unbelievable. On the stage beside me was a young lad named Noel Collier. Little did I know what I had let myself in for. Noel started slagging me off as he is a mad Walterstown supporter. Suddenly, in front of the large crowd, he asked me for my tracksuit! I eventually agreed to give it to him on one condition – that he start supporting Seneschalstown! So he agreed. Later, as we boarded the coach to our final destination of Navan, I could hear Noel shouting over and over again, 'Up Walterstown!'

It was a long day but we made it into Navan far earlier than we had in 1996. This was largely due to Fintan Ginnity who had the hard job of getting players on and off the stage as quickly as he could. Like me in Kentstown, it can be very difficult to get a fella off stage when addressing his own townspeople. You tend to get carried away by it all. The Meath supporters are fantastic and I will never forget that year. For most of us the celebrations continued on right throughout the winter. In December, the entire Meath team was invited to the All Stars awards sponsored by Eircell. As always, the event was held just before Christmas in the Burlington Hotel. I was given a nomination for the full-forward position and was hoping for my second such award.

In the course of the evening, I saw several of my team-mates win awards, so there was a little pressure on me. I did not have an outstanding year by any means and so there were real doubts as to whether I would win one. As the envelope was opened my heart was pounding. When I heard my name, I was thrilled. It was my second All Star but it was even more special than my first. I now knew that I was one of only a select few to have won an award in two different positions. My first was for the half-back position and this was for full-forward.

Meath players picked up a staggering seven awards that night. That is almost half a team! Mark O'Reilly and Darren Fay were great all year in the full-back line. As ever, John McDermott was a giant in midfield. What more can you say about Trevor? Alongside me in the full-forward line, Ollie Murphy was deadly. I was particularly delighted for Paddy Reynolds too. He won an award for right half-back. Not only had he worked his socks off for us on the field and in training and so deserved his award, but he also made history. There are not too many father and son winners and Paddy was following in the footsteps of his father Pat. I think I am right in saying that his father was Meath's first ever winner of this prestigious award back in 1973.

As a proud captain of that 1999 side, I would also like to pay tribute to the rest of the team. Cormac Sullivan did a fine job between the posts. Fay and O'Reilly could not have achieved their awards without the help of Cormac Murphy alongside them. Hopefully the time will come for Hank Traynor in the half-back line and that also applies to Nigel Crawford who has a great future ahead of him in midfield. Evan Kelly and Nigel Nestor were excellent alongside Trevor in the half-forward line and Donal Curtis more than deputised for Tommy Dowd in the corner. In fact, in the final, Kelly scored three points and Curtis weighed in with one. Richie Kealy, Tommy Dowd, Enda McManus, Jimmy McGuinness, Paul

Shankey and Barry Callaghan all helped out enormously in that campaign.

The climax of all the fun and partying came in January 2000 when the team travelled to South Africa for two weeks. We stayed in a beautiful location on the Indian Ocean for a week. Our second week saw us in Cape Town, where unlike the controversy surrounding the 2002 All-Ireland winning teams, we had a relaxing and trouble-free holiday. The locations we stayed in were stunningly beautiful. Something nearing a party of 100 was there and it was relatively quiet. We virtually had the run of the hotel to ourselves. The most exciting thing that happened, from a personal point of view, was taking part in a 'bungee jump'. A few lads could not wait to try it out with only Niall Kelly from Dunshaughlin opting out! What an adrenalin rush! It was my first time to do it and I think at its full stretch, I went into a freefall of well over 200 metres. The only thing that beats it is winning an All-Ireland and now I had two safely strapped under my belt. Returning home to Ireland soon afterwards, it was that comfort and the memories of a fantastic 1999 which would warm my heart through the rest of that winter.

# 9 The Pride Before the Fall

Sean Boylan had a very pleasant surprise in store for us prior to our National League semi-final with Kerry in 2000. Instead of bringing us down to Thurles on the coach, he organised a fleet of four or five stretch limousines to carry us down! It was a very strange and unusual thing for someone of Sean's character to do. I suppose he was trying to get the message across that we were the All-Ireland Champions and as such, we would travel in a way befitting champions. The crowd must have been wondering what was going on with these big dazzling cars outside Semple Stadium! Obviously, the Kerry lads did not like it one bit. In no time we found ourselves a few points down. They were trying to ram it home to us that, although we were 'The Royals' and had travelled like royalty, they were Kings of 'The Kingdom' and were really spelling it out to us on the pitch that day.

Things just went from bad to worse for us. When we found ourselves 10 points behind with time running out, there were a lot of red faces in the Meath camp. There was no way back and Kerry were going to send us home with our tails between our legs. I then scored a goal to give us just a glimmer of hope. A few moments later we scored another goal, one of the very best that I have ever seen. I remember Donal Curtis picking up a loose ball and drilling it towards the goal. The ball never rose more than a few feet off the ground and then Ollie Murphy got on the end of it. He connected with it first time and it fairly flew into the back of the net. Kerry still had a good advantage and it looked like a case of too little too late. Barry Callaghan then came on as a substitute and when he scored a goal with time almost up, we were desperate to give our all in the hope of salvaging something from what seemed an impossible position. The Kerry lads were now in panic and you could see that they were desperate to hang on. In the end, I simply do not know how we did it. We popped over a few points in added time and actually won the game by two points!

What a match! We were into the National League final in the most dramatic of circumstances. Our blushes had been spared. If we had been thrashed, as it looked likely for so long, we would have been so embarrassed returning home in our fancy cars. In fairness to Kerry, it can happen to anyone. When you are so far ahead you tend to take your foot off the pedal. But once again we had not given up and were rewarded. The mood in the dressing-room after that game was fantastic. We all worked our socks off and there was a tremendous team spirit. They all agreed that it was as fine a match as they had ever been involved in. Some probably went a bit far in saying that it outweighed the All-Ireland win. But I would agree that it was one of the best matches I have ever played in.

Sean also deserves much credit. He did some strange things in his time like bringing us all to Wales when half the world was asleep, but the limousine story beat all else. Thinking about it now, he probably psyched out both teams and even all the crowd who were present. He knew that the entire crowd and the Kerry team would see us and our luxury cars. Obviously, it would spur them on. At the same time, he knew that if we were behind and then lost, we would not want to sit our arses into those plush seats on the long journey home. So it actually helped us and was another master stroke from Sean Boylan.

I could now look forward to playing in my second League final having won it in 1994. It was also great to be back in Croke Park for another final after our super September win over Cork. As All-Ireland Champions, we had also franked the form and shown our true worthiness as the best team in the country. Derry were our opponents in the 2000 League final. They were obviously a big and strong side and would prove very difficult to beat, typical of teams at this level. Nevertheless, I was confident that we could win. The team spirit, especially after the win over Kerry, could not have been better.

On the first Sunday in May, Meath and Derry lined out for the first major GAA final of the new millennium. There was lots of talk back then, in all sports, about who would be the first to win such and such of the new millennium. I suppose it was some sort of incentive but it is really only for the record books and statisticians. At the end of the day, all any team wants is the silverware and the title. That final turned into a disaster for me. I was sent off, leaving me and some of my team-mates fuming because I did not deserve it. It involved myself and Derry's Kieran McKeever. In fairness, the referee was not really to blame as he saw nothing untoward and the game continued on. But the linesman, Paddy Russell, called him over and the next I knew, I was off.

The controversy occurred when a high ball went in towards the Derry goal mouth. There were many players under it and there was a bit of scrimmaging for the ball. Out of the pack came McKeever with the ball and I ran to try and wrestle it from his grasp. As I made contact with him, he fell to the ground like a sack of spuds, holding his face in his hands. As I said, the referee, Michael Curley, saw nothing wrong but then Paddy Russell waved him over and a short consultation began between them. My impression is that the referee thought it was an accidental collision which it genuinely was. Then I heard Russell tell the referee that I had elbowed McKeever in the face. So I was sent off and was very, very angry. I was livid with Paddy Russell. I was off in the National League final because of a wrong decision. McKeever also made me angry – there was no way I had touched him and by falling down clutching his face, he had cheated in order to get me sent off. However, it did not end there. My anger towards the Derry player landed me in more trouble.

On the way off the field, I called McKeever a 'wanker' and it was caught on camera. That landed me up before the GAA, which I will talk about shortly. I had to sit and watch the rest of the game from the dug-out and was worried about our chances. In the end, and with 14 men, we again showed our guts and courage to hold out for a draw. The game was tied at 1–12 apiece and we would have to replay. As things stood, I would not be able to play in that match. I was now banned but determined to appeal and clear my name.

Immediately after that drawn final, Tommy Dowd confronted Kieran McKeever. The Derry corner-back admitted that the whole thing was an accident and to his credit, he did apologise. But that was not going to do me any good and I had to appear before the Games Disciplinary Committee. I would not be able to appeal until I heard what action the GAA were going to take against me. I was on trial on two counts – 'striking' and 'verbal abuse'. The Derry goalkeeper, Ciaran McClusker, was also on trial with me that day. He was up on a charge of verbally abusing the referee. Thankfully, justice was done. The video of the incident clearly showed that it was an accident and the panel threw out the charge against me. But for verbally abusing McKeever, I was given a two-month ban. I was a little disappointed at this outcome. I felt that the abuse was due to me feeling wronged at the dismissal. So because I had been cleared, I felt that they should have been a little lenient and perhaps even let me off. Rules are rules and because this charge carried two months, I did not have a leg to stand on. Incidentally, the Derry keeper also got two months for his abuse of Michael Curley. A two-month ban was very expensive and worrying for me and everyone in the Meath camp. It meant that I was going to miss the replay and the opening Leinster Championship match.

Derry really rubbed it in when the two sides replayed the final in Clones. It was very painful having to watch from the sideline as Derry totally outplayed us. It was so frustrating knowing you were powerless to do anything about it. Anthony Tohill lorded it over us that day. I think it was especially disappointing as I felt that we were the better side in the first match prior to my sending off, and I feel we would have won. Credit to Derry in the replay. They took full advantage of the situation and deserved to be crowned League champions.

We could really have done without that replay. It now meant that we only had two weeks to prepare for our first match in Leinster and that would be minus my services. On top of all that, one of the last teams we wished to face were Offaly. They were to be our opponents and were somewhat of a bogey team for us. Once more I had to watch from the dug-out and there was a certain air of apprehension that day. We had some really tough encounters with Offaly in the previous few years and this was going to be another severe examination. At stake were our Leinster and All-Ireland titles and Offaly would relish the chance of another crack at us.

Donal Curtis took my place in the side. It was clear right from the start that it was not going to be our day. Offaly were really revved up for the game and they all played so solidly and gave nothing away. Their half-forward Colm Quinn had a very good game. He scored over half of Offaly's total as they ran out winners by 0–13 to 0–9. Make no mistake, it was a real body blow. In the space of a couple of weeks we had suffered double blows. We lost the League final to Derry and now we had relinquished our Leinster and All-Ireland titles. It was a bitter pill to swallow and I firmly lay the blame for that at the feet of Paddy Russell. Our miserable year in 2000 was all down to him. To this day I will never know what he was thinking as he stood on the sideline in that League final.

\*\*\*\*\*\*

Another long hot summer had to be endured by the Meath players and supporters. But this can also bring about opportunities. Previously, when Meath had exited from the championship early, I had taken off overseas. On this occasion, there was an offer on the table to go to Chicago to play with one of the big Gaelic football clubs out there. Val McMahon, originally from Meath, got in touch with me and asked if I was interested in going over to play with Wolfe Tones for six weeks. I did not make up my mind immediately and told him I would think about it. The funny thing is that Val had only hung up when another guy rang representing St Brendan's Club in Chicago and he also invited me over. In Chicago Wolfe Tones and St Brendan's are fierce rivals. The guy from St Brendan's actually offered me more money. But because Val had rung first, and he was from Meath, I decided to go over to him. I saw this as a good chance to get away. After all, sitting around all summer would only have brought constant reminders about what might have been. Another good reason for going to Chicago was that I could keep up my level of fitness and my match sharpness. It would help me for the forthcoming League campaign at the end of the summer and, in general, I would just be kept on the go. To have some sort of competitive match action under your belt is far better than having none at all.

The matches out in Chicago were certainly competitive. For instance, in our first match we faced the big rivals, St Brendan's. They fielded seven or eight county players from back home in their side. Niall Buckley from Kildare was probably the best known but they also had the O'Hare brothers from Clare who had played with London. The rivalry between the two clubs is unbelievable. On the surface it can seem fairly good-natured and friendly but underneath it is deadly serious. It is actually 10 times worse than the rivalry between Dublin and Meath. There was also a lot of pressure on us because we had to win this match to stay in the competition.

There are no real statistics for those matches and I have to go by memory. But I played fairly well in that first match. I scored a few points and created a couple of goals. We ended up winning by about five points. In our next game we played Parnells and railroaded them by about 10 points. That meant we were into the final where we now awaited the winners of the Parnells and St Brendan's match. With the rivalry the way it was, St Brendan's were desperate to reach the final and so get a crack at us. So much so that they brought over two more very well-known players for that clash with Parnells; Sligo's star player, Eamonn O'Hara arrived along with Derry's Sean Marty Lockhart.

Even that move could not help them beat Parnells. The match ended in a draw which meant that on points difference St Brendan's were lucky to get through to play us. So the two big rivals went head to head and even though they had struggled to get there, we knew that this was a real tough match. They also had a team full of talented players. Eamonn O'Hara must have suffered from a bit of jet lag in that drawn game. If so, then he really acclimatised well because in the final he was superb. He and Niall Buckley played brilliantly and totally dominated the middle of the park. By half-time, we were 10 points or so behind!

Before that final, we were all a little annoyed that O'Hara was allowed to play. He had been sent off in the clash with Parnells for striking an opponent. In Ireland, that would mean him automatically missing the next match. Then we were told the rule did not apply over there, which we felt to be very unfair. I would have thought that GAA rules are the rules no matter where you play.

The second half was a different story. We knuckled down and got to grips with their domination in midfield. We whittled their big lead down to just two points. But in the end our gallant efforts were all to no avail. They held out to win but we had at least made it an exciting finish. We also had several good chances near the end but it was not to be our day.

During my time in Chicago, I was looked after and treated very well. I had a great time out there and it was all thanks to Val and to a man named John Ganley. He organised a bit of work for me where I was staying in Oaklawn in the suburbs of the city. One of the watering holes I visited was 'The Goalpost'. It was a very popular bar and I met many people there, including a guy from Roscommon, Chris Keaveney. He and his friends were the salt of the earth and by the welcome they gave me, you would never have thought they were fierce St Brendan's followers!

One memorable moment from my time in Chicago came when I was out on a drinking session with John Ganley and some of his friends. We were at it all night and not being able to stand up any more, we headed back to John's house. Needless to say, we were absolutely jarred and so John let me sleep in a basement room while he slept upstairs. In the middle of the night, I was awoken by someone crawling into bed beside me! It was a woman, yet I had no idea what was happening. Suddenly the woman shot out of the bed, not knowing who I was or where I had come from. In the cold light of day, we all had a right laugh about it. It turned out that it was John's wife Anne who could not sleep with his loud snoring. So she decided to sleep in the spare bed in the basement not knowing that I was there!

\*\*\*\*\*\*

Two very exciting things happened in the months between my coming home in September and Christmas. Firstly, Amanda became pregnant again and all going well I would become a father for the second time. Then in the draw for the 2001 Leinster, we were pitted against our own fierce local rivals, Westmeath. In January 2001, I enjoyed a very eventful trip to Dubai to say the least. I travelled with the entire Meath panel and there must have been well over 100 of us on that trip. Despite a stay of just five days, so much happened in that short space of time. Going to Dubai was not a first for me. I had been there the previous year and know quite a few people there. Paul McCabe, a brother of former Meath and Seneschalstown stalwart Mattie, lives and works there. My uncle's sister also lives there, so it was like a home from home for me.

The main purpose of our trip was to promote Gaelic football in areas where Irish people reside. There are thousands of Irish living and working out there. Many are nurses, doctors, teachers, construction workers, and those working in the horse racing industry. It was also an occasion for us to let our hair down after all the hard games and training. Naturally, in our mini-break, we were determined to make the most of it before jetting back to a hectic schedule of League, training and then the Leinster.

While we were there, I lined up for the 1999 All Stars in a game against the 2000 All Stars. Most of the lads who took to the field that day were half jarred! That was reflected in the result which read more like a cricket score. I think there must have been around 10 goals scored and, although it was almost impossible to keep the score that day, for the record I did finish on the losing side.

On another day, Trevor Giles and myself, along with Mark O'Reilly, went jet skiing. Right from the off, things went badly and got much worse. Definitely, there was a gremlin in the works when my jet ski would not start. I then had to go and get a replacement but as fate would have it Giles drove into Paddy Reynolds and damaged his machine! As we tried to straighten up the front bumper on Trevor's, to our horror we discovered a big hole just under the back of Paddy's machine! We left it back hoping that nobody would spot it, but as we were about to walk away, we were called back and asked to explain the damage caused. Our general good humour at the incident soon turned to frowns and grimaces when told the estimated cost of the damage. It would cost £2,500 to fix! That soon wiped the smiles off our faces and we were now worried men. Then one of us remarked that you could buy a brand new jet ski for that price so eventually we all agreed on a figure of around £200! That experience proved more expensive than propping up the bar all day!

On the day we departed, we were all sitting by the hotel swimming pool when something far more disastrous almost occurred. What started out as a bit of fun soon turned to a good deal of alarm and anxiety. Amanda and myself were lying on sun loungers beside the pool, as were Mark O'Reilly and the Kerry quartet of Páidí Ó Sé, Darragh Ó Sé, Fergal Ó Sé and Tomás Ó Sé. Most of us were wearing shorts, swimming trunks or tracksuit bottoms. A couple of journalists then arrived and Mark made a rather tempting suggestion. Both Jim O'Sullivan of *The Examiner* and Brian Carthy of RTÉ Sport were very smartly dressed and had just checked out of their hotel rooms. Mark suddenly whispered to the rest of us that we should throw them into the pool. So we thought nothing of it and a few seconds later we lifted them up and threw them into the deep end! The big problem we had overlooked was the fact that Brian Carthy could not swim! Amid all the laughter and excitement, we had all failed to notice this until Jim O'Sullivan swam towards him to help. Well alarmed by now, Mark jumped in and went to his rescue. The atmosphere suddenly changed as all we could see was Brian's arm outstretched while he was thrashing about and struggling. They got to him in plenty of time but the high jinks were now over and the mood turned very serious. All I can say is that it was some hours later before Brian could raise a laugh about it.

\* \* \* \* \* \*

After all the relaxation came to an end, it was back to the football. Our minds were very much focused on the Leinster clash with Westmeath. Going into that very important match, I think we had a psychological edge over them. Earlier in the year, we got the better of them in a very close O'Byrne Cup meeting in Mullingar. But that win was thanks to a very late goal and we knew this was going to be a very stiff test. This was a huge game. The O'Byrne Cup win meant nothing as the League and all sorts of other challenges are all geared up to the big day of the All-Ireland Championships. Despite the fact that they are our nearest neighbours, we were also wary that as each year goes by, they are eager to lay the ghost of never having beaten us in Leinster.

Westmeath got off to the perfect start. Ger Heavin put the ball in our net and there was barely a minute gone. This was a dream start for them but there was still a long way to go. It is not as important as scoring a goal a minute from the end. We did not panic and knew we just had to knuckle down and concentrate on our own game. They were the better team in the first half but after the break it was a different story. I was playing with much more confidence and making a lot of runs. In one particular run, I tried to latch on to a high ball which came in towards me. Out of the corner of my eye, I could see their keeper coming towards it as well but I managed to get there first and fist it to the back of the net. That goal was part of a double whammy for Westmeath. When Ollie Murphy also scored a goal, the writing was on the wall for them. To their credit, they gave their all, and in the end they were far from disgraced. They had caused us much trouble in that first half but we took over after that.

I think the one-point win for us was a little more comfortable than the score of 2–12 to 1–14 suggests. As regards my own performance, I was also more than happy. I played well and scored a goal and two points.

That defeat was tough on Westmeath. They had played so well. But the two goals we scored really knocked them back. Once again, just as in the O'Byrne Cup match, a late goal from us finally brought about the end of their very brave challenge. I was marking Dave Mitchell. I had been with him in Chicago with Wolfe Tones the previous year and felt sorry for him. After the game he could not hide his disappointment, telling me how the referee did them no favours. But Dave and the rest of the Westmeath team still had another chance. The new format brought in by the GAA meant that they could still reach the later knockout stages of the All-Ireland. They went into the so-called 'back-door' system.

We were now into the semi-final of the Leinster where we would meet Kildare. Kildare again had us running around and really made us earn our corn. They played very well but by now we knew how to handle their usual running and hand-passing style of play. They actually led in the early stages of the second half but in truth, and a bit like the Westmeath game, we never felt we were going to lose. Everytime they went a point or even two points ahead, we felt comfortable within ourselves. I cannot explain it but I just knew we would peg them back. Maybe it has something to do with our many comebacks from far greater deficits. But that game was really a story of two players – Kildare's Glenn Ryan and Trevor Giles. Glenn was a real doubtful starter for them before the game. It was obvious that he was not fully fit as he struggled throughout. In contrast, the ever-reliable Trevor Giles had a real barnstormer of a game. He scored no less than a goal and five points and also set up a lot of other scores for us. I also played another good game and scored four points in our 1–16 to 1–11 win.

We had reached yet another Leinster final and it more than made up for the misery of the year before when we fell at the first hurdle. Again we had a final with Dublin to look forward to. It was another mouth-watering prospect and I could not wait. Although we had their measure in recent years, these games are always so close and this would prove to be no exception. People talk about 'swings and roundabouts' and that 'everything that goes around comes around'.

In fact, that really applied to the 2001 Leinster final between Meath and Dublin. It was also remarkably similar to the 1994 contest between the sides. Only this time, the game was to swing in the opposite direction. Just as many people were shocked by the inclusion of Micky McQuillan in goals for us in 1994, so many Dubs must have been surprised by Davy Byrne's selection in the Dublin goal. It certainly raised my eyebrows as he had not been their regular keeper during their League campaign.

To make matters worse for Davy, he made a terrible mistake at the very start of the game which allowed me to capitalise. I think it was Ollie Murphy who sent in a high ball towards the Dublin goal. Davy slapped the ball down in a way which suggested he was unsure or maybe lacked confidence. Perhaps he was even a little unsettled by the big match atmosphere. In any case, I was on hand to dive at the ball and I just got my fingertips to it. Then I looked on anxiously as it trickled into the net. As if in slow motion the ball took its time to cross the line. It was a great start for us but must have been terrible for poor Davy Byrne. Just as there had been a strange goalkeeping change in the '94 match, so too there had been one in this game. Just as there had been a monumental goalkeeping error back in '94, so too there was a huge 'boo-boo' from a keeper. What a strange set of coincidences! Also, McQuillan's error had cost us dearly and although we tried our best to get back in the game, in the end we lost. In just the same way, Davy's error now made Dublin's task all the harder. They did make a bit of a fight but when Richie Kealy scored a second goal for us, the writing was on the wall for the Dubs. We ran out winners by 2–11 to 0–14 and I was thrilled to have won my third Leinster title with Meath.

Games are won and lost on errors such as that made by the Dublin keeper. But it would be grossly unfair to attribute our success to that mistake. Dublin had plenty of time to come back from that early blunder and they did make a match of it. I thought our win was due to the performances of Ollie Murphy and Richie Kealy. Richie only came on as a substitute. You could say that because of our strength in depth and panel of players, he was yet another case of a player unlucky not to start games. Richie always had to wait for his chance to come and on this day he really made the most of it. He performed well in challenges and in training and was as good as any of the other lads. When he came on against

Dublin, he played very well and caused them all sorts of problems. Indeed he proved what a good player we all knew him to be.

After bagging my third Leinster medal, I was hoping that I was now on the road to landing a third All-Ireland. With the new system in place, instead of going into the semi-final we were now into the All-Ireland quarter-finals. Only this new back-door system threw up Westmeath as our opponents! We knew from our first match with them in Leinster that they were going to be tough to beat. They would be itching for another crack at us. Furthermore, they would also have their tails up because after losing narrowly to us, they then went on to beat Mayo by a point.

True to form, Westmeath started the game like bats out of hell. We did not know what hit us in that first period. We simply had no answer to Westmeath. They were running us ragged and we could not get a grip at all. Three goals were put past us in that first half as Westmeath led by 3–7 to 1–6. Not surprisingly, Sean had a few serious words to say at the interval. He told the midfield to tighten up and to fight hard for any breaking ball. That actually made a lot of sense as Westmeath were enjoying all the freedom in the middle. They had been running right through the heart of us. Next Sean told the defence to smarten up and to get the ball into the forwards quickly.

The second half started as the first had ended with Westmeath in the ascendancy. Gradually, Nigel Crawford got the hang of things in the centre and as a result, we clawed our way back to three points behind. Westmeath responded but amazingly, they could not capitalise. They had five or six chances to put us away once and for all but they failed to do it. Even so, they probably did not worry too much. As long as they were having possession of the ball, they knew we could not do anything about it. They also knew the clock was running down and so time was on their side. I remember turning to an umpire and asking him how long was left. He told me there were around three minutes to play. As I was speaking, Westmeath were on the attack again and so I had a word with Ollie Murphy. I told him that when the ball came back down towards us, we had to go for goal. He nodded in agreement. There was no other way. We were three points behind and time was almost up.

Seconds later, the ball was cleared out from our defence to Nigel Nestor. He sent a hopeful ball in towards the Westmeath penalty area and I got to it. I went to fist the ball across to Ollie but it fell behind him. So I managed to retrieve the ball and then tried to cut inside their defence. But they slammed the door shut and so I fed it back to Ollie who was on the Hogan Stand side of the Canal End. He buried the ball in the back of the net and next I remember, the crowd went wild. It was virtually the last kick of the game and seconds later the final whistle blew. The score of 3–9 to 2–12 meant we had to do it all again. The Westmeath team were gutted. It was a match they should have won easily but their misses proved costly. They were punished for those wasted chances. For the umpteenth time, we had fought back to save our skins. At one stage in that second half, Westmeath were nine points to the good. This was not to be the last time when we would come back from the dead. It not only amazes me, but I have a feeling that all GAA followers are equally amazed by the huge deficits we have overcome in the past. No doubt it will continue to happen well into the future. There is no secret. We just play for the full 70 minutes and beyond.

******

On the very weekend of our important replay with Westmeath, Amanda was due to give birth to our second child. On the Friday morning, the day before the replay (held that year on a Saturday), I brought Amanda to the hospital for a CT scan. She was already two weeks overdue and we were all getting a little anxious in case she went into labour on the day of the Westmeath match. The midwife who gave Amanda her check-up was actually a niece of Mattie Gilsenan, a former Meath player. At this stage Amanda was close to giving birth and the midwife asked if we could return the next day. When I told her I was playing in the All-Ireland quarter-final the next day, she replied: 'Oh well, we'll have to look after you so!' On our way back to Athboy we stopped off for tea with some friends of ours – Pat and Marie Smyth. While we were there, the midwife rang me and asked us to come back in that evening. Amazingly, on the way to the hospital, Amanda started going into labour! I went to stay with a friend of mine, Paul Donohoe, and for hours I was hanging by the phone thinking the call would never come. Finally, the midwife rang and asked if I would like to come over.

At around 9.50 pm on 10 August 2001, the day before our match against Westmeath, Amanda gave birth to our second child,

Lauren. I was now the proud father of two daughters. With all the waiting and worrying over, it was time to focus properly on the big game. Although it was not the ideal preparation for me, I was bursting with pride and ready to give my all. On a personal level, when you are full of pride as I was at that time, everything else seems irrelevant. So going into that replay, less than 24 hours after Lauren was born, I had nothing to lose. There was no pressure on me whatsoever; I could just go out there and express all my joy and delight freely.

\* \* \* \* \* \*

For a change, it was Meath who actually started off the brighter. To cap a memorable few days for myself, I scored a goal after seven minutes. It was just the kind of start we had hoped for. Then around 10 minutes later, just when we thought it was going to be our day, we were reduced to 14 men. Hank Traynor had already been booked in the early stages. Somewhat clumsily, he fouled again and so the referee had no option but to show him the red card. That gave Westmeath a boost and you could see them raise their game after that incident. The half-time break could not have come sooner and this gave us a chance to regroup and reassess things.

But it was Westmeath who edged in front after the break. Then I was switched back into midfield and that move worked to our advantage. I started to win a lot of breaking ball and as a result I could lay off ball and pass it in quickly to our forwards. It was a great individual effort from Ray Magee which eventually settled the game. From about 25 yards out, he let fly and the ball hit the back of the net. It was a cracking goal and Westmeath had no answer to it. Although we won by five points, the 2–10 to 0–11 score was much tighter than it may suggest. Westmeath must be given great credit for both displays. I think they left their form way behind after the first game. They were just not the same side in the replay and you could see that after the first 10 minutes. Hank's dismissal gave them hope but in reality, a nine-point lead from the first game must have had a bad effect on them. It is very hard to pick up the pieces after that and the selectors and management must have had a huge task in trying to lift them.

All-Ireland champions Kerry were next up in the semi-final. Beforehand, people were saying that we had not a prayer against this Kerry machine. They had been so impressive in both their previous matches. Only two late Dublin goals had stopped them in the penultimate match but in the replay, Kerry won easily. That Kerry had the measure of Dublin in both matches, and did it in front of the fanatical Dublin support, was proof of the difficult task we faced. Typical of the vein of form they were in, Kerry began as if they were going to hammer us. Suddenly, and looking back now it did seem like it happened in an instant, the Kerry juggernaut came to an abrupt halt. Without any resistance at all, we took over and never looked back. I will never really know what happened to Kerry that day. It was so strange to see them with their tails up one moment and a few minutes later down flat.

I think it was one of the weirdest matches ever seen. Maybe they were overconfident before the game. Maybe they had no stomach for a fight. I just do not know and I find it hard to fathom. Kerry had always shown great character as well as their undoubted skill down through the years. We really had no opposition and won as we liked, 2–14 to 0–5! Even allowing for Kerry's non-showing, you cannot take anything away from our performance. The points still have to be put over and we showed great application to the job. I thought the whole team performed brilliantly but especially the back lines. A miserable day for Kerry was completed when they had a man sent off. The final score was also very unusual for a semi-final. At that stage of a Championship, the matches are very closely contested and it is rare to see such a huge winning margin. Kerry also went into the record books that day for all the wrong reasons. It was their heaviest defeat in the All-Ireland since way back in 1934!

Galway were the only team standing in our way to another All-Ireland title. But they would be looking to go one better after losing to Kerry the year before. The side from the west had shown similar guts and courage to us. They had only lost out on winning Sam the year before after a replay. Also, in their semi-final with Derry, they came from five points behind to win, thanks to a late goal. That semi-final looked like a replay with both sides level, 1–11 to 0–14. Then Galway earned the right to meet us in the All-Ireland final with that killer goal.

I could now harbour dreams of placing my newborn baby girl, Lauren, in the Sam Maguire Cup – the same as I had done with

Sophia in 1999. In two previous finals, I had ended up a winner. I was hoping that this would be three out of three. Quite apart from winning in '96 and '99, most of us also had more experience. Most important of all, we had the experience of winning. There was nothing unusual in our preparations this time. We did all our usual training routines and of course there was a great buzz all over Meath with all the bunting, the razzmatazz and the cars and houses decked out in the Meath colours.

We gathered at the usual meeting points and then it was on to Croke Park. Some of us took the time to go out into the stands and watch the Minor final between Dublin and Tyrone. The dressing-room was pretty relaxed and there were no special instructions and no special cases to look out for on the Galway team. We had seen it all before and nothing could be said or done that hadn't been said or done before. After the team photos, the parade and the National Anthem, we took our positions. The referee threw up the ball and there followed a few minutes of frantic football, typical of any side in a final. Things settled down a little after both sides registered their first points. We started off fairly well but then Galway started to take over and at the break were a few points in front.

There was no real panic in the dressing-room at half-time. We had been here before especially against Mayo in '96. We began brightly and matched Galway but in the second part of that first half, we were very slack. I felt that we allowed Galway too much time and space. That was the main thing we had to improve on after the break. Obviously unknown to us, Galway were about to make a big tactical decision. Padraig Joyce was playing full-forward for them and Darren Fay more than had his measure. But running out after the interval, Joyce moved into the corner where he was now marked by Mark O'Reilly. It was a move by John O'Mahoney and his selectors which was to prove decisive. Padraig Joyce ran amok in that second half. It seemed to lift the rest of the Galway team leaving us unable to cope with them. They were superfit and lightening fast. I think Joyce scored a whopping nine points in that second period and it was literally the difference between both sides. We had no answer to them. They were simply too good for us on the day and they won the All-Ireland by 0–17 to 0–8.

My fellow Meath team-mates and I were devastated. For the first time in an All-Ireland final I knew the pain of the losers' dressing-room. I felt that we had not just been beaten – we were humiliated.

Galway played us off the park and were a class above us in all departments. We had crumbled in much the same way as Kerry had fallen to us in the semi-final. There were strange parallels and similarities in the defeats of Kerry and ourselves. Both of us had started off brightly but then fell flat.

All credit to the Tribesmen for the way in which they dismantled us. Padraig Joyce was a sensation and it is hard to remember a better individual performance in an All-Ireland final. I could hear the sheer delight echoing from the corridors as Galway celebrated. I knew how it felt as I sat there in the stony cold silence of a pride-bashed concrete room. The loneliness of the losers' dressing-room is a really miserable and horrible place to be. No amount of cheap words could console us. Now I knew how Mick Lyons felt when Alan Nash tried to cheer him up all those years before. In four All-Ireland finals I had played in at Croke Park (five if you count the League), I had been a winner in them all. Now I was a loser. Not only had we lost, we had put up no sort of resistance at all. It was difficult to stomach. In hindsight it would be easy to make excuses and maybe say that Darren Fay should have been switched to counter the threat of Joyce. But there were no excuses. We had 15 able and experienced men but we were outplayed and outclassed on the day.

Making my way out to the Meath coach, I found it hard to raise a smile. I wished I could have crawled under something – anything to avoid facing the press and above all our friends, families and supporters. I felt we had let them all down badly and had underperformed. I also felt part of one of the worst ever Meath performances in an All-Ireland final. When confronted with facing the music, however, we were all given such a surprise. Our supporters were just fantastic and lifted our spirits no end. Outside the coach, outside Croke Park and in the City West Hotel, they were all there. Fair play to them. They were obviously as disappointed as we were but they tried their very best to cheer us up.

In retrospect, it is hard to console yourself and put things in context. Someone did not die and besides, I had won two Senior All-Irelands out of three. I took heart from the well-known lines of the song: 'Don't be sad 'cause two out of three ain't bad'. Tens of thousands of players, living and deceased, would give their right arm to even reach a final. On further reflection, we did not do a great deal wrong in that final. Galway just never gave us an inch. They were superfit and Padraig Joyce had a day to remember.

# 10 Decisions and Disappointment

It was now time for me to consider my future. After the defeat by Galway, John McDermott finally hung up his boots. He had come out of retirement to help Meath in the 2001 campaign and had been a great servant to us. Without him in the middle of the park, we would have been a very weakened side. And so I sat down with Amanda, between the defeat by Galway and the 2002 season, and we discussed my future. It was no longer a case of how much more I could offer Meath or how much more I could achieve. My family and my career were now the main issues on the table.

Amanda had always been a great support to me but it was time for me to start supporting her now. I had to start living a normal life and help my family. I had two young daughters at an age where I could start watching them grow up and Sophia was just about to start school. My livelihood was another issue. I had a business to run and had to bring in the money. After weighing up all the pros and cons, there was a unanimous result. It was decided my footballing days with Meath would come to an end. Even if it were only a temporary break from the game, the year 2002 would see me leaving the Meath set-up.

We were drawn to meet Westmeath in our first match of the Leinster Championship. They had proved very tough in our previous matches and this would be no exception. I was really hoping that after the decision I had made, we would not fall at the first. Above all, I was desperately hoping that my last match would not happen to be Westmeath's first-ever Championship win over us! As it turned out, we never had a moment's worry. The big crowd that attended the game in Portlaoise must have gone away disappointed. If they were expecting a cracker, then they got a very one-sided result. We strolled to an easy win by 1–12 to 0–11.

It is hard to know the exact reason why Westmeath never performed that day. Perhaps they never got over the heartbreak of the previous defeats we had inflicted on them. They had built up handsome leads against us in the past only to let them slip. Perhaps they had no appetite for another tasty clash with us and lost the game before they trudged out onto the pitch. There was any number of reasons. I certainly know that we did not perform miracles that day. We did not play all that well. I thought our backs did well, but even then there were no fireworks. Regardless of past results between two neighbours, you always expect a rousing encounter.

In fact, the Westmeath team we played that day were the poorest I have ever seen. There were also rumours going around about Ger Heavin. In the days and weeks prior to the big clash, I was talking to Westmeath supporters who told me that all was not right within the camp. They were saying that there was a bit of a falling out between their star player and the management and selectors. If that were true, then it would surely have caused great tension and disruption right through the team. These things do happen and it is a fact of life in sport. It is how those situations are handled which is the key. The fact is they were only a shadow of the team we knew.

Next up in the Leinster semi-final were Dublin and we would have to brighten up considerably. If the Westmeath team were one of the poorest I had seen, then our next opponents having suffered a lot at our hands in recent years, would surely provide a really stern test. Yet another Leinster encounter between Dublin and ourselves and I was hoping we would reach another Leinster final and a chance to play for my fourth Leinster medal. It was not to be, however. Dublin dashed my and Meath's hope of another Leinster title. I thought it was a fairly even match with nothing between the sides until Dublin scored two killer goals. In the end, those goals made the difference and we argued long and hard afterwards that one should have been disallowed. In particular, I remember a Dublin player kicking a ball in towards our goal. Possibly, it was Ray Cosgrove who went up and punched it towards the net, but in the process he collided with our keeper, Cormac Sullivan. The ball ended up in the net but we felt that Cormac had been fouled.

However, when I recall it now, I have to say that the Dublin player did well to get his hand to it. To be fair, I can also remember a certain Colm O'Rourke bundling John O'Leary into the back of the net many years earlier. So I suppose it all evens out over time and they got the rub of the green this time. Dublin had their dander up after that and were very hard to peg back. They went on to lift the Leinster by 2–11 to 0–10.

Despite the disappointment, it was not yet time to hang up the boots. We were now in the back-door system and Louth were the next door we were aiming to come through. The big trouble with this game was that we had only less than a week to prepare for it. Sides like Louth are vastly improved and the days of Leinster being dominated by Dublin and Meath are fast coming to an end. Twenty or 30 years ago people would have laughed if you told them Offaly would win the Leinster title followed by Kildare as happened in 1997 and 1998. We found it hard going against the Wee County. I think that mentally and physically it was tough to motivate ourselves after the Leinster final only six days previously. We were not ready for it but beggars cannot be choosers and a second chance was better than a long summer of inactivity.

One of the biggest crowds, if not *the* biggest, turned up at Páirc Tailteann to see us face Louth in the All-Ireland quarter-final. Truth be told, there is actually a lot of bitterness between Louth and Meath – more so than any other county in Leinster. Much is made about Dublin and ourselves, but that is all nonsense. That is friendly rivalry, similar to that with Westmeath. In fact, the Dubs and ourselves have the utmost respect for one another. With Louth there has always been a certain bad feeling, which is hard to pinpoint. Suffice to say Louth people have never had anything good to say about us. If I am totally honest, we never really have had anything good to say about them either. All I know is that we got off on the wrong footing somewhere along the line.

On the day of the Louth game, I was attending a wedding in Co Wexford. The match was on Saturday evening so a helicopter was arranged to bring me to and from the game. It only took half an hour to fly from Navan to Wexford where my friend, Richard Lynch from Kentstown, was getting married to Wexford woman, Margaret MacDonald. After the ceremony and all the sober celebrations, I flew back to Navan and arrived there in plenty of time for the game.

The rest of the Meath team had gathered in Bellinter and that's where I landed. As the game got underway, it was obvious that we had not recovered fully from our exertions the week before. Louth got off to the best possible start and for the whole game we were chasing their shadows.

As full-time approached, suddenly all the drama started. I seem to recall Richie Kealy scored a goal giving us a glimmer of hope. Entering time added on for stoppages, most of us thought that there were three minutes injury time to be played. Suddenly, I sensed that Louth were becoming a little panicky. You could see that they were desperate for the referee to blow up. They were ready to celebrate a famous win. I remember Nigel Nestor got the ball who in turn passed it to Ollie Murphy. Hoping the ball would be passed to me, I put up my hand and drifted back off my marker. Ollie then drilled the ball across in my general direction. I latched onto it, rushed through on goal and blasted the ball to the back of the Louth net.

It was more instinct than anything else. The whole place went wild. I remember I was so excited in that moment, I took my shirt off and waved it around my head! Ollie was behind me and waving his shirt as well. We were all on a high. I can never recall such mad scenes like it before. We had won with the last kick of the game and were so relieved. Just another famous Meath comeback from a seemingly hopeless position had seen off Louth by 3–8 to 2–9. The Louth players and officials were livid. They claimed that there should only have been three minutes added on and that the referee had actually played five minutes. It was not the first time I had been at the centre of controversy involving Louth. Everyone was over the moon in the dressing-room. Sean congratulated every single one of us amid an unbelievable buzz. However, silence then fell upon the room when the Louth boss came in to congratulate us. Paddy Carr was almost in tears. He could barely get the words out and you could see he was a broken man. We knew something of the way he was feeling after our defeat to Galway the previous September.

The celebrations were just beginning for me after that last-gasp win over Louth. Pat Smyth drove me from the grounds back out to Bellinter where I got the helicopter back down to Wexford for the remainder of the wedding. The hair still stands on the back of my neck when I remember the reception I received. We touched down beside a lake and when I jumped out, you would have sworn it was me who was getting married. All along the balcony of the hotel, and along the embankment in front of the lake, people were applauding and cheering me. It was a very touching moment. Then I began hearing all the different stories of the game from various wedding guests. Some of the funnier accounts had me in stitches. Some people were listening to RTÉ Radio while others were tuned into LM FM Radio. Apparently, a poor reception made the commentary very hard to hear. Other people were on phones and mobiles to try and find out the score or else bringing up the teletext on the television. By all accounts, there was bedlam and mayhem in the hotel. Louth people were saying that they had held on while Meath people were saying that they had snatched it! Neutrals at the wedding also chipped in with their opinions on the matter. Some said there was a replay while others said there was extra time! It sounded like things were as frantic there as on the pitch. It was a weekend I'm not likely to forget for many years to come.

In the draw for the next round of qualifiers, we faced Laois. We had not played them for a few years but were all too aware that they were a big danger. Previous Laois sides were always big and physical. They relished a challenge with us and were hoping to put us on our backside as they had done in '92. Back then, that was very embarrassing for Meath, especially considering the number of All-Ireland finals we had reached in the late Eighties and early Nineties. Just like the Westmeath tie, we never had a moment's anxiety. We strolled to an even easier win, 1–15 to 0–7. The stature and physical aspect expected from Laois was just not there. They were a quite young side and had very few big fellas on the team. They had all the hallmarks of a team looking to the future and in the process of rebuilding. After the game, I received the Man of the Match award for my efforts.

A week after that, on 21st July, we faced Donegal. Because we had not faced them in a long time, we were confident of beating them. Who could blame us? We were on such a roll and our confidence was sky high. Donegal were very sharp, however. They played a Kildare-like game only with more zip and hunger. I remember that I struggled to cope with it. I was playing in a midfield and full-forward role and the ball bypassed me a lot. Even so, we started off fairly well and I thought both teams were evenly matched. Then we made a monumental mistake.

They were attacking our goal midway through the first half but the move broke down and our backs got possession. To our horror, Cormac Murphy fumbled the ball. The Donegal forwards pounced and despite Paddy Reynolds' best efforts, the ball ended up in the back of our net. Our backs were now very much to the wall. I was very disappointed with Murphy. He should have just hoofed the ball upfield. It proved to be a very costly mistake. Hard as we tried after that, it gave Donegal greater confidence and we just could not bridge the gap. We did manage one last-gasp effort as Donal Curtis ran onto a through ball. He flicked it with his hand and it seemed time stood still as we watched it move towards the net. Agonisingly, the ball went the other side of the net and wide. That was the last action as Donegal held out to win by 1–13 to 0–14.

Afterwards, the dressing-room was like a morgue. I knew it was my last game but did not want to say anything. In any case, it would not have been the right time and I certainly did not want any big fuss made. My last game against Donegal was a disappointing way to bow out, but career-wise I had little to complain about.

The following day, Sunday, the newspapers ran amok with speculation. In essence they were saying that I had retired because of threats made to my family and me from rival fans. It was incredible the things they said, and thousands would be led to believe them. Great Meath footballers like Tommy Dowd and John McDermott had hung up their boots and there was not a dickey bird about it. But because it was me, and I had been at the centre of so much press activity down the years, they decided that there was another possible story here. That is why I appeared on RTÉ's *Six One* sports news the following evening. I wanted to get everything off my chest by talking to Eamon Horan.

The story that Amanda, my kids and I had been threatened by rival fans, to the extent that I decided to call it a day, was a total fabrication by certain tabloid newspapers. Of course, we get abuse from the terraces. My Meath colleagues and I have been called everything under the sun. What's more, we've had coins and objects thrown at us from the stands. But you have to blot it all out and just get on with the game. If you did not, then there would be no games. It is just a fact of life in sport and you have to be thick-skinned.

There were also rumours flying about that I had a blazing row with Sean Boylan. I have had my fair share of disagreements with Sean over the years but it never once stopped me from lining out with Meath. Come to think of it, I would say that most of the players have had their say with Sean. In the heat of the moment you spit out what you feel and then it is forgotten. We all know the story of Beckham, Ferguson and the flying football boot. It's just another fact of football life.

For the record, the worst abuse that I can recall actually came from on the field and not from the stands. It came in the Donegal game as the referee blew the final whistle. As I was swapping shirts with a Donegal player, all sorts of people were running wild onto the pitch. To my astonishment, a Donegal selector ran to me and shouted:

'Go on back to Meath, you fucker!'

'What did you say?' I asked.

'Ah, go and fuck off,' he bellowed back.

I was very angry and wanted to confront the guy. But he got away and someone actually grabbed me before I had time to make the headlines for all the *right* reasons! There I was, in my last match and in a moment of despair, actually swapping shirts with an opponent when that happened. I thought it was terrible to kick a man when he is down. Later I talked to Donegal's Mickey Moran and brought up the matter. He apologised to me and went to get the selector in question. This time the selector was contrite, apologising and claiming he just got carried away in all the excitement!

As I stated earlier, some Irish journalists are now becoming just as bad as some of the English gutter press. One journalist who really gets up my nose is Roy Curtis of *The Sunday World*. His newspaper was the real culprit with respect to my retirement and he has been on my back for years. In fact, Curtis has written all sorts of nonsense down through the years. Many people, especially friends, would ring me and tell me that there was something about me in the paper. After reading it, I would usually feel dumbfounded. I do not know where Roy Curtis got his information from, perhaps he rang other journalists who had *actually* talked to me or else he was just putting his own slant on events. The truth is that in my whole career with Meath, Curtis has never once made contact with me to arrange an interview or otherwise, despite the fact that I have read a whole heap of stuff under his name. I have never ever met or even talked to the guy.

I will also hold my hands up and admit that sometimes I have been my own worst enemy. Clearly, the Irish media had a field day with me after my racist comments in Australia in 1999. Over the years my constant moaning and bickering on the field have also landed me in trouble. That was all truth and fact. But it is the lies about me that are hard to stomach. These reporters have been constantly on the lookout for me, and so when I announced I was quitting on 24 July 2002, it was yet another case of 'Get Geraghty'.

\*\*\*\*\*\*

My retirement from Meath Senior football brought some unexpected good news. A week after that television interview, Tom Purcell from Buccaneers Rugby Club rang me. To my surprise he asked me if I would be interested in playing rugby. I told him I would have to think about it seeing that I had never played rugby before. But as I had stated quite consistently in all my interviews, I was ready to try something new after the over-burdening load of Gaelic Games. Navan Rugby Club also got in contact with me but, although they are very conveniently located, Buccaneers are a famous club. Speculation still continued about my future, however. According to one newspaper, I was all set to join a League of Ireland soccer club!

Having finally made up my mind, I rang Tom Purcell back and told him I would give it a go and see how things went. A few weeks later, I travelled to Athlone to train with them. I must admit, I found the training very hard to get used to. I had played with the round ball all my life. Suddenly I was faced with the crisp passing of an oval ball and it would take time to learn the moves and calls.

Training with Buccaneers, there were other things which were totally different to football. The most obvious difference was the physique of the players. In football, most of the players are tall and lean, while in rugby the lads are smaller and of stocky build. There were also so many strange foreign accents. The club is made up of players from the four corners of Ireland and there are also players from New Zealand, Australia, France, South Africa and Britain. New Zealand must be the most represented as there are at least four Kiwi players at the club. Chief among them is John McKee, a New Zealander who has coached in Australia. He joined Buccaneers as director of rugby from Montferrand in France. His invaluable experience is a huge advantage to the club. Naturally there has been much excitement and expectation as a result.

Playing rugby, I did not feel in any way out of my depth. After all, I am a quick learner and have pace and ability. Having been at a soccer trial in England and not disgracing myself at Arsenal, I was eager for a new experience. There was also no pressure on me. If I made the grade, fine, but if not, it would be no big deal. Essentially, I had nothing to lose. Before me, Gaelic footballers have made the grade at Buccaneers. One of the most experienced players at the club only happened to be a highly respected footballer with Offaly. Mike Devine, known as 'Deviner', has played rugby for Connacht and was the club's Player of the Year in 1997. Being somewhat of a veteran at the club, he has won three Connacht Senior Leagues and has more National Rugby League appearances with Buccs than any other player currently there.

Buccaneers took me on for my speed and pace. They were obviously looking at me as a winger and before long they tried me out in that position. I was put in their reserve side to play in the Oval Cup which is a Junior competition. My first ever rugby match came in Arklow, Co Wicklow. I came on at half-time and although I did not score, I really enjoyed my first run and could not wait to get another chance. In my next outing, I actually scored what I thought was my first 'try'. But it was disallowed as the line judge said my foot was 'in touch'. I was getting better with more experience and after we won the Oval Cup, I was to get my first taste of the Senior ranks.

My big day came on 15 September 2002. We were playing at home in Ericsson Park against Galwegians in the Connacht Senior League. This was a local derby between two very famous names in Irish rugby. They are both steeped in tradition and history and so I felt it was an honour to line out that day in the famous black and amber colours of Buccaneers. The colours are exactly the same as

Kilkenny; the only difference being that the stripes on our jerseys run horizontally and we wear black shorts. Galwegians have produced many fine players down through the years. Probably the most famous in recent years has been Eric Elwood. He was a fantastic points scorer for Ireland in the mid to late Nineties with his great kicking abilities. Obviously, there is a lot of rivalry between both camps and everyone was expecting a close game.

I was very nervous before the start. This was my first game of rugby at this level and, with many eyes on me, I really wanted to look the part. I did not want to do anything stupid or silly which would make me look totally out of place in the side. So you could say there was a fair bit of pressure on me. I need not have worried. It turned out to be a dream debut for me, but there was a bitter taste and twist all the same. Playing as a winger, I saw quite a lot of the ball and scored a nice try. Many reports stated that I had made a big impression in my first Senior match. The *Irish Independent* even printed a colour photo of me in a real action shot of a winger. Sadly, it was to be our only try. They ended up scoring two tries and won the game by the narrowest of margins, 23–22.

It was a losing debut, but at least I scored our only try and we did go down fighting. Whatever else happens, when I look back one day on my sporting career, I can always tell my grandkids that I scored a try in my very first Senior rugby match. In subsequent matches, I played well without scoring. Then I missed lots of training. I was helping my club Seneschalstown reach the semi-finals in Meath and coming up to the Christmas period, the pub was extremely busy. I also went to Chicago for a week's break with Amanda. As a result, rugby took a back seat and I was not surprised or disappointed to be dropped to the reserves.

In reality, I was never really going to figure prominently at Buccaneers. They have vast resources and so have many players from all over the world who have been playing the game all of their lives. I could never have expected to rock that boat. In their pre-season programme, they had pen-pictures of over 50 players including myself. So the competition for places was immense. Even allowing for all my missed training and matches, I got quite a few games in the reserves. I really enjoyed playing the game, despite all the cuts and bruises and the aches and pains which go with this most physical of sports.

# 11 Rules Rows Resurface

Australian Rules, or the International Rules to give it its correct title, is a marvellous game. There's no denying it was a fantastic move by the GAA to introduce it to this country. It has worked so well and, if anything, the popularity of the game is on the increase. The competition itself began back in 1984 and I feel privileged to have followed in the stud prints of many Meath greats who have lined out for Ireland in this code. Colm O'Rourke was the star of that very first Series. Although Ireland lost by an aggregate of 222–208 at Páirc Uí Chaoimh in Cork and twice in Croke Park, Colm ended up top scorer with 45 points. He achieved such a high score because at that stage the competition was run over three matches. The current format of two matches was agreed in 1998. Nonetheless, it was some feat by Colm. In that Irish panel he was joined by fellow Meath stalwarts, Liam Hayes, Mick Lyons and Joe Cassells.

When the Series was played again in 1986, Colm and Mick were again involved but those matches were better known for all the wrong reasons. In the First Test in Perth, Pat Spillane and Pat O'Byrne, along with three Australian players, were sent to the line following violent scenes on the pitch. Those infamous but well-known scenes actually brought the Series into question and it looked doubtful if it would ever be played again. After all, it was at an experimental stage. Ireland won that Series, 2–1, and so gained revenge for losing at home in Ireland two years before. Australia did the same the following year by winning 2–1 away in Ireland. Jim Stynes of Dublin was top scorer with 38 points, but in fact was playing with Australia and not Ireland, as you would have expected. Back then, as a young lad watching those games at home on television, I hardly imagined I would become embroiled in the now infamous 1999 Series when Jim was part of the Australian management.

Representing Meath in that loss to the Aussies in '87 were Mick Lyons and Liam Hayes again, who were joined by Robbie O'Malley and Bernard Flynn. A gap of three years ensued until the next phase of matches in 1990. Robbie O'Malley captained the Irish team to a 2–1 victory and Bernard Flynn ended as the tournament's top scorer with 29 points. Then a huge gap of eight years – for reasons best known to the GAA – followed until the next Series took place. These matches were very much tried and tested, which took enormous effort and organising, especially with the long away trips Down Under. Also, the huge amount of money involved was quite a significant sum back in those early years. In 1990, for example, when Robbie captained Ireland, the teams played in Melbourne, Canberra and Perth. That meant they were away for over a month so you can imagine the costs accumulating with hotels, food, drink, travel and so on.

In those early years the matches were also known as 'Compromise Rules'. That was because the Aussies agreed to play with our round ball rather than their oval-shaped one, which we would not have been used to playing. In return, we had to play by their rules and all the rough and tumble it brings. In the years that followed, we may have wished that the compromise was the other way around, as the brutal nature of their game almost led, on more than one occasion, to the whole thing been scrapped.

All those early teething problems seem to have been ironed out and now a very successful formula has been found and put in place. There are no more month-long tours and no more inconsistent gaps in the years when the Series is played. Certainly the huge and growing popularity now seems to have secured its future. The game is now played between both countries on an annual basis. There are now just two Tests instead of three, with one country playing at home one year and away the next year. When it came to the new format of two matches in 1998, the score from previous Tests stood at 2–2. But the strange thing about it was that both wins, for both countries, were recorded away. So in '98 at Croke Park, when I had failed to make the panel from the trials, we were under pressure to redress the balance and stop the habit of the away team winning.

Things looked to be fitting the same pattern, which did not look good for Ireland, when Australia won the First Test by the narrowest margin, 62–61. Meath players who lined out that year were Darren Fay and John McDermott. They were to end up on the winning side as Ireland won the Second Test by 67–56 which meant they had won on an aggregate score of 128–118. The hoodoo had also been broken and Ireland had at last won on home soil.

Trevor Giles got his big chance along with myself in 1999. As I already pointed out at length, that Series made the headlines for the wrong reasons with my racist comment totally overshadowing everything else that happened. For a guy making his debut in Rules, Trevor took to it like a duck to water. He notched 10 points in Ireland's First Test win but it was Galway's Jarlath Fallon who was to prove our hero. He scored the killer goal in a personal tally of 19 points.

In the Second Test, John McDermott scored a very important goal worth six points. We had our backs to the wall at that stage and were 19–7 behind, coming to the end of the first quarter. But John's goal left us just six behind. We gradually chipped away at their lead until the final score of 52–52 gave us the Series. The win also gave us a 4–2 lead in the entire Series since it began.

In the Millennium Series in 2000 at Croke Park, I had a particularly good game in the First Test. We got off to a good start and led 12–0. Midway through the second quarter, we had a lead of 14 points but then the Aussies cut the deficit to nine points at half-time. A few minutes after the restart, I scored a goal which put us back in the driving seat. Trevor actually made that goal for me and at that stage it looked like we would go on and win easily. That was not to be the case, however. But then again that is the beauty of this game. It is so unpredictable and all can change in a flash. In our game a three-point goal is seen as precious, so you can imagine what six pointers do in this game.

The Australians fought back so well that they went on to win the First Test, 55–47. To be honest, I don't think it was so much a case of them winning as us tiring badly. In the match Justin Leppitsch was top Aussie with 17 points. But it was no consolation that I ended up top Irish scorer with 10 points.

When the Second Test came, we were up against it from the start with an eight-point deficit to overcome. Things went from bad to worse and we could never strike a blow. Australia won by 68–51 to win the Series by a whopping 25 points. An indication of just how bad we were was that for the entire game, I only managed two 'behinds'. Two points is a really poor showing from someone in my position. But Trevor only hit one behind so all in all it was a disaster, especially for the 57,000 who attended only a day after the Kerry v Galway All-Ireland final.

My return to Australia in 2001 must have been closely watched by a number of people. To say I was afraid to open my mouth would be going too far, but I was conscious of what I was saying! Thankfully, everything passed without incident and I was determined to let my football do the talking. Having only played in a friendly game at the Melbourne Cricket Ground in 1999, I was really looking forward to playing there in the First Test of 2001 and to savour the atmosphere. This is a ground that once held a crowd of 110,000 for an international cricket match which gives you an idea of its sheer size. Before the game started, there was all the razzmatazz expected more of a big American football game. There was music and a fireworks display and given that it was at night, it was an amazing spectacle. Running out on the pitch, the ground was hard but very slippery from the dew.

Determined to have a good game, I remember I started slowly but I improved as the game progressed. We led by a few points after the first quarter which was largely due to Brendan Devenney who was having a 'stormer'. Australia hit back to lead by six points at half-time. Then on the restart, I scored two overs which brought us back level. In a ding-dong battle, Australia went clear again. It couldn't have been more exciting as Anthony Tohill scored a goal to leave the scores at 41–41 going into the last quarter. Kieran McGeeney scored a goal in the final quarter which seemed to hand us the advantage as we had a nice lead. But the home side battled back and, even though I hit another over, we were hanging on. We were left to count our blessings as Australia were left to rue missed chances. They hit three or four wides in the closing minutes and so we hung on for a 59–53 win. There were several outstanding performances in that win. On a personal note, I was thrilled with my 10 points which was the perfect way to respond to my misery of

1999. But Brendan Devenney had a dream debut in Australian Rules. He ended the match as the top scorer with a haul of 14 points. Tohill came a close second with 13 points.

We were halfway towards another Rules victory and the question now was whether we could do it to give us an unbelievable record of four wins from four away in Australia. That is a statistic which is hard to believe, seeing that it is extremely hard for any team, in any code, to win even one match away. Football Park in Adelaide was the venue for the Second Test. A crowd of just over 30,000 turned up, which is small – even Croke Park would be guaranteed to pull in at least 40,000. I opened the scoring but it was only a 'behind' that was quickly cancelled out by the Aussies. Then Anthony Tohill scored a goal and we opened up a bit of a gap midway through that first quarter. They came back strong, leaving only a point in it at the end of that opening period. I scored a goal on the restart and that gave us a bit of leeway as we went six clear. But no sooner did I score than they went straight up the other end and also scored a goal! They were determined not to lose at home again and by half-time, they led by a point, 33–32.

Donegal's Brendan Devenney had a fantastic couple of debut Tests and thanks to scores from him, we went ahead in the third quarter. A bit like wounded animals, the Aussies responded but their kicking was a bit wayward and they could only manage one-point scores. When Devenney popped up with an over inside the last quarter, it looked like were were home and hosed. We were 15 points ahead. Two goals from them would have given them hope, but in the form they were in that was never going to materialise. We won the Second Test, 71–52 which was all very easy in the end. Amazingly, we had kept our record of never having lost a Series in Australia.

Tadhg Kennelly, another impressive newcomer to the game, was top scorer in that game with 15 points. But without question, the man of the Series was Brendan Devenney. His consistency in both games meant that he ended up top Irish scorer with 22 points. Devenney outscored my own 21 points and Tohill's 19 to prove his worth. His scores in both games were turning points. He is a player with a great future and Australia 2001 was a proud moment for him. But there are so many other quality footballers worth a mention – players like Westmeath's Dessie Dolan and Dave Mitchell and Tipperary star, Declan Browne. That said, it was great to see Brendan go into the record books as the top Irish player in 2001 – even if he did pip me to it!

Selectors are very often forgotten but I think they must be praised after our magnificent win in 2001. Generally, when you are picked to represent your country at any level, you are the cream of the crop. Therefore, the best players do not necessarily have to come from the best counties. There are so many talented players who play with the weaker counties and it is good to see them recognised.

I have a theory regarding our feat of winning all of our Rules Series away from home. Remember also that Australia won on their first two visits here. I believe that when you are away, you want to express yourself. You want to show people what you can do. You are in a different location and can relax a little too. Playing at home can often be a little monotonous; doing the same thing all year in the same places.

In 2002, Evan Kelly was called up to the Irish team and so he joined Trevor Giles and myself. This continued the fine tradition of Meath players to have worn the green jersey. I was delighted for Evan and once again the men who picked the team did a fine job. They leave no stone unturned in trying to find the right players. His nippiness, pace and scoring ability would be an asset in the front line.

In the relatively short history of this great competition, I do not think there was ever a Series played in wetter conditions than in 2002. It never seemed to stop raining for the entire two weeks. There were floods all over the country and none more so than in Dublin. Luckily we had the superb draining system of Croke Park's new 'Desso' pitch. But for that, the Series would have been in doubt. With that in mind, the people who trudged into the ground for the First Test should have been given medals! All you could see in the stadium stands were people huddled together in a sea of waterproofs and umbrellas. The weather failed to dampen our enthusiasm and we got off to a good start. At one stage we lead 38–19 which was a huge and almost unassailable lead.

The nature of this game, as I pointed out before, is that with six-point goals the situation can change in an instant. To our horror that is exactly what happened. The Aussies finished strongly in the final period and went away to win 67–58. We tired visibly in that final quarter and it is hard to know if that was really the case, or if it was once again the 'away' factor.

Conditions for the Second Test were even wetter than the first game. They were so bad that people struggled to get to Croke Park on time because of serious flooding. That did not stop over 70,000 from turning up, which I think was a record attendance for a Rules match. The crowd would not be left disappointed, however, and there would be plenty of incidents to warm them up. We made the better start but I was disappointed I did not do a lot better. I made a few good runs but some of my team-mates failed to find me. Then the few chances that did come my way, I failed to take. After that came the moment which took all the gloss off the occasion. I was caught up in a bad-tempered moment but could do nothing about it.

While we were on an attack, one of our players was fouled. It happened right beside me, where out of the blue their Brisbane Lions star Brad Scott grabbed me. He got a firm hold on the neck of my jersey and kept yelling at me: 'Go on, go on – hit me.' 'No, you hit me,' I replied. To my complete surprise, he did. The next I knew I was on the ground! Looking back, I am glad I kept my cool and did not retaliate. Perhaps instinct kicked in, seeing how much I had suffered in the 1999 incident, or maybe I was following Mick Lyons from memory all of those years ago. In any case, it proved to be very costly for Scott. The referee sent him off and we had a free right in front of the posts. We duly scored a three-point over which put us around 10 points to the good. Many people may feel it was good thinking on my part that I had just fallen down to get him off and so get the free. But what would be the point in that? When he was sent off we had the ridiculous situation of another player coming on to replace him. I did not fall down intentionally. When he let loose, if you look at it again, I was leaning back to try and get out of the way. So I was a little off-balance and when he connected with my jaw, I could not keep upright. In fact, I was a little dazed and a little numb for a few moments afterwards. It may not have looked a hard punch, but I can tell you it was!

Like a carbon copy of the first game, they battled back well and finished the stronger in the final period. With a few minutes to go it turned into a thriller. Either team had one hand on the Series in those last minutes. But it was the Aussies who finished with a flurry. They hit score after score and even denied us the win at the death. The match finished in a draw, 42–42 and so they won the Series by seven points. Many people said that when we looked likely winners in both games, we tired badly. Perhaps they have a case. But we train just as hard as any professionals and in my view the Aussies just put in a supreme effort in the late stages of those games. We were also left to regret a lot of missed chances – just as Australia had done the previous year when it was us who finished the better.

On another day, we could have scored four or five goals in that match. Dessie Dolan, Padraig Joyce and myself were all guilty of missing good chances. Moreover, I was also angry and very disappointed with our management. I was on from the start, then taken off and then put back on with just five minutes left. I felt they got it badly wrong. As an athlete, when you are taken off your body calms and cools down. Even without the damp conditions, the body loses all of its adrenalin and warmth. So it is next to impossible to get up off a wet bench and then be expected to perform for just five minutes or so. Everyone knows that a player needs time to get his muscles tuned up. That is the reason why you see the substitutes running up and down the sidelines before being brought on. They are warming up the muscles and getting the circulation going. I was stone cold getting off that bench to go straight on. A better and more professional approach should really be taken in the future.

That was yet another away win in the Series and meant that Ireland now led 5–4 since it began. In 2003 Ireland headed to Australia, hoping to keep our own magnificent away record going. Somehow I felt that the Aussies would move heaven and earth to make sure that didn't happen, and they succeeded by winning the series on points.

Just before Christmas 2002, an International Rules Tribunal summoned Brad Scott to a meeting. Obviously, I was not going to travel halfway around the world for a hearing, so Croke Park officials organised a telephone link-up to Australia. In the event, I was not needed. Apparently, Scott told them that he was provoked by me! Thankfully, the referee also gave evidence. He stood up for me and said that it was the Aussie who was the aggressor in the incident. As a result, they came down fairly hard on him. He has been banned for three matches. That rules him out in 2003 and the first match in 2004. The ban probably means he will never represent his country again. In truth, he may not have played in any of those matches anyway. He is easily replaceable as the Australians introduce a large batch of new talent each year.

People may also wonder at the severity of his sentence in comparison to mine. He got three matches for striking while I got only one for a racist remark. The GAA appeased the Aussies in '99 by giving me one match ban and we also issued apologies. In Scott's case, the Australians knew that the GAA have always been sensitive when it comes to violence. They knew that the GAA took such a serious view about violence on the pitch. Moreover, they were well aware of it because the GAA had actually informed their counterparts Down Under that if something was not done about violence, they would consider pulling out of the Series altogether! Under those circumstances, Scott got a stiff sentence.

The message coming out was loud and clear. With millions watching on television, and major sponsors like Coca-Cola to consider, the Irish and Australians are united in safeguarding the future of this exciting spectacle. No longer will thuggery or racism be tolerated. I can see heavier sentences handed out in future with possible carry-overs to the offending player's club or county. But I do feel that in future, players should be reminded about their responsibilities before they participate.

An apology was issued by Brad Scott. In contrast to my fairly long statement, his was short. It read: 'I regret my actions. I accept there is no place in any code for that kind of behaviour.' Of course, I have no sympathy for him. What he did was stupid and he has to bear the consequences. Unlike my situation, he had time to respond and knew what he was doing. He spent some seconds engaged in dialogue with me and all he had to do was keep a hold of me until players rushed in to break it up. Why he lashed out, I do not know.

Rules governing the International Rules are generally good. However, there are a few changes I would like to see made. When a player is sent off, then the rules should be the same as ours. A team with a player off should be minus a player. It is ludicrous to send off a player and then to bring on another man in his place. The whole appointment of referees should be looked at as well. Some of our players have been subjected to very high and rough tackles over the years. In my opinion, the Irish referees are very fair overall. In contrast, Australian referees tend to favour Aussie players and therefore seem to be oblivious to high challenges. On the plus side, I think we can take something from their game and apply it to our own. A player incurring the wrath of the referee is sent to the 'sin-bin' for a cooling-off period of 10 minutes. That is a great idea and it could take the place of our warnings, name-taking and yellow cards. Truth be told, the yellow card was never part of our game anyway and was only introduced here a few years ago from soccer.

Overall I think everyone agrees that the International Rules has been a great success. It has had its ups and downs but nonetheless has survived the growing pains and is becoming so popular – just look at the record-breaking attendance at Croke Park during the floods! It has also meant the start of a good relationship between Ireland and Australia. The game is a huge favourite of mine and, who knows, the GAA one day may even decide to introduce the game here under a new governing body at club and county level.

Following a tough encounter with Mayo, the Meath Senior team win the 1996 All–Ireland Football Championship.

Graham is voted GAA Personality of the Month by National Irish Bank in September 1996, showing (left to right) Jean Geraghty, Graham, Amanda Egan, and Ger Geraghty.

The summer of replays in the Leinster clash 1996 – Graham attempts a hand pass surrounded by Kildare players.

The Big Day mode of
transport for Graham –
helicopter!

Graham and Amanda
Geraghty following their
wedding ceremony at St
James' Church, Athboy, 19
September 1997.

Central Division GAA finals in Gaelic Athletic Park, Chicago, 20 August 2000 (St Brendan's v Wolfe Tones) – front row (left to right) Adrian Ruane, Rory Mone, Damien Browne, Padraig Raftery, Conor Mone, Frank McCarthy, Gary Mason, Pat Kealy, Bernard Keaney, JP Rooney, Pat O'Riordan, Timber Tony. Back row (left to right) John Conroy, Danny O'Donnell, Paddy Browne, Sean McLaughlin, Tom Culkin, Graham Geraghty, Barry O'Hagan, Peter O'Dwyer, Martin Rafter, Peter McGinnity, Sean Folan, David Mitchell, John Kerley, and David Martin.

Brad Scott throwing a punch at Graham in the controversial Australian Rules Series, 2002.

Versatile sportsman – Playing with Buccaneers, Graham tackles Galwegians' Peter McDonagh in the Connacht Rugby Junior Cup semi-final in May 2003.

Daughters of a champion –
Sophia (left) and Lauren
Geraghty.

Vintage Geraghty in control – whether playing for his club Seneschalstown
against Kilmainhamwood (above) or his county against Tyrone (below).

# 12 State of the Game

Since I started playing football, things have changed at a rapid rate. In this modern era of professionalism, where we have seen the amateur ethos of rugby and even athletics all but disappear, so too change is happening within the GAA. This can only be for the better. Top brass in GAA headquarters are obviously wary of what is taking place, but even they have been powerless to prevent change. Probably the most significant move came in 1999 with the setting up of the Gaelic Players Association (GPA). By acting as a voice for players, I suppose you could say it is like a small union representing its members. The move was spearheaded by some famous faces from the playing field, including Kilkenny hurling legend DJ Carey and Dublin footballer Dessie Farrell, their main spokesperson.

Undeniably, the GPA have made their presence felt and have had some success, but honestly they don't impress me at all. They claim to represent players and from the outset were going to address the big issue of 'pay for play'. To my mind, they have remained on the fence, largely inactive on that controversial subject. But my main bone of contention is the fact that they never consulted me or my Meath team-mates. When we captured the All-Ireland in 1999, I was captain and photographed on almost every front page in the country. We were the best team in Ireland and had some terrific players like Darren Fay and Trevor Giles. At that time the GPA were in their infancy and canvassing for members and the support of players. But as far as I am aware, not one Meath player was approached by them! The whole thing is a bit of a joke. They are always on about their several hundred members and yet have never once approached the best team and some of the best-known players in Ireland. You could easily picture someone like Trevor Giles as a fine ambassador for our sport. Then, on 14th October, GPA chief executive Dessie Farrell was delighted to announce that Meath footballers had finally signed up and become members of the organisation. He also said that it was a huge relief to him and to his members to finally have Meath on board. However, it has taken four years for them to make an official approach to Meath. In 2003, Dessie made contact with Darren Fay, and as a result, some Meath footballers signed up. For the record, I am not a member of the GPA, nonetheless, up to early October this year, around 20 Meath players had joined.

Overall, their lack of consultation is very unprofessional. Maybe they genuinely overlooked us but it all seems rather bizarre, to say the very least. The bottom line is that, as a whole, the All-Ireland Champions of 1996 and 1999 have never been consulted with regard to becoming members of the GPA. Maybe the GPA have achieved certain goals behind the scenes, but to my mind, they have really only had one success and even then it could be questioned. When the Cork footballers and hurlers both rebelled late in 2002, the entire affair was given much coverage in the media. There were all sorts of threats flying about and it was said that the Cork County players would go on strike. But the GPA were really only bit part players. Essentially, they were just looking for publicity as those troubles had been ongoing in Cork for several years.

All this talk of better treatment for players is well and good but I feel the GPA are not really achieving much. Truth be told they are a bit of a shambles. You only have to look at the length of time they have been talking about expenses or an allowance for players. It is all falling on deaf ears as the powers-that-be in Croke Park just brush it aside to deal with more important matters. On the subject of payments for players, I do not agree with it at all. Beyond all doubt, the money is just not there. Even if the money were there, it would need to be in constant supply and for that reason it cannot and could not work. Take a look at the situation in soccer across the water. Clubs are struggling so much and the situation is only getting worse. In the next few years it is likely that dozens of clubs will go to the wall.

In Britain, the reality is that there are only a handful of clubs who are well off. The rest are hugely in debt. So if payments were to be made in Gaelic Games, in both codes, then many clubs and counties would suffer. When I say that, I am talking about the widely touted figure of €130, which is the proposed amount payable to a player as an expense allowance. It simply would not work. A fair number of questions would also arise. Who do you pay? Do you pay the Senior players only and, if so, do you pay only those that appear on the pitch or do you pay the entire panel? I mean, on a playing day you could have 15 players and maybe three subs getting a game. But I know that there are around 32 players on the Meath panel! For one game that would amount to a lot of payments in expenses. What would be the cost if you add up Championship, League and O'Byrne Cup games? Also, what about Senior matches at club level?

Great care would also have to be taken over who is on the payroll and who is not. Then you have the smaller and improving counties like Laois and Sligo. They would have to be paid the same as the bigger counties or else there would be trouble. There are far too many questions, far too many pitfalls and no concrete solutions. At the end of the day, the money is just not there. I know people will talk about the GAA's millions stashed away and all the money that went into the rebuilding of Croke Park. But most of that money came from the Government and remember that the GAA are also in debt. At the last count, it was reported that the GAA were in debt to the tune of over €70 million, and were looking for another €40 million from the Government. It is also costing over €4 million to run Croke Park each year. If all that is true, then I cannot understand why the GAA will not open up Croke Park to other sports and events.

I would dearly like to see Croke Park opened up to other sports like soccer and rugby. The GAA have to start moving with the times and get rid of their backward attitudes. With regard to Australian Rules, they have shown that they can relate well with other foreign sports bodies. They should now start building up relationships with those closer to home. It does not take a genius to work out that with the GAA losing money hand over fist, they simply have to open up their magnificent stadium. It does not make much sense in the current financial climate to have it lying idle from September to St

Patrick's Day. More important than money, it has to be used to its full potential and especially for the benefit of the Irish people.

The rule which forbids the playing of those sports is known as Rule 42. Like myself and so many other people, Roscommon and recently St Joseph's of Milltown Malbay in Clare would also like to see a change in that rule. But would you believe there has now been a ban imposed on any more talk or submissions on Rule 42 until GAA Congress meets in Belfast in 2004! By that stage, who knows what sort of debts the GAA will have incurred? In March the Hogan Stand and the Canal End (a favourite Meath haunt) were completed after 15 years of work. But that is not the end of development. There are now plans to knock down Hill 16; in its place a new terrace will be built at an estimated cost of €23 million.

The general feeling out there is that other sports will eventually be played on the hallowed ground. Much of that stems from the expectations people have of the new GAA President, Sean Kelly. On RTÉ's *The Late Late Show* on the weekend of Ireland's Grand Slam showdown with England, some well-known personalities from Irish rugby appeared. Former Ireland great Moss Keane was heard to say: 'I know Sean Kelly well. He comes from around five miles from where I live and I can tell you he has a fairly liberal attitude. I can see the day coming.' Tony Ward and Keith Wood also agreed with that view. But it was the colourful George Hook who really received the applause when he stated: 'It's not the GAA's stadium – it's the Irish people's stadium. As long as it has taken one cent of Irish taxpayer's money to go into the building of it, then it belongs to the Irish people.'

I was in the North Stand in Lansdowne Road on that disappointing day back in March when Ireland collapsed 42–6 to England. Thousands of people were looking for tickets for that game to no avail. The GAA would have doubled the crowd that turned up for that match. Rugby is so popular right now and the GAA would do well to capitalise on that. The same is true of soccer. Lansdowne is an old stadium which simply cannot hold the numbers of people that want to watch sports there. Ireland have never had a more popular soccer manager than Brian Kerr. As a young man he played Gaelic football, and other great soccer names like Kevin Moran, Niall Quinn and Denis Irwin also had their roots in Gaelic Games. In finishing on this subject, the GAA will have to wake up and take action. Some of their rules are so ridiculous and others, in this modern era, have been in place for over 100 years!

\*\*\*\*\*\*

All over the country Gaelic football fans like to know what the future holds for their particular county. From years playing against footballing counties, I'd like to share my own opinions on the state of the game. Needless to say, I'll start with my own beloved Meath, seeing that Meath folk are forever coming up and asking me about our future. In 2003, we had an up and down League campaign but Sean was really trying out young lads. Trevor and Darren are still there and luckily we always have had a conveyor belt of talent to choose from. But it is very hard to pinpoint a particular name for the future. Just because a young fella is brilliant early on, it does not follow that he will make it at Senior level.

Our future will also depend on who is in charge. Those with short memories were calling for Sean's head after the Donegal defeat in 2002. I actually thought he was going to follow me and call it a day. He did give me that impression because he has a young family and, like myself, he would like to spend more time with them and watch them grow up. So that begs the question of who will eventually take over from the legend. I would definitely rule out Tommy Dowd. He would be a very popular choice but I doubt he would take on the task. All of this is only my opinion but I would narrow it down to two candidates – Colm O'Rourke and a dark horse, Colm Coyle. O'Rourke is Meath through and through and I feel he is the obvious choice. He has vast experience which would stand him in good stead. One of Meath's all-time greats, Colm's knowledge of the game, as he has shown in his media roles, is second to none. Crucially, he has also managed the Ireland team in Australian Rules.

My friend and Seneschalstown team-mate, Colm Coyle, also has the experience. He has proved himself at club and county level and is also the manager of Monaghan. I would not rule out another potential candidate, Eamonn Barry, either. He has done a fine job in getting Dunshaughlin to the All-Ireland Club semi-finals in 2003. On 3 November 2003, Barry challenged Boylan for the second time for the position of county team manager but was beaten by 69 votes to 19.

It would be an honour for me to be boss of Meath. I would like the job some day and I would be more than capable of handling it. But although I have a lot of experience as a player, I am only learning the ropes in the coaching and training department. I am currently helping Clan na Gael, a newly formed and amalgamated club in Athboy. But I do realise I have far more to learn. All told, I would like to be in charge of Meath at some stage in the future.

Elsewhere in Leinster, Dublin will always be the team to beat. Without doubt, it is always one of the biggest games of the year if we meet them. Apart from in 2002, we have had the upper hand on them over the last seven years. But Dublin have some really good young players like Ciaran Whelan, Ray Cosgrave and Paul Casey, and they are almost always the Leinster favourites. I remember watching from the stands as a youngster and seeing some really famous Dublin stars who gave us much to think about in the famous battles of the past. As much as I really idolised our own stars like Colm O'Rourke, Mick Lyons and Martin O'Connell, you had to admire some of the Dublin idols as well.

The fair-haired Keith Barr was known as something of a hard man. Therefore, he was a real hate figure and a big target for abuse from Meath fans. But I know Keith very well and he is a real gentleman. Like many Meath players, he was given an unfair tag of being a dirty player. That was unwarranted as he played fair but was as tough as nails in the process and hard in the tackle. In truth, Keith Barr was one of the best ever centre-halves and there have been few of his like since.

When I mention the name 'Charlie', Dublin people will instantly know that I am not talking about a former Taoiseach. Charlie Redmond was the darling of the Dublin supporters. A real favourite on Hill 16, he was along with our own Brian Stafford, one of the best free-takers the game has ever seen. Brian popped over a lot of easy and straightforward frees but Charlie hit them over from all angles. If he was the finest of free-takers, Dublin fans will need no reminding that he was also a real culprit when it came to missing penalties. He certainly missed some very important spot kicks in front of the television cameras. One of the best things I can say about Charlie, however, is that he is now living in Ashbourne, Co. Meath, so we can claim him as one of our own!

Everyone knows that we have had our problems with the goalkeeping position. Dublin have always been blessed in that regard and in 2003 their young keeper Stephen Cluxton was voted the Young Player of the Year. He was following in a fine tradition of Dublin keepers with John O'Leary surely the greatest of them all. Certainly, he was part of the old Dublin rearguard who came straight into the new modern era. A fine keeper and a great shotstopper.

'Jayo' was an integral part of that new era too. Of course, I am referring to the man who arrived on the scene with pop star status, Jason Sherlock. He had flair and because of his small stocky frame and his pace, he caused all teams great problems. Dublin would not have won the All-Ireland in 1995 without him. There is no such thing as a one-man team but everything revolved around getting the ball into Jason as quickly as possible. He also had great strength and determination and would lean in against defenders with his shoulders as if he were almost barging his way through to the goal.

Tommy Carr played and managed for Dublin like an army man. He was very regimental and very strict, always with a very serious look about him. I have met and talked with him but still find him very standoffish and a bit aloof. It does take all sorts to make the world go round, though, and I feel Tommy did a very good job with Dublin. He got a raw deal and never got any credit for all the good work he did with Dublin. Then he was effectively 'shafted' to make way for Tommy Lyons. What Tommy Lyons has inherited today is all down to the good and hard work of Carr. In contrast to Carr, Lyons is very happy-go-lucky, but it hides the credentials of a man well equipped to land Dublin another All-Ireland. He came close in 2002 and took the defeat by Armagh on the chin and with a smile to boot. If he ever does bring Sam back to the capital, it could not happen to a nicer man.

Kildare are a funny side. Over the years they have had the players and shown that they have what it takes. But they never seem to go through with their effort when it really matters. There is clearly something missing and I am unsure whether it has got anything to do with their running style, which can and did weaken them. Many Kildare people were disappointed and angry when two of their star players deserted them in the Eighties. Larry Tompkins and Shay Fahy transferred to Cork and later were rewarded by winning All-Ireland medals. I do not blame them and that is no disrespect to Kildare – after all, when Cathal Sheridan could not get his place in the Meath team, he transferred to Kildare!

It is just that if you have the talent, then you are not going to get that coveted All-Ireland medal by staying with a weaker county which Kildare were at that time. I mean if I was a talented footballer, and I was living up in Antrim, I would do my level best to get a transfer to one of the bigger counties. Tipperary's Declan Browne is an exception. He could take his pick of counties but he chooses to stay with his beloved Tipp. It all depends on what you want.

Offaly are going nowhere at the moment. They have been at a standstill since 1997 and I cannot see them doing anything, believing their bubble to have burst. Westmeath could still be the county we have to fear and their bubble has not burst just yet! They have given us some mighty scares in the last few years and I think they are still good enough. They also have players coming through from the younger levels. In October 2003, Westmeath appointed Páidí Ó Sé as their new manager. They could be a force to be reckoned with for the next few years.

Laois under magical Mick O'Dwyer have now become one of the big powers in Leinster. After they lost this year's National League final to the eventual All-Ireland Champions Tyrone, they went on to frank the form when they won the Leinster. Their win over Kildare (2–13 to 1–13) was their first such title in 53 years. The legendary O'Dwyer has now managed Kerry, Kildare and Laois to Senior titles. With their Minors and U-21s also doing well, all eyes will be on them next year and they will be a tough nut to crack in Leinster.

Until 2002, when they were so unlucky not to have dumped us out, Louth had really done nothing over the last 20 years. But apart from that year, I do not see them with any immediate future. The same is true of Wicklow who have really gone backwards since the early Nineties. I think the club scene revolving around Eire Óg has destroyed Carlow. When one of the top clubs in the country refuses to allow its players turn out for the county, then there is only one outcome. That is very sad for Carlow.

When dormant counties like Laois and Louth suddenly start to wake, you have to be beware then of Longford and Wexford. Longford have some really good players, and in Paul Bardon they have one of the best forwards in Ireland. On a good day they will push anybody. Wexford also have to be watched. A few years ago you could afford to send your second team down there but not anymore.

\*\*\*\*\*\*

Connacht football was in a state of crisis not so very long ago. It was so poor that, like Connacht rugby today, people feared for its very future. Those days have long since passed and now it has never been in a healthier state. Galway and Mayo always had things their own way, but now there are a few very serious contenders to the title in the West.

Always the team to beat in Connacht, Galway will therefore be knocking on the door of the All-Ireland, even despite this year's defeat against Donegal. Michael Donnellan must be one of the most under-rated players around. For me, he is the engine room of the Galway team. He does so much unseen work. He is a great all-rounder and has a real touch of class about him. So influential is his presence that when he was absent from their team, Galway were not the same.

Along with Sean Boylan, John O'Mahony must be one of the best managers of the last 20 years. A recent poll among footballers actually put John way ahead of Sean! Interestingly, both have actually travelled on very similar paths. For O'Mahony to build Galway up for an All-Ireland title was some feat. But to fall on hard times only to come back and win another was a measure of his skills.

They trounced us in the 2001 All-Ireland final. We had no answers to them that day. There was no postmortem afterwards. No banging of tables, no questions and no answers. Other counties may try and analyse things but that has never been our style in Meath. You can call it a really amateurish way of doing things but it is, after all, an amateur game. The simple fact is that on the day, Galway were the better team and were fitter, faster and stronger. One thing I do remember about that defeat, and there are not too many things that I care to remember about it, was something that happened outside my home in Athboy. When the family got up next day, we discovered that someone had painted slogans reading 'UP GALWAY' on the road outside the house. It was obviously some Galway person living in Athboy who was trying to ram it down my throat – again!

Galway still have the same core group of players with the likes of Donnellan, Fallon and Joyce. With others undoubtedly coming through, they are a huge threat to every team in Ireland. I will never forget them wiping the floor with us, which is the threat that remains. Definitely more Connacht titles for Galway.

Talk of Galway and their fierce rivals Mayo are sure to figure in any conversation. There is also plenty rivalry between Mayo and Meath and I am not talking about '96. In fact, the rivalry stretches back to the Land Commission when thousands of Mayo people settled on lands provided for them in Meath by the Government. John Maughan, the man who put them back on the football map, is now back in charge after a spell away. With his superfitness and his tanned legs, he would not look out of place on the catwalk! He loves to strut his stuff up and down the sideline. Being serious, though, he was very unlucky not to land them an All-Ireland win on two occasions in the Nineties. Come to think of it, he is probably the greatest manager never to have lifted the Sam Maguire yet.

As a result of all that heartbreak, Mayo's spirit has been broken. It will be a good while before they trouble the likes of Galway in Connacht. Crossmolina's heartbreaking loss to Nemo Rangers has also set the county back. I can actually see other counties posing a much bigger threat to Galway.

Roscommon shocked both Mayo and Galway to lift the Connacht title in 2001. However, Galway beat them easily that same year in the back-door system. Roscommon have not been the same since and their problems were compounded with the suspensions resulting from their holiday hotel frolics when several players were playing 'naked pool'! Despite having great players like Frankie Dolan and All Star half-back Francie Grehan, I cannot see Roscommon causing a stir.

Since beating Mayo in their great hour of the Connacht final in 1994, Leitrim have fallen into a slump. Things were not helped by the departure of their star player Declan Darcy soon afterwards. He left to play with Dublin in a transfer over work. They are surely the weakest county in Connacht right now.

Once the weakest link, Sligo have risen so much that they are perhaps the biggest danger to Galway now. They have been playing to a consistently high level over the last couple of years and, despite not really performing this year, they are still improving. One of the most exciting teams in the country to watch, they play to the final whistle and so never know when they are beaten. Sligo have exciting players especially in midfield with Paul Durcan and All Star Eamonn O'Hara – a great combination. It will not surprise me to see them keep their tails up. If they do, then Yeats' County is not too far away from achieving great things in Connacht.

\* \* \* \* \* \*

Traditionally, Munster has always been a two-horse race. With few exceptions, the title there is almost always fought out between Cork and Kerry. Of course, everything depends on the draw but, even if they do meet, the winner will no doubt go on to lift the Munster crown.

The name of Kerry is legendary. They stand on a pedestal above all others. Talk to any football supporter and ask them to name the greatest player ever and you can be sure that a Kerry player will be the most popular. Names like Mick O'Connell, Jack O'Shea, Pat Spillane, Mikey Sheehy, Páidí Ó Sé, Eoin 'Bomber' Liston and Maurice Fitzgerald are just a few of their all-time greats. Kerry will always be the team to fear. There is never a bad Kerry team and they are generally strong. The same applies to all of their underage sides. They will win more All-Irelands in the coming years and there is no doubt about that. They did not really perform this year and that could have something to do with all the controversy behind the scenes. The talent they have is frightening as they have players coming through in abundance. If you were to count the number of All Stars that Kerry have collected over the years, then I would say they have won at least twice as many as the next best county. They have already won more All-Irelands than any other county.

The retirement of Maurice Fitzgerald is a huge loss. At the Manager of the Year awards earlier in the year, I talked to RTÉ's Jimmy Magee, who told me that Maurice was making a comeback to the Kerry team in 2003. It did not happen and he has since called it a day. Maurice was one of the most naturally gifted and skilful players you were ever likely to see. We all remember his famous equalising point from the sideline against Dublin in the All-Ireland semi-final in Thurles, which has been played over and over again on television. But I can remember him scoring from both sidelines! A player like him only comes along every decade or two. He always looked to be in slow motion as the players around him were flat out. It is such a pity that just as he was reaching his prime, he decided to end his career. He is a pure genius and I would dearly like to meet him some day and get his views on football.

Another one of the all-time greats is the former Kerry manager and player, Mick O'Dwyer. He won so many All-Irelands with Kerry and then proved his genius by guiding Kildare to a Leinster title. For so long Kildare looked like beating Galway in the All-Ireland final. Now he is applying his vast knowledge and experience to Laois, and the magic worked again as they reached the League final in 2003 and won the Leinster title!

One of the greatest characters the game has ever known and certainly the best character in the game today is Páidí Ó Sé. Micko is also no doubt proud that one of his best players from the Seventies and Eighties has gone on to guide Kerry to All-Ireland success as a manager. Páidí would probably make a great soccer manager as well. He is a great believer in the squad 'rotation' system. Something that Maurice Fitzgerald was none too happy about! If you are a Kerry player, you can never be too sure that your place on the team is secure. Indeed, he is a firm believer in the old Jack Charlton motto of 'no prima donnas'. Television loves Páidí and vice versa. He is always so good humoured and game for a laugh. I remember hearing about an advert he made for Kerry Radio a few years ago which really bears this out. The particular advertisement endorsed an animal food product and Páidí's line was: 'It's so good, I'd ate it myself!'

That said, I think Páidí went to great lengths to antagonise the Kerry people. It was beyond me why he called the Kerry supporters 'the worst kind of fucking animal' recently. He caused a right rumpus and a lot of people were calling for his head on a plate! Then there was the dispute between himself and John O'Keeffe, and more recently he toyed with the media and no doubt many staunch Kerry supporters over the fitness of Darragh Ó Sé. Páidí stated that the media were inventing all sorts of stories about Darragh's injury. With a cheeky grin, Páidí added that all Darragh had was 'a glorified ankle injury' and that he could make the Munster final against Limerick, but in his opinion Darragh would not. Of course, Páidí was right and Darragh had to sit out the Munster final on the sideline. I like Páidí a lot, but feared for his future as Kerry manager, which inevitably came to end in October. His appointment as manager of Westmeath was certainly a surprise. He was given a two-year contract by the Westmeath County Board at a meeting on 15th October. It will be interesting to see if he can bring success to Westmeath. However, it will certainly freshen things up and add a lot of impetus to the Westmeath GAA. But whatever he achieves, it will be on the back of some excellent groundwork already laid down by Luke Dempsey. The now ex-Westmeath manager did a very good job and I felt that, in the end, he was 'shafted'.

Pat Spillane is very outspoken and many people have no time for him. Personally, I have a lot of respect for him because of what he has achieved as a player. He was part of Micko's great side that lifted six or seven All-Irelands. I also admire his frankness because he calls things as he sees them, which also makes for very good television. But he can be very hard on young players and probably does not realise it. I think Pat may forget how young and inexperienced players can be and such comments can harm their careers. Besides, I feel that he has no great love for Meath. Maybe that is just winding up Colm O'Rourke but Pat always seems to get in a dig!

There is only one player in the Kingdom whom I do not particularly like. I hope he does not take me up the wrong way on that! It is not so much that I dislike him but more a case of him 'bugging the shit out of me'. You see, the player in question is Seamus Moynihan and every time I played against him, he gave me a right roasting! Without doubt, he is one of the very best footballers in the country. He has struggled of late, and people are now asking questions of him, but his class was always there to see.

In contrast, Cork are a funny team. Some years they can be brilliant and others they can be brutally bad, as was the case this year. They have won many All-Irelands, but for the biggest county, I feel that they have the resources at their disposal to do far better. In fairness, having a top-class hurling team may also count against them. On the plus side, they are probably the best county, and streets ahead of the rest, with regard to the total number of All-Irelands they have won in both codes. Undeniably, Larry Tompkins has done a fine job down there, and his decision not to seek an eight term as manager has signalled it's time for change. Going back to his playing days, he was a player you would love to hate. But he was also a huge influence and motivating factor behind Cork. Many people forget that he actually came from playing football with Kildare and certainly made the right move in applying for that transfer. He will probably always be remembered for his great free-taking ability.

Their star player is Colin Corkery. He has been a fantastic servant to Cork, despite getting a lot of unwarranted abuse from Pat Spillane and other members of the media. Who will ever forget his stunning display which got Nemo Rangers out of trouble and on to victory in the All-Ireland Club Championship in 2003. It was a Man of the Match performance!

If Kerry or Cork slip up in Munster, then there are really only two other counties who can push them. Clare with the help of some big strong fellas in the side won the Munster title in 1992, when they caused one of the biggest ever shocks, slamming Kerry 2–10 to 0–12. That was a great day for Clare but there is far more required today, aside from the physical game. Truth be told, Clare have slipped away altogether. On the other hand, Tipperary reached the Munster final the following year, 1993. They gave Cork a match and scored 1–10 before going down with their heads held high. But Tipp are still a threat and will be there if either of the big two slip up. They nearly caused a sensation when they drew with Cork in the 2002 Munster final. We actually played them in recent times in a challenge and were very impressed, having previously dismissed them as just a hurling county. Declan Browne, who plays under both codes, is their most influential player and a very good forward.

If Cork or Kerry have one of their bad days, then Tipperary could take advantage. After all, they gave Kerry a mighty fright a couple of years ago when they had a perfectly good goal disallowed and Kerry held on.

The other county who can cause a shock, should Tipperary falter, is Limerick. They have improved in leaps and bounds. Munster is, as I said already, between Cork and Kerry. If not, then Tipperary and Limerick will be waiting in the wings.

\* \* \* \* \* \*

Ulster football is without doubt the strongest in Ireland after Armagh's title win in 2002. Over the last 10 years we have also seen the strengths of Down, Derry and Donegal, who put Meath out in 2002. And in 2003, Tyrone won the National League and Armagh went on contest the All-Ireland final, which Tyrone won for the first time in their history. All of them are very formidable. Football there was dormant for years, but now it is a real force and has produced many outstanding footballers. I think Crossmaglen has been a huge boost to Armagh. One of the best club sides over the last 10 years, it certainly had an effect on the Orchard County. What can you say about Oisin McConville and Diarmuid Marsden that has not already been written? They proved their All-Ireland winning form by getting to the League semi-final and again reached the All-Ireland final in 2003. But whatever comes out of the North, it will be a mighty team that beats them. It can be argued that Armagh have also been the most consistent of Ulster teams over the last three decades.

Derry have gone off the boil. They have done it before and now a lot of their big players are no longer with them. Anthony Tohill was one of their greatest players but he is now approaching the end of his career. Because of that, Derry are in the process of having to rebuild. Before Tohill, Joe Brolly was one of their great stars. He had a great left foot and now has a great gift of the gab on *The Sunday Game*!

Down have really gone downhill since their golden spell in the early Nineties landed them two All-Irelands. James McCartan was probably the fastest or nippiest forward ever seen in the modern era.

They are presently trying to find more players like him and so are rebuilding. It will be a while before Down make their presence felt.

After the glory of 1992, Donegal really faded badly. But after knocking us out in 2002, their appetite has been whetted again and they are back. They were very unlucky not to beat Dublin in this year's semi-final and face Armagh in the final.

This year Donegal knocked out Galway in the All-Ireland quarter-final with ease. Then in the semi-final they gave Armagh the runaround before losing it in the final 10 minutes. They are going to be a huge threat to Armagh, Tyrone and all concerned in the next couple of seasons.

Cavan are still living off their history. They were one of the truly great sides of the Fifties and Sixties. They also blow hot and cold and in recent years have followed some great performances by some forgettable ones. Inconsistency is the curse of any good team. They have some big, fit and fast players but it is hard to see them having any sort of impact.

If John Maughan could not achieve things with Fermanagh, then I don't know who can. What I do know is that their reaching the League semi-final did not surprise me and it was great to see them finally do something and then do us! They have had some fine players through the years, most notably the Brewster brothers, Paul and Tom. They are really outstanding players but it is still hard to see them troubling the leaders in Ulster.

It would be marvellous to see my very good friend, Colm Coyle, achieve something with Monaghan. He recently gave a television interview where he said he was very impressed with the set-up. The standard was as good as any he had seen, which is high praise coming from an All-Ireland winner. He also remarked that it will be very hard for him to trim down to a panel of 30, such is the level of interest and commitment up there. That is praise indeed and we will watch very keenly. Meath beat them in the qualifier where I scored a point. But they had beaten All-Ireland champions Armagh in the first round in Ulster so they are not to be taken lightly – though I doubt they will trouble Tyrone, Armagh or Donegal in the next few years.

\*\*\*\*\*\*

So that's my view. However, there are a lot of other good and positive things about this great Irish sport of ours – a sport we should be proud of but which we take for granted very much. Gaelic Games are a great way of meeting people socially. I have met people from every county in Ireland as well as overseas. As a result, I have made countless friendships. Most people are born with an ambition to travel. In that respect, I must have travelled every highway and byway of Ireland as well as seeing many countries around the world. The GAA have given me great memories from my times in America, Australia, South Africa and the Middle East.

Then there is all the recognition that success has brought me. It is nice to be recognised wherever you go, and although I am no Roy Keane, people have come up to me many times and asked for my autograph. A funny incident actually happened last year when I went to the Galway Races. I enjoy horse racing and I accompanied a friend of mine, Sean Higgins, there. Afterwards we went for a few pints and later to Supermac's in Eyre Square for a bite to eat. As we left the fast food outlet, someone shouted my name from behind me. I stopped to look back and there was the manager running towards me. I was a little surprised and wondering what was up. But he just smiled and said: 'Graham, let me shake your hand. I'd just like to thank you for coming in.' Sean and I could not stop laughing our heads off about it. You would think I was some big personality. In reality, the manager was probably a huge GAA fan and the only one sober enough to recognise me in a place full of intoxicated racegoers!

Another friend of mine, George King from Kentstown, told me that he was over at Old Trafford in 2002 to see Manchester United play. After the game, he had the pleasure of meeting Roy Keane. George told me, and I have no reason to disbelieve him, that Roy asked him where he was from. When George answered, 'Meath,' apparently Roy replied: 'You know, that Geraghty fella is getting more publicity than I am!' If it is true, then I suppose Roy was referring to the time between 21 July and October in 2002. In July came the rumours of threats to me and my family, followed by the announcement that I was quitting the game. Then in September I was brought into the Ireland team to play Australia while in

October I was 'floored' by Brad Scott! So I suppose I did get my fair share of publicity but nothing in comparison to what Roy got!

Roy is one of the best players that Ireland ever produced. But the entire country was divided over the 'Storm in Saipan' incident. Unquestionably, it was the most famous row ever to erupt in Irish sporting history. Weighing up everything, my feeling is that Roy was right. I am not just saying that because I am a player. You have to remember that Roy was complaining for years about the facilities provided for them. He is a real professional and is used to top-class facilities in Manchester. As a manager, Mick McCarthy handled things badly. As any boss knows, if you have a problem you sort it out and do not air your views to others about it. What a pity that both of them could not have sorted out their differences for the good of the team and the country. If that had happened, then there is no telling how far Ireland could have gone. As it was, the loss of Roy was colossal in terms of his ability and his presence. Even more to blame than Roy and Mick were the FAI. Over the years, they have had plenty of opportunity to sort out problems raised by Roy and others. They only made half-hearted attempts at doing so and were always just sitting on the fence. The Genesis Report also found lots of faults with the FAI. Hopefully, lessons will be learned from it all because, in the long run, it does the image of Ireland no good.

There are nice things about being a successful footballer, but it also has its fair share of drawbacks. I think the worst thing about being a footballer is the fact that people expect the same thing of you day after day. To keep up the same level of performance game after game, month after month and year after year is impossible. You can be carrying a restrictive injury or playing in a match when not feeling too well. You might have a cold or flu or a stomach bug or even had a poor night's sleep. There are many reasons why a player may not be performing as expected and, with that in mind, supporters should really give the benefit of the doubt.

There is also the situation where you may find you are not in the same league as somebody else. If that is the case, then you could be given the runaround. Some players may find that hard to take but it is a fact of life. There will always be people better than yourself – just look at someone like Maurice Fitzgerald – or there will be players who are stronger and fitter than yourself. You just have to accept it in the same way as there are those with less ability than you.

One thing that I will always remember, and of which I feel really proud, was trying to help a young player who sought advice from me some years ago. You can win all you like but there is something really special about trying to help a young player who seeks you out. It was an honour for me to be asked. The young guy in question was actually a Dublin Minor player. He rang me at home one day and explained that he was on the Dublin Minor panel. He just wanted some tips from me on how to improve his game. I cannot even remember what advice I gave him but I was impressed by him. He obviously had plenty of ambition for him to ring me at home and tell me about his hopes. To all young lads like him, I would probably give him the same words of wisdom that many teachers and coaches would no doubt give. Play as much as you can, when you can and above all, look, listen and learn. Practice does make perfect but you can also learn so much more by watching players on television or, better still, going to see them play in the flesh. Try not to miss training as that would be like missing a day at school or college.

It does help to have the support of family and friends and I have been lucky in that regard. To have a wife like Amanda, who has always been a big Meath supporter, is a huge bonus. My father Ger and my sisters Sandra, Karen and Lisa have been great to me, and I know they are all proud of what I have achieved. But undoubtedly two rocks for me are my mother and grandmother. Many match reports, which my late grandmother kept for me in a scrapbook, were of invaluable assistance in helping me recall all those memorable games down through the years. All the time she spent cutting out match clippings and other items of interest from newspapers, certainly proved well worthwhile and her great efforts did not go to waste. My mother was a huge influence too. She always backed me up when I was playing underage football and was there to offer words of encouragement. In and out of football, I would often find myself talking to her beforehand. The question that immediately comes to mind when asking her advice was, 'Do you think I'm doing the right thing?'

# 13 Rumour and Innuendo

In my footballing career many things have been said and written about me, often lies and wild exaggerations, but nothing compares to what has been written about my private life. Rumours of wife-beating and violence have plagued me and my family for years and it is high time to set the record straight once and for all.

After my marriage to Amanda Egan in late September 1997 and our subsequent honeymoon in Africa, there was only one thing of paramount importance to deal with on our arrival home. We immediately had to start searching for a home of our own. Prior to our wedding, and for a good deal afterwards, we were living with Amanda's mother, Kathleen, in Higginstown situated on the Delvin–Mullingar Road outside Athboy. We both knew that things could not continue like that. Everyone needs their own space and we really needed to find our own nest. A few months later in 1998, I managed to find a small house for us to rent. It was situated in Beauparc outside Navan and, although it was not as yet the ideal situation, it did at least offer us a place of our own and our independence. That was very important to me, not least because Amanda was now pregnant and expecting our first child.

With a family on the way, and an extra mouth to feed, for once football was not to the forefront of my mind. I knew that the little house in Navan would only serve as a temporary stop. It would give us both time to have a look around and find the home of our choice. When our daughter Sophia was born in September 1998, we were still living at Beauparc. Our new child only served to strengthen our resolve to find a new house. In the current climate, it is not at all easy to find a new home – especially when you are a first-time buyer. It was certainly not easy for us either, but in the winter of 1998 a few months after the birth of Sophia, we found what we were looking for.

In Higginstown, just down the road from Amanda's mother, there is a well-known pub called 'The Bawn Inn'. On the site of this pub are Athboy Pitch and Putt Club and two soccer pitches, which are the home of Athboy Celtic Soccer Club. A few hundred yards further down the road, we found the site where we wanted to build our new home. The site was located on such a small piece of land that the locals and its owner referred to it as the 'wee field'. But it really caught our eye and was everything we had hoped for. Conveniently, it was just a stone's throw from Amanda's family home and near my work in Athboy. Best of all, it was only 12 miles from Meath's training pitches in Navan. We purchased the site from the owner, Bart Cassidy, and then sought out the services of local builder Pat Smith, who set about the construction of the house. When the work was eventually completed, we could not have been happier. It was a beautiful and spacious dormer bungalow and we decided to name it 'Paircwee', meaning the 'wee field'!

In July 1999, we were ready to move into our new home and began shifting our personal belongings and household goods across to Athboy. A week before we moved in, without thinking and without any warning, disaster struck. One day, as we arrived from Navan with another load of furniture and belongings, we were horrified to discover that the house had been burgled! The thieves had gained entry through a window at the back of the house and we lost a lot of valuable items. Among the list of possessions stolen were a television, video recorder, stereo system and worst of all, many of our wedding gifts.

It was a terrible start for us. At least if your home is gutted by fire, you still have the site and you can start again from scratch. But it is a horrible feeling knowing that a person or persons have gone through your home and your personal items. Your home is your sanctuary and your refuge, and it is not a pleasant feeling knowing that it has been plundered. That invasion of our home and our private life was only just the start of things to come, however.

From personal experience as a high-profile Gaelic footballer, I know that people always want a piece of you and will talk about you in different ways. Throughout the country, many GAA fans think the worst of me and some of my Meath team-mates. Even in Meath, people have different opinions about me. That is fine by me and I can handle it all. But when they involve my wife, it can be particularly nasty and very upsetting.

Even before Amanda and myself got married, rumours concerning our relationship started to circulate around Meath and beyond. Over the years I got to hear nearly all the stories – and believe me I'm still hearing them! Family and friends would tell me what they heard, but more often than not it was left to Amanda to tell me the latest scurrilous piece of information. Naturally, it caused her a great deal of upset.

Looking back now, perhaps I was a little flippant about her concerns. I would probably have laughed it off or told her not to worry or let things get to her. That has always been my nature. I guess I have heard so many things out on the field of play that I just pass it all off as just words. It's a case of 'sticks and stones may break my bones but names will never hurt me'. Out on the green sod, if someone said something unpleasant to me, it would not even register. In fact, I felt as though I must have been playing well to get a reaction. In that case, I would feel a bit of a boost and would step up my performance level as a result. But for Amanda, I know it is much harder and, bearing in mind the things she has told me over the years, it has been very traumatic and worrying for her.

When Amanda and myself started seeing each other, I remember her telling me that friends of hers, and even complete strangers, told her to steer well clear of me. Apparently, I was a real hothead and treated women terribly. Rumour had it that I had even beaten up my ex-girlfriend very badly!

Shortly before our marriage, Amanda rang me from her workplace very upset. Her Granny had rung her at work concerned for her well-being. After Amanda had told her to calm down, her Granny let her know that a neighbour had called to her with news that I had broken Amanda's nose! Her Granny was so alarmed that when Amanda arrived home from work, we had to go around and reassure her that everything was fine and that it was all just malicious gossip. I think after that episode, Amanda and myself realised the depths that some people will stoop in order to cause maximum harm. So much for so-called neighbours. If memory serves me well, the next thing that occurred was on our honeymoon in Kenya. A well-known Irish tabloid newspaper went around looking for photographs of our wedding. They wanted to see if it was true that Amanda had two black eyes, which I was supposed to have inflicted upon her a few days before our marriage!

The vicious rumours started before we got married, when we were getting married and have continued into our married life. A very well-documented story happened in August 1998, a year after our wedding. Amanda was shopping for groceries in Dunnes Stores in Navan. As she began to pay for the goods at the checkout, she could hear two women behind her talking. At the time, Amanda was eight months pregnant with Sophia. Apparently, one woman was telling the other that Amanda was my wife and that when she was in having a check-up in the maternity hospital, she had told some woman that I had beaten her up and as a result had suffered a broken arm and had lost the baby! That day I will always remember as I was out playing golf with my father at Royal Tara. Amanda rang me on my mobile in a distressed state. She had just stormed out of Dunnes Stores highly upset, leaving her shopping behind. I rushed home from the golf course to calm her down. These sort of rumours, apart from the hurt and pain caused, bring huge disruption to a normal day.

Before I get on to the next ridiculous rumour, I think it is time to draw breath here and just reflect on what nonsense has been put about. If I had beaten up an ex-girlfriend, you would have thought Amanda would have 'sussed' me out before tying the knot with me. If I gave her two black eyes before the wedding, then you would have thought the hundreds of invited guests would have noticed something and that surely would have been the end of any wedding. Above all, if Amanda had suffered a miscarriage and a broken arm at my expense, then surely that would have been very noticeable indeed – especially when a broken limb requires a cast for a good few weeks.

As I have already stated, if these comical stories did not involve Amanda, then it would all be like water off a duck's back to me. I have heard so much of this sort of stuff in training and in competitive play. Believe it or not, I tried hard to remember some of the things that players say (apart from the obvious swear words) and

I could not recall anything out of the ordinary – apart from one quip which involved me and another man's wife!

During a Dublin v Meath Championship game in Croke Park, a Dublin player, in the heat of the moment, snarled at John McDermott saying: 'You fucking eejit – you don't even know that Graham Geraghty rode your wife.' All I can say is that, because of the nature of the remark, time stood still for an instant for both John and myself. After all, this was no ordinary remark. This was a sucker punch below the belt and involved his wife. Great credit must be given to 'Big' John. He was never the sort of player to retaliate anyway, being such a gentle giant. But he knew it was a wind-up and never even once discussed the matter with me.

Perhaps as each year goes by, and as the competition intensifies, commonplace remarks do not work so players have to find more hurtful comments to direct at an opponent. Just as a Mayo player tried to wind up McDermott by placing his fingers where the sun does not shine, so this Dublin player tried something to rattle John. It is a measure of how high John stood as a player and as a gentleman that opponents of a lower standard tried to get at him, but ultimately failed.

Even more ludicrous was the next rumour. The incident in 1999 was alleged to have happened on the eve of the Leinster final. Word got around that I had beaten Amanda up and down the central area of Navan known as 'the Square'. I was then arrested and thrown into jail in Navan for the night. Next morning, Sean Boylan had to come and bail me out in time to play at Croke Park. It was ridiculous stuff; even funny if it wasn't so serious. What sort of half-wit makes up such a story? Can he or she not see that it does not even stand up before it is spread about? For one, a Meath player would be banned from drinking the night before a match – never mind a Leinster final. But 'banned' is even the wrong word as a player just would not do it anyway. Second, at the hour of the night it was supposed to have taken place, a player would be trying to get some sleep ahead of the big game.

In the millennium year 2000, we had a couple of friends over from America and so we all travelled up to Dublin for the All-Ireland final between Kerry and Galway. The match ended in a draw and Kerry went on to win the replay. Amanda was 11 weeks pregnant at the time but the happy weekend that we were all enjoying soon turned into a nightmare. Without warning, Amanda began to feel pains and was rushed to the Rotunda Hospital. Sadly, the doctors told us that there was nothing they could do. She had suffered a miscarriage and we were all devastated. Even though only close family and friends knew about it, the word and rumours began to spread. Once again, it was rumoured that I had beaten Amanda and as a result she had lost the baby. So where was I supposed to have carried out the assault? In front of 68,000 people at Croke Park? In a quiet moment away from the couple who were with us? Or in the Burlington Hotel, having spent all our time with our friends? It was bad enough losing a child, but having to put up with that scandalous story made it all the worse. I just do not know how anybody can be so insensitive at a time like that. Why could they not let us grieve and get over our loss?

On the pitch I can take mostly anything that is thrown at me – physically or verbally. I have to admit that hearing all those stories, particularly the one about me beating Amanda so that she lost our child, really tested my patience. There is only so much you can take and I found that my peace of mind was severely jolted. Many times you hear these stories from friends or admirers. Most often they tell you that someone approached them because of their links to Amanda and me. Having ascertained that such and such was a friend of ours, then they would ask something like: 'Is it true that he beats up his wife?'

Over the years we have found out the sources of these rumours and identified many of the conveyors. On the very rare occasion, you will actually find someone saying it directly to your face. Other times you find someone who is 'under the influence' and will blurt it all out to you. As a pub manager, and one who is used to dealing with intoxicated customers, that is no surprise. One such incident immediately springs to mind. When Amanda and myself attended Jody Devine's wedding to Emer McNamee, we met many interesting people to say the least. One guest, a female, approached me and we got into a discussion about something or other – possibly to do with football. The chat soon turned into a bit of a debate whereby she started to become a little agitated and loud. The next thing I knew she just came straight out with the line: 'Do you still beat your wife up?' I was absolutely livid. So I went over and fetched Amanda and brought her over to this woman, who by now was looking quite sheepish and embarrassed, and said to her: 'Why don't you tell my wife what you've just said to me?' Not surprisingly the woman backed away but not before Amanda vented her own anger. The very next day, the woman in question rang and apologised.

There is no doubt that all the rumours began in Athboy. Many people will wonder why I am a target and why so many people are spreading malicious gossip about me. I have no idea why it is continuing unabated, but my gut feeling tells me there is a simple answer to it. It is not because I am from Navan and definitely not because I am a Meath footballer, it all goes down to the green-eyed monster himself – jealousy.

One incident in particular confirmed my suspicions. On a social outing to Navan one evening, I was verbally abused by a rugby player. Amanda and myself were in the lounge of the Newgrange Hotel, having a quiet drink and minding our own business. Navan were after losing in the Towns' Cup in rugby, so there were a lot of people – particularly rugby players – on the premises. A guy came swaggering over to us, obviously thinking he was Mr Invincible. Typically, he was a big strong and rounded fella and, with all the confidence in the world, he put to me in a rather patronising and insulting way the following questions:

'Are you still playing that pussy game?' he asked.

'What game is that?' I replied.

'That Gaelic football shite,' he spat back at me with a touch of venom.

'I am, but I thought you were asking about the rugby I am playing,' I said.

'Who are you playing with?' he asked.

'Buccaneers... who are you playing with?' I enquired.

'Navan second team,' came the response, at which I smiled at Amanda. Then he asked: 'Is that your wife – are you still beating her?'

I think we were about to get up and leave when the hotel porter came over and asked the rugby player to leave the premises. Obviously, they had been watching him closely.

Before our recent heartbreaking loss to Fermanagh in the All-Ireland qualifiers, there was a story doing the rounds that I was drunk the day before that match. That game was on a Sunday and I was at a wedding the day before. A girl who works with us in Doran's told us that a friend of hers was over in Kells and had heard that I was drunk at the wedding. It was true that I was drinking at that wedding the day before the match. I had four bottles of Becks non-alcoholic beer! On the eve of such an important game, when I actually felt we had every chance of not only winning but going all the way to win the All-Ireland, there is no way I would be drinking. So people will no doubt ask why was I attending a wedding in the first place when there is always such a temptation to drink? Well, if you recall, earlier I wrote about attending a wedding in Wexford in 2002 – on the day of the qualifier against Louth. A helicopter whisked me up to the game in Navan. I then scored a goal which broke Louth hearts and then the helicopter brought me back down to the wedding. I can also say that I did drink quite a bit after that – and a lot were bought for me!

If I had been drinking at these weddings, there is no way I could have scored a goal and played well. Any PE instructor, any doctor or any athlete will tell you that alcohol inhibits your performance levels. If I dared to drink, I would also be putting my place in an already very competitive team in grave jeopardy. Also, my zipping pace, which I consider one of my strong points, could not be used to its full effect. Although we lost to Fermanagh, I challenge anyone to look at the video and tell me I had been drinking the day before. I actually played quite well, especially in the first half when we had a slender lead. I set up a few points and scored one myself. None of us played well in the second period as Fermanagh went on the rampage.

On the subject of alcohol, I do know that Sean Boylan has received a number of phone calls over the years about players supposedly drinking before matches. Most of them were hoax calls, however, I would say that there were a few valid cases. But they were never true of me; I value my fitness and above all everyone connected with the Meath team. It would not surprise me if someone started a rumour to say that my arrival back in the Meath team caused a bit of discontent in the camp. That is just the sort of thing these small-minded people say to make excuses for us exiting the Championship. Nothing could be further from the truth and in fact we all get on and gel so well. Even the new additions to the team welcomed me back. Maybe we need a bit of 'aggro' in the camp to give us that little bit extra.

In all my time with Meath, I have only had one major disagreement with fellow players. That came when I first started out in my attempts to make the Senior side. The incident happened when I was a member of the Minor side and we were playing in Croke Park the same day as our Senior team. We won our match fairly comfortably but the Seniors, and in particular Bernard Flynn, had a tough encounter with Laois. I remember that Flynn was playing in the corner-forward position and was giving his marker a torrid time. The Laois fella could not take it anymore and so threw a punch at Flynn and was duly sent off. When the Minor and Senior teams attended the Beechmount Hotel in Navan later that night, I wanted to talk to him and the other players. We really looked up to them. They were our idols. They had won two All-Irelands and it was my big ambition to follow in their footsteps. I wanted to get to know them and pick up as many valuable tips as I could. I remember, as I made my way over to them, that Bernard Flynn was standing in a group along with Brian Stafford, Martin O'Connell, Terry Ferguson and their partners. Clearly, I remember saying to Bernard Flynn, in a half-joking sort of way:

'Have you any black eyes after today?'

To my surprise, he went mad and Brian Stafford asked me to go away and leave them.

A few people gathered around to see what was happening and Terry Ferguson responded: 'What the fuck did you say? You better leave!'

I left with my tail between my legs. As I did so I could hear Ferguson's wife say: 'Come back and talk to us when you have two All-Ireland medals under your belt.' I felt a little down after that. All I wanted to do was to talk to my idols for just a few minutes. I think Flynn was a little upset after their match with Laois. After the player was sent off for striking him, he had to endure a good lot of abuse from the Laois folk in the crowd. To make matters worse for him, he had to head home to Laois. He was living and working there, being a partner in a pub called 'The Pedigree Corner'.

Worse was to follow for me. Shortly after that, I joined the Meath Senior team for the first time and found that I was isolated. None of the Senior players would talk to me or come near me! I felt it was all very childish. Colm O'Rourke then got wind of what had happened in the Beechmount and one day he took me to one side. Colm told me that I had to make an apology to the Senior team. I was not happy at all about that and I told Colm that I had done nothing wrong. He agreed with me but he also made me see that I was on the verge of breaking into their tight-knit group and they did not like it one little bit. To them I was a smart, cocky little git and had to come down a peg or two. He told me if I did what he asked, then I could win them over. Reluctantly, I went along with what Colm said. I apologised to Flynn for upsetting him and he immediately accepted my apology. Then Brian Stafford came over and slapped me on the back and said that I had done the right thing. Thankfully, it worked and after that, I never looked back.

That Meath team from the 1980s were a totally different bunch to the teams that I have been playing with up through the 1990s to the present. They were a hardy bunch of lads, many with reputations of being 'hard men'. So much so that there were often rumours of rows and fisticuffs on the training ground. One such story which I remember concerned none other than Bernard Flynn. In his playing days, Bernard was a real nippy forward. He was a real marksman and a targetman in much the same mould that was to produce Tommy Dowd. Bernard has now made a nice little niche for himself in the media. He writes a column for a top newspaper and has a slot on RTÉ's *The Sunday Game*. He looks all dapper and smooth as if butter would not melt in his mouth. Looks can be deceiving. I felt his wrath in that late night incident in the Beechmount Hotel, but he also had a big bust-up with the most famous Meath hardman of them all – Mick Lyons. One evening at training in Navan, a bit of a tussle developed between Lyons and Flynn. Suddenly, and totally out of nowhere, Flynn blew a fuse and threw a punch at Lyons! Mick was furious and tried to get back at Flynn. Fortunately, for Bernard's sake, four or five lads grabbed a hold of Lyons and held him back. The surprising thing was that, far from backing down or keeping quiet, Flynn actually kept taunting and goading Mick until it all eventually died down!

That sort of thing has not happened since I became a member of the Senior panel and the old guard had all but disappeared. Right up through the 1990s to the present, I cannot think of a single incident either in the dressing-room or out on the training pitch. We are all a very close team. Sometimes I think we were far too close and could have done with a bit of a flare up to fire us up. Definitely we could do with some character and a bit of boldness from the class of '88.

However, the rumour mill was still grinding as far as I was concerned. On 29 June 2003, *Ireland on Sunday* ran a front-page story under the headline: 'GERAGHTY – MY SMEAR NIGHTMARE'. Just above it a sub-headline read 'GAA stars agony at claims of violence against wife and stranger'. In the report, they detailed the various rumours of wife-beating which I have already related. However, they also wrote about me hitting a young lad because he drew all over my daughter's face with markers in Doran's. This story was going around Athboy for what seemed like ages. As is the general trend of rumours, there were all sorts of flowery bits added on, resulting in many variations of the story. Apparently, this lad hit me and then I hit him back. Then I was supposed to have broken his nose. There was also a lot of blood and an ambulance had to be called to whisk the lad off to hospital. The newspaper in question obviously got wind of the story and sent a reporter and photographer to Athboy. They arrived out to Paircwee, which I was none too happy about. They just swanned their way into our driveway, wanting the whole story and to take photographs. Naturally, we refused; and if you look at the article you will see it contains no present-day photos of me.

On the front page they used a small photo of me holding Sophia in the Sam Maguire Cup – that was from 1999. Then on page 5 they had similar past photographs – of me holding Lauren and of me in a scuffle with an Australian Rules player. The only photos they printed from their day in Athboy were Doran's on Main Street and a small inset of a reluctant Amanda at our front door.

On Friday 4 July, 2003 I visited my solicitors, Regan, McEntee & Partners in Trim. They were confident that I had been libelled in the article penned by Valerie Hanley. I then instructed my solicitors to instigate legal proceedings against *Ireland on Sunday*. On receipt of my solicitors' letter, William Fry Solicitors acting on their behalf stated that they would be standing by their story and would be making no apology. Thankfully and eventually common sense has prevailed. I am happy to confirm that this legal issue between *Ireland on Sunday* and myself has been resolved to both Amanda's and my satisfaction.

Amid all the stress and hassle we faced in recent times, it was like a breath of fresh air and a huge sense of relief when we received some surprising letters of support. The day after the story appeared in *Ireland on Sunday*, a letter arrived from the parish priest of Dunboyne, Monsignor Ted Dunne PP: '*Just a few lines to assure you of my total support during these difficult times... Remember, Graham, that you have an artistry in football which they have not got...* They were lovely and very kind words from Monsignor Dunne. If that letter was an unexpected pick-me-up, then the next day brought yet another pleasant surprise. Fr Michael Sheerin, parish priest in Lobinstown, Navan wrote us an equally eloquent and uplifting letter. When I read his words, the hairs literally stood on the back of my neck: '*I have found the men of Meath to be men of honour, decency and best of all, courage when the time comes for it.*' Good wishes and letters like that, especially from people who are looked up to by the public, are a real tonic and an antidote to the sickness you feel from the garbage written about you. Thankfully, the clergy are not alone in their lending of support. We can always count on family and friends as well as colleagues at work, our regular customers and the real genuine Meath supporters. As Fr Sheerin so rightfully said, these true Meath people are full of honour, decency and courage, especially the kind of people like those in the townland of Coolronan. They showed their true colours when the gutter press tried to get them to talk during my difficult time in Australia in '99.

So what about the public? Here is a question I will put to you. In all the years you have seen me play, in all the rough treatment I have received – and I got a lot against the Dubs and even Westmeath in 2003 – have you ever seen me display violence or dish out a really dirty tackle in response? Over the years I have received cuts, bruises, broken bones and even had teeth chipped. If I did not even show a hint of violence in response, how could I show violence towards my wife or a young stranger in an unprovoked situation? Remember the last Australian Rules match at Croke Park? The Australian player Brad Scott taunted me. I ignored him but he floored me. I did not retaliate. Even then it was not over as he tried to blame me at the hearing! The committee did not listen to him and he ended up with a hefty ban.

Whether it is fellow players or the public or the media, I feel I have been misunderstood for my entire footballing career. I would like to be remembered for what I have done and achieved rather than for what I am supposed to have done. I am proud of having won everything at every level that Gaelic football has to offer. I have won two All-Irelands and was the proud captain on the second occasion in 1999. I have also won two All Star awards and have represented my country in International Rules. But all this seems to be overshadowed by the negative stuff said about me. I feel the lines from a well-known 1960's hit by The Animals is very apt: 'I'm just a soul whose intentions are good / Oh Lord, please don't let me be misunderstood.'

Others will say that this is the price of fame. The price you pay for all your success and for being in the public eye. Again I disagree. The real price of fame is something that professional soccer stars like Keane, Irwin, Quinn and Duff must be laughing at. We get a dinner and a few drinks after a match, or if we are lucky enough to win a Leinster or an All-Ireland, then we may be treated to a foreign holiday. Recently, our travel expenses were increased from 35 cent a mile to 50 cent! I mean it is a complete joke and even if the GPA get the €127 expense allowance for players, it still falls well below our true worth. Gaelic players are as fit if not fitter than any professional sports people and yet we get such a poor return. I know a lot of people will say that we do it for the love of the game. That is just bullshit! Of course we do it for love – the same as all professional sports people do. We are now living in the 21st century and yet expected to play like professionals while working and bringing up families. Add to that the travelling, the training, after-match drinks and foreign trips, buying gear and getting injured (not to mention up and coming legal fees!) and then I ask you – what value or what price would you slap on that? I am not saying that the GAA should start forking out money. I have already stated in an earlier chapter that I do not believe that would work. I am just saying, in mine and many other cases, that is the price of fame, which is a huge price to have to pay.

# 14 *The Comeback*

Despite intense newspaper speculation that I would make a return to the Meath team for the League campaign in early 2003, it was never going to happen. After my retirement, it was far too early for me to be drawn on making any decision. In any event, I was really enjoying rugby with Buccaneers. But every week it seemed like there was a journalist on the phone enquiring about whether I was making a comeback or not. For example, in the second week of January, it was Paddy Hickey of the *Irish Independent*. He thought I was returning to the Meath team as I had filled in for Sean Boylan at the Manager of the Year awards earlier in Dublin. In the *Irish Mirror*, Colm Keys suggested that I was certain to make a return for the first round of the Leinster Championship. He felt that there was no way I would turn down the opportunity of facing our neighbours Westmeath on 1st June. However, what many of these journalists overlooked was that as I was no longer part of the Meath set-up, Sean and the selectors had to find a replacement. In mid-January, Sean signalled his intentions by fielding a Meath team which contained only four well-known and regular players.

On 15th January in an O'Byrne Cup quarter-final against Longford, only Hank Traynor, Darren Fay, Donal Curtis and Ollie Murphy were Meath stalwarts that played. That day there were many new faces in the Meath team and a few of them impressed greatly. The match ended in a shock result, however. Longford won by 1–11 to 0–11. The match was also played in Navan under the floodlights and impressive facilities at Simonstown Gaels. Nonetheless, I would say that Sean was very pleased and satisfied at how well some of the new guys fared.

Nobody likes losing in any competitive game – and especially at home. But one new guy really signalled his intentions in that game.

Daithí Regan was Meath's top scorer with 0–5. A corner-forward, Daithí was sending out a clear message. He could more than hold his own at Inter-County level and was ready to fill in for me or any of the other Meath forwards. To many in Meath, Daithí and several others in the team are well known. But to the general public and the County scene, he was a new kid on the block. With the National League just around the corner, it would be very interesting to see how Daithí and several others would perform against stiffer opposition.

Meath were in Division 1B which was fairly competitive and strong. The group comprised Laois, Kildare, Mayo, Sligo and the three Ulster counties of Cavan, Down and Fermanagh. The first match against Laois would prove a real test. Under the legendary Mick O'Dwyer, Laois were coming under intense scrutiny from the media microscope. The press, and indeed the whole country, were fascinated about whether the legendary Kerry maestro could bring success to Laois. After all, he had done so with his great Kerry sides and also with Kildare. The game was played in Páirc Tailteann, Navan on 2nd February. It was not a good start for Meath as Laois won fairly comfortably by 0–11 to 0–7. In contrast, it was a great start for Micko and in the coming weeks and months, he would go on to achieve great and historic feats with Laois.

The following week, things went from bad to worse for Meath when they met Cavan away in Breffni Park. Cavan thrashed the Royals by 1–16 to 0–7. I know it was just the League, but after that shocking 12-point defeat to Cavan, the distress signals were out. There simply had to be an improvement and it did come in the next match against the Lilywhites. Meath got the win they badly needed – but only just. It was a close-run thing but Meath scraped through in Navan by 0–13 to 0–12. When they followed that with a great 0–13 to 1–9 win over Sligo in Markievicz Park, it seemed like things were coming right.

One of the reasons for this was Sean adding some of the more experienced players to the team to aid the youngsters. Then, just as the tide seemed to be turning for us, Meath suffered another humiliating defeat. The 3–9 to 0–12 defeat at the hands of Fermanagh – again at home in Navan – raised a lot of questions. The dogs in the street were barking that there was no future for this current panel of players. Even though Trevor Giles would mark this

League campaign with a return from a long lay off through injury, many staunch Meath followers felt that the blend of old and new would not work. There were wicked whisperings that many of our best players were finished and that Meath's best days were firmly behind them.

Heavy home defeats to Longford, Laois and Fermanagh were one thing, but there was another worrying trend. In the O'Byrne Cup game and the first five League games, Meath had failed to register a goal! This was an astonishing fact. Meath have always scored goals and have always had the players to do it. It was also an embarrassment that after five games in the group, every other county had scored at least three goals.

In getting prepared for the Championship ahead, Sean and his selectors must surely have worried over this. In Meath's last two matches, the goal drought was quenched but there were no fireworks. On 23rd March in Navan, Meath beat old rivals Mayo by 1–16 to 0–12. In their final outing away to Down in Newcastle, Meath tallied 1–11 but lost out by a point to the Mournemen's 0–15. It was a mediocre if not poor League campaign with an awful lot of work to be done. The likes of Daithí Regan and the McKeigue brothers had created favourable impressions but there was very little else for Meath folk to get excited about. There were very real worries that we had very little going for us ahead of the big Leinster clash with Westmeath on 1st June.

As Meath football was lying a little flat and deflated, my rugby career was going from strength to strength. From my very first match with Buccaneers when I scored a try, I was gathering momentum. Moreover, I was learning all the time. So by the time Buccs reached the semi-finals of the Heineken Connacht Junior Cup, I was really pumped up and eager to do my best. In that semi-final, we faced Galwegians. It proved to be a very tight match and we just squeezed through to the final. I was delighted with my performance in that game. It was my finest display in the Buccaneers' colours. I had an all-round good game and ended up scoring the winning try. After overcoming a strong Galwegians' side, we were now the hottest of favourites to win the Cup. We were very much expected to easily brush aside the challenge of Ballinasloe in the final.

The match took place in Crowley Park, Galway on 11th May. The outsiders played well above themselves and only trailed 12–8 when a penalty, deep into stoppage time in the first half, gave us a 15–8 lead at the break. It took two late tries from us, when the score was 22–13 in our favour, for us to finally fight off the challenge of a brave Ballinasloe. We won 34–13 but the scoreline was very misleading. Once again, I had a great chance to score the winning try. We created a fine flowing move and as the ball was moved across the line, I was the last man and had just to receive the ball to score. But the pass was a wild one and the chance of my crowning glory went astray! Nevertheless, I had won a Connacht Junior Cup and that was a fine feat for my first ever season in the game. Having never ever played rugby before my retirement from football, and when you consider that so many start out in rugby when they are young and at school, I was very proud of my achievements.

A few players of that winning side are worth a mention as it is quite possible that one or two of them will go on to achieve even greater things. First, I will mention Adrian Hanley. He is a backrow player and was Young Player of the Year at Buccaneers three seasons ago. He is a real favourite at the club. Anthony Nash, affectionately known as 'Nashy', has propped for Leinster Youths and the Irish Youths as well as Connacht U-21s. Next, Robert Keady is a real clubman. He is the proud possessor of two Connacht Senior Cup medals and was also a tower of strength as Buccs achieved the Junior League and Cup double last season.

On the day of that final with Ballinasloe a funny thing happened. As you will recall, in 2002 I was flown by helicopter to Navan for the Leinster clash with Louth as I was at a wedding in Wexford that same day. Well, on the day of the final with Ballinasloe, I was also required to play for my club Seneschalstown. We were playing a very important game against Simonstown Gaels. So the idea of getting a helicopter to accommodate both games surfaced once more. However, in the end, I made the journey to Galway in a four-seater plane! The plane was owned by a friend of Seneschalstown selector, Frank Sheridan. I suppose it is all a case of planes, trains or automobiles – get there how you can! On this occasion, however, it was going to be a bit of a rush. Weddings may go on all night and into the next day and so there is no real rush or hurry. In this case, the rugby final was scheduled for 3 pm and I was due back to play for Seneschalstown at 7.45 pm. Plenty of time you would think – but the rugby match would finish around 4.30 pm and the airport in Galway closed at 5 pm!

When we beat Ballinasloe, I could not even hang around for the presentation of the cup and medals. I grabbed my bag and stuffed my gear into it and then Tommy Kennedy from Kentstown and myself made for the airport as fast as we could. Thankfully, we made it there in time meaning I would get to Navan in plenty of time for the 7.45 kick-off. But not before I experienced a few hairy moments in transit. Unlike helicopter trips, flights in small Cessna-like planes are far from smooth. The chopper may not be as fast but at least you do not experience turbulence! I felt seasick after that plane journey. When we landed in a field in Stackallen, around four or five miles from Navan, Frank Sheridan was there to pick me up. I was so relieved to go to his house for a cup of tea before the game with Simonstown! Somewhat surprisingly, considering all that had gone on that day, I played fairly well in that game. I actually scored a few crucial points and we won. But that is as good as it got for me and Seneschalstown. Personally, it was a year which will be remembered for all the wrong reasons and one which I wish to forget.

It now seems like a nightmare, but in the course of playing for my club this year, I was sent off no less than three times. Once I was actually sent off a few minutes after coming on as a substitute in another match with Simonstown! When I was sent off for the third time – in a match with Ballivor – I actually pushed and jostled the referee but did not hit him. It looks likely that because of that incident, and taking into account the previous two red cards, I will be facing a lengthy suspension.

In mid-April, while playing with both Buccaneers and Seneschalstown, I knew that there was going to be a big void in the weeks and months ahead as the rugby season was fast coming to a close. There was also great excitement and great anticipation in Meath about our opening Leinster clash with Westmeath. Nobody talked about anything else; especially in Doran's the subject was on everyone's lips. For this reason, the idea of rejoining the Meath panel became an appealing and appetising one indeed. There is something very special about the advent of summer and the All-Ireland Championships. There is a great buzz around and because of that it helps to create a great atmosphere. It is something that the whole nation looks forward to and, with all due respect to Buccaneers and Seneschalstown, they just pale into insignificance by comparison.

It finally began to dawn on me that there was no way I could just sit and watch my team-mates in action against Westmeath. Whether I watched it at home, in the pub or most likely at Croke Park, it felt almost criminal for me not to be involved. With the press hounding me as well, everything was swaying me towards a return. My heart strings were been tugged from all angles and the turning point came when Darren Fay visited me in the pub one evening. He asked the inevitable question to which I replied that I had not fully made up my mind – yet. But I hinted that I would like to come back. Darren responded by telling me to come to training and left it at that.

A few days later, Sean Boylan rang, having heard that I had been talking to Darren. First, he declared that he was not going to ask me back or put any pressure on me. He said he would leave it up to me to decide. Next, he stressed that if I wished to come back to the Meath team, then I had to genuinely want to. Nonetheless, the final thing he did say was: 'We're flying out to Portugal this Sunday and I have your name down.' That was pure Sean and that sealed my decision. Later, I rang Owen Lynch, as Sean had advised, and confirmed my seat on the trip to Portugal. When I arrived at Dublin Airport on Sunday, 20th April, it was great to see all the familiar faces again. There were big smiles everywhere – especially on the faces of Giles and Curtis. We were like classmates going away on a school trip, so full of the joys of spring were we. But this was to be no holiday – it was all serious business.

There was little or no craic in Portugal, which was a good thing as we really had to get focused and 'psyched up' for the crunch clash with Westmeath. In previous encounters with our closest neighbours, the stakes were always the same for both counties. Win, and you could walk down the streets of Mullingar with your head held high. Lose, and you would not feel like walking down the street in Navan. In Portugal, we were up every morning at 8 am and did some very strenuous and serious workouts. An expert in physical fitness, Gerry Loftus from Kildare was our fitness instructor and has been working with us for some time now. In fact, Gerry participated in the physical endurance programme, *Milk Superstars*, shown on

RTÉ television many years ago in 1982. As part of the training session, Gerry had us doing a form of Thai Chi, including a lot of breathing and stretching exercises. After breakfast, we all headed off to a football pitch where we trained for the rest of the day. In the evening we had dinner followed by a meeting where we were told the agenda for the next day. All of us were in bed around 10 pm and by that time, we could not wait to hit the scratcher! It was non-stop but we knew we could only benefit from it.

When we arrived back from Portugal, a few challenge matches were arranged for us in May. The first match was against Sligo in Enfield. We won that by five or six points but I remember I was very rusty. Although I was playing rugby and club football around the same time, and I was very fit, the match sharpness against good county players was not yet in tune.

We then played Colm Coyle's Monaghan in Navan just a few weeks before our big Leinster opener. We won that hands down by a very wide margin – some 16 or 17 points – but all the talk at that time was about the injuries suffered by two of our key players. Ollie Murphy broke his shoulder and Nigel Crawford received a very bad injury when his thigh muscle had torn away from the bone. The injury was so bad that it could have spelt the end of his career. With Murphy out, Daithí Regan had earned his place and was duly called up for the Westmeath match. There were also five other new faces who were handed their Senior Championship debut. Four days before the big game, on 28th May, Sean announced the team. Tomas O'Connor, Charles McCarthy, Shane and Niall McKeigue and David Crimmins were the men given their big chance to impress.

In the case of Niall McKeigue and David Crimmins, they had appeared as subs the previous year but this was their first taste of the full 70 minutes. With Shane McKeigue also carrying a niggling injury, I remember that a lot of Westmeath supporters were ribbing us about all our problems. In such circumstances, allied to all our new faces, they were very confident of victory. I was also named in the starting 15 at full-forward. As the big day approached, I was nervous but that was only to be expected. On the way up to Dublin, you could see the streams of cars everywhere. You see all the colours – the maroon of Westmeath and our green and gold, and suddenly it hits you. You then realise the importance of it all and you know you cannot afford to let your side down. Naturally enough, I was also worried as to how I would perform. I knew that all eyes were on me – especially the media – after coming out of retirement. There was so much to contend with and yet so much to play for. When the referee Michael Curley threw up the ball, I was ready to give my all. I was hoping that I would not let anyone down.

We got off to a dream start. After only a minute, Hank Traynor cut through the Westmeath backline like a hot knife through butter. He blasted an unstoppable shot to the back of the net and we had the perfect start. I think that goal must have given our newcomers a lot of heart and confidence. After Hank's great goal, they played brilliantly. Daithí Regan and Shane McKeigue were outstanding in the forward line. Both got on the scoresheet and were causing the Westmeath defence all sorts of headaches. And Charles McCarthy was having such a great game at midfield that you would have thought he was playing there alongside McDermott and McGuiness all his life!

I wish I could say the same about my own performance. I was finding the going very tough indeed. You can play all the challenges you like, and you can be as fit as a fiddle from playing in other codes, but Championship football is totally different. For starters, it is 10 times faster than Club or even League games. Every player on the field has been built up to this level. They are all so finely tuned and ready to burst blood vessels. I simply could not get involved in the match. Everything seemed to be bypassing me, which as usual was making me frustrated. I felt like a spectator rather than a player. Aside from that, we led by 1–10 to 0–8 at the break, but that was largely thanks to the debutantes.

At the break, we could not believe our five-point lead. It was making for an exciting game. We had six new faces in the side and we were playing live on television. That was some lead when you consider the players we had injured and me playing in limbo. I remember thinking that if we could keep this going, and if I could get a footing, then we would coast to victory. Up in the television gantry, the panellists from RTÉ's *The Sunday Game* were voicing their concerns about me. All three of them – Michael Lyster, Colm O'Rourke and Tony Davis – agreed that I was very rusty and not in the game at all. They were too right and echoing what most spectators, including myself, were feeling! My great mentor and fellow Meathman, Colm O'Rourke, made the following comment: 'Graham Geraghty has never been the type of player that dominates a match. But he is the type of player who just needs one chance and he can turn a game.'

As I took to the field, I knew I had to try and get into the game. If I did not, the critics and the supporters would be out for my blood. If the first period was a little stale and one-sided, then the second half would become so full of drama that, if not one of the best games seen in years, then it would certainly become one of the most talked about. I do not know what Luke Dempsey said to his players at the break, but if we thought our cushion was enough to carry us through, then we were in for a very rude awakening.

Westmeath were totally transformed after the interval and played quite stunning football. They were awesome and majestic and suddenly we were the ones in trouble and very much on the back foot. In the first 15 minutes of the half, they scored two goals. While not taking anything away from Westmeath's play, both goals were defensive howlers on our part. Cormac Sullivan was at fault for the first. He failed to collect a simple enough cross and the ball bounced off his chest into the path of the waiting Dessie Dolan. Dolan then had the easy task of palming the ball to the net. Following that, Westmeath were scoring points from all directions and we simply had no answer to it. Their second goal was a real farce on our part. A Westmeath player struck the ball towards our goal but the shot was blocked. Still the ball came back in again and once more, Sullivan failed to gather it. The ball slipped through his hands and then through the legs of Nigel Nestor behind him. It seemed like slow motion as the ball trickled across the line. At that stage, it also felt like 'curtains' for us.

By the time of that second goal, we had failed to add to our half-time tally and Westmeath scored two goals and four points to lead, 2–12 to 1–10. We were the team now trailing by five and it did not look good. In 19 previous Championship games between both sides, Westmeath had never beaten Meath. All that looked set to change. We had to respond and we did. Three points without reply brought us back to within two points. There was still 10 minutes plus injury time so we had plenty of time left. That was when all the drama started to unfold and I finally got my act together.

Before that, I was genuinely worried about my performance. I was starting to get annoyed and agitated. Sean then beckoned me over to the sideline. Contrary to what many thought at that time, he was not telling me to calm down because I was already on a yellow card from earlier in the game. It was just a positional switch and in fact, he was telling me to tell another player to go into a certain position.

Another reason for my rather inept display up until the final few minutes was the close marking of the Westmeath defenders. There seemed to be two or three of them going for the ball with me and I was getting some rough treatment in the process. If you remember early in the first half, I was bearing down on their goal when several of their players came in hard on me. The legs were swiped from beneath me and my ankle badly bruised as a result. All this would never wash with eyes watching me. I had to get in on the action fast as time was running out. If I did not do something, then my place in the side was also in grave jeopardy. When Sean made a series of substitutions with Kealy, Curtis and Murphy all coming on, I remember looking over anxiously to the line. I thought my time was up and that I was going to be called off.

Thankfully, they persisted with me and it paid off. With only around five minutes remaining, Cormac Murphy, who had just come on, sent in a high-hopeful ball towards me. Instinctively, I knew that their keeper would come for it as well, so I just latched on to it with my fist before he did. To my delight, and the delight of all connected with Meath, the ball ended up in the back of the net. I had come good in the nick of time and once more we were out of jail.

That goal put us a point in front, 2–13 to 2–12, and time was almost up. In truth, it was a lucky enough goal. First, it could have gone anywhere, including over the bar for a point. And second, when Cormac passed the ball to me, it was actually too high for me and I had to reach up and flick it. It was a fantastic feeling to see that ball ripple the net. The relief all around the ground, among players and supporters, was enormous.

Seconds later, we were quickly brought back down to earth when Donal Curtis was given a straight red card for head-butting Martin Flanagan. It was a silly thing for Donal to do as there was no need for it. He knew it but it was all in the heat of the moment – and it was to cost him a three-month ban. To make matters worse, Dessie then levelled with a great point from a narrow angle. With the scores tied at 2–13 each, many of us thought the referee would call a draw. But more drama was to follow.

Westmeath went on the attack again but they lost the ball and Hank Traynor took it away. The next we knew, the referee blew and gave Westmeath a free straight in front of the posts. In his judgement Hank had picked the ball off the ground. We went berserk and I was absolutely livid. I could not believe Michael Curley could make such a decision at such a late stage. It was cruel and he had effectively handed Westmeath the match on a plate.

As Dessie Dolan got ready to kick, I was still fuming with Curley. When asked how long was left, he said there was a minute and 40 seconds. I did not think there was that much time left. But then it dawned on me that even if Dolan scored, we still had the chance to go down the other end and perhaps snatch a draw. Dolan ran forward a few paces and kicked. As I looked at the curling flight of the ball, I remember thinking, 'that's gone wide'. We all looked anxiously at the linesmen and referee and when it was waved wide, we could not believe it. Again we were spared men! No question about it but Westmeath should have confined us to the back-door system.

It was great for us that we now had a second chance. But it was also sad that the game had to end like that for Dessie Dolan. He was their Man of the Match as he had played brilliantly throughout the 70 minutes. The way he was playing, I doubt anyone thought he would miss that relatively easy free. Who knows what was going through his head as he stepped forward to kick? Some people suggested that I shouted something at him, which was not the case.

None of us played particularly well. We would have to show great improvement in the replay. Apart from the goal, I did nothing. Nevertheless, it was heartwarming to hear about some generous compliments which were paid to me after the game. Colm O'Rourke was certainly prophetic with his half-time comment but his fellow analyst, Cork's Tony Davis, said a really nice thing about me (probably the nicest compliment I ever received from RTÉ panellists!). Tony said that I had 'killer instinct' and that I was 'a born winner', which I must admit was very flattering.

Next day a fantastic action photo of that goal appeared on the front page of *The Irish Times'* sports supplement. The photographer, Dara MacDonaill, did very well to capture the moment when I beat the keeper and punched the ball to the net. The photo shows Westmeath keeper Aidan Lennon and myself jumping for the ball. His arm has pushed my head right back and it looks as though I am about to suffer a broken neck – or even decapitation! Also in *The Irish Times*, Ian O'Riordan wrote: 'Graham Geraghty reminded everyone exactly why he can walk straight back into the Meath team. Set up perfectly by Cormac Murphy, he produced a one-handed fisted goal in the way only Geraghty can, and so Meath were back in front.'

It would be unkind, unfair and untrue to say that I walked straight back into the Meath team. Nobody is ever really guaranteed a place and this was no different. Four days before the game, I was named by Sean Boylan in the Meath starting 15 – at full-forward. But on the day, I started at centre-half forward and that was testimony to the tremendous abilities and potential of those eventually picked in the full-forward line.

I do not know what the statistics or the record books show, but I would venture to say that a new record was created that day in the Championship. Would I be right in saying that it was the first time that three newcomers, all playing in the full-forward line, all managed to score – and score more than one point? Daithí Regan had already shown us what he could do, and did not let us down on that day. He scored three points from the right corner. Shane McKeigue scored two points from the left corner and David Crimmins also scored a brace from full-forward. For the replay, we were hoping they would carry on that form and show even more improvement. As regards myself and some of the others in the team, we had to show improvement in leaps and bounds.

The replay, in Portlaoise the following Saturday, resulted in a very one-sided affair as we ran out easy winners by 1–11 to 0–5. It could so easily have been a different story. Westmeath actually started the better and had two excellent goal chances early on. They also hit a number of wides so it was actually a tighter game than the scoreline suggests.

At half-time in that game we lead by three points but in the second half, Westmeath had a glorious chance to get back into the game. They were awarded a penalty but Dessie Dolan fluffed it badly and Cormac Sullivan smothered it easily. Once again, many people suggested that I had said something to Dolan as he stepped up to take the kick. I was nowhere near him and, in any case, anyone who knows anything about football knows that you cannot be near the kicker. However, I did have words with him just a few minutes before that. As he was lying on the ground, I bent down and said to him: 'Dessie, you are a bigger man than that – get up!' I felt that he was play-acting and looking for a penalty after Paddy Reynolds ran into him.

Fair dues to Westmeath, however. They really put it up to us again, but again they had nothing to show for it. They should have beaten us in that first game but history will only remember them for *never* having beaten us in the Championship. Daithí Regan had another outstanding game for us, as he hit six points in that replay and David Crimmins chipped in with a goal. They are great finds and they must surely have a bright future ahead in the Meath jersey. For the record, I was happy with my game as I scored two points.

On Saturday, 14th June, we played Kildare in the Leinster semi-final. For drama and excitement, it could never reach the heights and the thrills and spills of our epic with Westmeath. It came quite close, though. This semi-final opened up with all guns blazing and another glaring miss at the death was to prove very costly. We could not have asked for a better start. We led by 1–3 to 0–1 but we also missed three glorious chances of a goal. There is a saying that if you do not convert your chances, then you will be punished. By the time the referee blew the half-time whistle, we certainly were made to pay for those misses. Kildare went on a real blitz and our defence had no answer to the bombardment. The Lilywhites scored 10 points without reply and went in leading 0–11 to 1–3 at the break.

To say we were shell-shocked at the interval would be a gross understatement. We blitzed Kildare in the first 15 minutes and could easily have been eight or 11 points ahead, if one or two of those chances had gone in. Instead we were five points in arrears.

Talk about a game of two halves – that first half with Kildare was a game of two quarters. In the second half we responded well. We showed the real never-say-die Meath attitude and had Kildare on the retreat. We were ahead in that half by 0–8 to 0–4 going into the dying minutes but we still trailed by a point. Daithí Regan then had a great chance to take the game to yet another replay but he missed. When the final whistle sounded moments later, it was joy for Kildare and despair for us.

Daithí was really down after that miss but you could not blame him for our defeat. He had been Meath's best player all year and had barely put a foot wrong. When you are young and scoring at will, it is inevitable that something will bring you back down to earth with a bang. It is all part of the learning process for him. I do not blame anyone for that defeat but we should really have been in the Leinster final.

We lost that semi-final in the first half when we sat back and just ball-watched Kildare. As a result they outscored us 10–0 and we were out of Leinster. At least we were still in the qualifiers and there we would meet Monaghan. This was a very interesting pairing as Monaghan were now managed by ex-Meath stalwart, and my old Seneschalstown team mate, Colm Coyle. It was also billed as 'the pupil against the teacher – Coyle versus Boylan'.

Playing Monaghan in Clones was a very difficult assignment. They had beaten All-Ireland champions Armagh in Ulster and had also vanquished our conquerors Westmeath in the previous qualifying round. So we were very much up against it, despite playing for the fourth week in a row. With the fatigue factor in mind, it was therefore a huge boost to get a fresh pair of legs, as Nigel Crawford returned after his bad injury.

Any concerns we had soon evaporated as we got off to a flyer. Leading by a point, I then scored my second goal since my return and there were barely 10 minutes on the clock. Trevor sent in a free towards me and it was like a carbon copy of the goal I got against Westmeath. It was the same again as I flicked the ball behind me and it finished up in the back of the net. In the lead by 1–2 to 0–1, we simply played Monaghan off the park in that first half. In fact, we were dominating in almost every position and then Crimmins sealed our dominance just before the break with a well-taken second goal.

Going into the dressing-room, we had a commanding 12-point lead, 2–8 to 0–2. At the break Sean decided to rest the excellent David Crimmins and sent out Evan Kelly in his place. I really enjoyed myself in that first half. I was moving well and getting plenty of the ball. I also preferred the position I was now playing in. In the first few matches I was at corner-forward and full-forward but now I was in the half-forward line. At the break Darren Fay said that if we got another four or five points in the second half, then it would be all over.

In the event we only got two points and it almost proved to be disastrous. Fair play to Monaghan for fighting back but we were all worried about this new development. In our last three games we were only dominating for 15 or 20 minutes and then we were being dominated by the opposition for seemingly longer periods. Maybe in the Monaghan game it was a combination of tiredness finally setting in and a bit of complacency. After all, a 12-point lead is virtually unassailable.

Monaghan won the second half by 0–10 to 0–2 but it was not enough as we won by 2–10 to 0–12. If you are superstitious, then there may have been another reason for our second-half collapse. I have often heard it said about such and such a team 'playing into the scoring goals'. In the first half, for example, the goalposts we played into meant that Monaghan only scored two points down the other end. Those same goalposts which Monaghan played into in the second half meant that we only scored two points at the same end as Monaghan played in the first half!

Overall though, we were pleased with the performance. A win is a win and we were into the next qualifying round. David Crimmins scored 1–3 in only 35 minutes of play, I scored a goal and a point and Crawford and Ollie Murphy returned after injury. After the game I shook Colm Coyle's hand and said 'hard luck'. All in all, Colm can look back on a great first year with Monaghan. Beating Armagh is a great boost for his CV.

A break of two weeks until our next match was ideal. In the meantime, we had a look at the videos of the Kildare and Monaghan games to try to establish just why we went missing for long periods in those games. We could not really find an answer other than that there will always be periods when other teams have a large amount of possession. So basically we put it down to that. When Fermanagh came out as our next opponents, I was watching the draw on the television in the pub. The attitude among all the customers and staff was that we would get past them without too much bother. I have to admit that I felt that way as well, although Sean and some of the other players were very cautious and tried hard to deflect us from that way of thinking.

On 6 July we faced Fermanagh and everyone in Meath was full of confidence. In a poor first half, when none of us really played well, we led by 0–5 to 0–3. Sean was not at all happy. He is not the sort to fling cups around but you could see the concern on his face. I remember him telling us to be sharper on the breaking ball and to get it into the forwards quickly.

The rest of that day was a nightmare as we had no answer to Fermanagh after the break. In fairness, they did their homework on us and played some magnificent football in the process. Their left-footed players kicked great scores from the left and their right-footed ones from the right. In the end we were left with egg all over our faces. We were down and out of the 2003 Championship as Fermanagh marched on, winning by 1–12 to 0–9. In the dressing-room afterwards, it was like a funeral. Looking back now, I feel a lot of regret that myself and the rest of the team underperformed. It was all down to sheer complacency and overconfidence. We let ourselves down, we let Sean Boylan down and, above all, we let the Meath people down. One of my last memories was of Sean Boylan and everyone shaking hands with him. Many felt it was going to be goodbye from Sean and that he would step down after that defeat. I was delighted when Sean indicated his wish to remain in the position.

On my way home, a funny thing happened. I stopped off in Oldcastle for a quiet pint and as I was sitting at the bar, reflecting on what might have been, a friend of mine came in and sat beside me. He is a Northern man and was wearing a Fermanagh jersey. Anyone who spotted us must have thought it very odd to say the least!

Two weeks later, I watched Kildare in the Leinster final but it was so hard to look at it. I knew that with a bit of better luck, it should have been us in that final. I had similar feelings when I watched Fermanagh playing again and that just about summed up my year with Meath. With all the fun and the fanfare of summer, I got back on the rollercoaster. I got a great buzz from the highs of the Westmeath and Monaghan matches, but felt sick to the pit of my stomach after the sudden plunge into the depths that the Fermanagh match brought.

\*\*\*\*\*\*

Just when I thought everything was over and that things could not get any worse, they did. In fact, the defeat by Fermanagh was to be followed by not just one more blow but a double whammy and without doubt the bitterest pill I ever had to swallow. On Wednesday, 6th August, John O'Keeffe, the Irish International Rules manager, dropped me from the initial panel of 67 players for the Series in October. To tell the truth, I was not that gutted with his decision. My wife Amanda is expecting our third child in February and, with the pub and everything else, I would not have gone to Australia anyway. Nonetheless, it was the manner in which he did it and the reason he gave which particularly annoyed me.

Having been a Series regular for the last four years, the least he could have done was ring me and tell me everything man to man. But I was to learn about the decision through the media. It was on the RTÉ Sports News that evening and in the papers the next day: 'GRAHAM RULES KO!' was the banner headline in *The Irish Sun* with a sub-headline 'Geraghty axed from Aussie trip – and that could end his international career'. When asked about my exclusion, O'Keeffe responded with the following words:

> *Graham's omission was a decision we came to. The same question could be asked of various other players, but what I'm keen to do this year is to bring in players who are on form this year – not last year or the year before or because they have reputations.*
>
> *We need players who are playing well right now. I'm particularly interested in finding new players. There are a number of lads who have played for the last few years but it's important to get enthusiastic players who are very keen to make this panel and who will take a lot of pride in an Irish jersey.*

That was all a load of bullshit from O'Keeffe. If that was the true reason – and I know for a fact that it was not – then why did he include my fellow Meath and Ireland players, Darren Fay, Trevor Giles and Evan Kelly, in that panel? After all, they are no spring chickens either and Trevor goes back as far as me in terms of Rules appearances. So as regards the Meath players selected in that panel, omitting me stood out like a sore thumb. In recent years, I have played well and my experience would rub off on others. Truth be told, the real reason O'Keeffe dropped me was because of an incident that happened before the First Test in 2002. He had gathered the panel of players at a hotel in Dublin, and I told him I would arrive later on that night as I had to organise an important charity function in the pub. But I got carried away with things in the pub and also had a few drinks. Seeing that I was over the limit, I chose not to drive to Dublin that night and decided to go first thing next morning instead.

Around 8 am next morning, I left for Dublin. Though I explained the situation to John O'Keeffe, he was none too happy. In fact he was so annoyed with me that he told me he was dropping me for the First Test! As manager, that was his decision which was fair enough. But I thought he could have been a little more lenient. I accepted his decision and knuckled down and did not do anything else wrong. However, it was plainly obvious that there were bad vibes between us and it spilled over to the Second Test. In running out for that match, I was delighted to be representing my country for the fourth year running. In the first quarter, I was happy with my performance and when Brad Scott floored me, we capitalised and went into a nice lead. Yet soon after that, O'Keeffe took me off. He did not put me on again until the final five minutes, which earlier in the book, I explained how pointless and futile that decision was. Now you know why I was sensationally dropped from the Rules side this year. O'Keeffe may also have had the perfect excuse to drop me after I was at the centre of another incident just as he was selecting and considering his panel of Rules players. This particular incident was to cost me very dearly, perhaps meaning that I have played for the very last time.

* * * * * *

In playing for my club Seneschalstown this year, I had already been sent off twice (against Simonstown and Skryne) prior to a crucial clash with Ballivor in Dunsany on 5th August (the day before the Rules panel was announced). Ballivor got stuck into us from the start and it was a very stormy game to say the least. I was also sent off in that game for two bookable offences but was only trying to get the referee to give me and my team a bit of protection, as there were lads literally clattering into us. To my mind, the referee and linesmen were doing absolutely nothing about it.

Reports said that I 'physically abused' referee Jim Smith from Dunshaughlin. I admit that I knocked his notebook out of his hands while I remonstrated with him 10 minutes before the end. I also admit that I verbally abused him as I followed him off the pitch at the end of the game. But I never physically abused or hit him. I am also led to believe that as I shouted at him in the dressing-room afterwards, a plastic drinks bottle was thrown at him and that was written into his report. However, I did not throw the bottle at him.

Because of my bad disciplinary record this year with Seneschalstown, and all the furore and rage with Jim Smith, I knew I was in trouble. In the calm and cold light of day, I was wrong and I deserved to be punished. At the very worst, I would have accepted a six-month ban. What I got from the Meath County Board was totally unjustified. Their decision was disgraceful.

On Monday, 8th September the Meath County Board unanimously agreed to ban me from playing any more football for 48 weeks, i.e. one year. I could not believe it. Naturally, I was angry and very, very disappointed. I was also hurt and felt badly let down. Similar to the O'Keeffe situation, the feelings of hurt, anger and disappointment were more to do with the way the County Board went about reaching their decision and their failure to recognise or understand my situation and feelings. For starters, they never even notified me to tell me that the meeting was taking place. Countless people asked me when was the meeting but I just kept telling them that I had not a clue! The County Board could also have taken into account, as most court judges would undoubtedly have, 'mitigating circumstances'. I had scored a crucial goal against Westmeath this year which helped spare the blushes of those who handed down that severe sentence to me.

I helped Meath win two All-Irelands – captaining them in 1999. Was this the way to treat an All-Ireland winning captain? I had also helped Meath to many other titles and this is how I was repaid.

A few days after the ban, I flew to Lanzarote for a week's holiday with Amanda and a few staff from Doran's. It was a welcome relief and some respite from all the talk surrounding the 48-week sentence, but in my absence an appeal was put in to the Leinster Council. The appeal was lodged on the basis that I was not notified about when the Meath County Board were holding the original meeting to determine my fate.

On the evening of Thursday, 25th September, myself, Francis Flynn and Seneschalstown chairman Micky Dillon were very hopeful that the ban would be reduced. However, within five minutes of us appearing, a member of the Leinster Council Management Committee told us they were upholding the decision of the Meath County Board. They gave no reason for their judgment, therefore, the ban stood and I will not play football again until July 2004.

\* \* \* \* \* \*

Had I not made it to the top in football, I really do not know what I would be doing. I am quite sure it would have involved something in some sporting field. Reflecting on my career thus far, I could not have achieved my goals and dreams without the biggest help of all – my Meath mentors.

Sean Boylan has been, without doubt, one of the biggest names in GAA over the last 20 years. For me, he has been a huge influence since I first got involved with Meath back in 1990. He saw my potential and, unquestionably, he turned me into a much better footballer. He is a real man manager rather than a football manager and that, to me, is the key. In essence, he has respect for all and is a pure gentleman.

When I first went into the Meath panel, Colm O'Rourke was one of the people who really believed in me. In one of my first crucial games against Dublin, Colm told me before the game that I was not to worry as I was well able for Niall Guiden. I was always a fan of Colm's so to play with him was a real morale booster. I will never forget how Colm helped me out during my torrid time in Australia. It was only then that I knew who my real friends were.

Though we all looked up to the hard man, Mick Lyons, in reality he was a 'gentle giant'. I played a couple of games with him and also played under him when he was a selector. I have already spoken about how Mick was a huge influence on my career. He is gone from the team but will never be forgotten.

Mention of my team-mates and I just have to start off with Trevor. Trevor Giles is the complete footballer. When I first saw him, we were playing in an U-12 match and he was only around nine-years-old. Even then he had his now familiar blond hair and big red cheeks! From the start I remember his very awkward style of playing. He was forever running with the ball and always looking up before he kicked it – he did not have to keep his eye on it as he knew instinctively where it was. Trevor still has that style today and all young lads should watch him closely. A real role model.

Tommy Dowd has also been a huge influence for players and supporters alike. I remember when I was in Chicago, a few Mayo people I was talking to asked me: 'How is the Charolais Bull?' referring to Tommy. After Colm O'Rourke, he became the player that led from the front. I can never remember Tommy having a bad game for Meath. A great and determined player.

A very good friend of mine is Darren Fay. He is a lot like Mick Lyons in that he is quiet and a man of few words. But on the field of play, he has plenty to say. So much so that he is – in many people's opinions, including mine – quite simply the best full-back playing the game. Without him we would be lost, as the case has proved in the past.

After all the happenings of late, I think it appropriate, as I come to the end of my book, to finish with a quote, which hopefully will go some way towards helping people understand me a little better. In his *Irish Times*' column, 'Sideline Cut' on 14th June, Keith Duggan wrote:

> *The engagement between Geraghty and one of the linesmen was some sight. There were times when the forward looked apoplectic with rage over some missed call or perceived slight and seconds later he was back playing*

*the game with his customary coolness. Away from the field, Geraghty is a polite and subdued figure in his public engagements, a personality utterly at odds with the lean figure constantly agitating with whatever official is close at hand.*

*Personally, I think nine times out of 10, Geraghty is worth the admission price alone. Along with the unfathomable and serene Trevor Giles, he seems to embody most – or at least some – of what Meath stands for. It is no secret his profile, from the blond hair to the bored manner he adopts when the ball is up the far end – infuriates opposition fans and frequently he is at the receiving end of their vocal displeasure. If it ever bothered him, it has long since ceased to.*

Next year, I will find myself in the unusual role of being a spectator at all Meath matches in Croke Park. Not since my school days have I been in such a position but I am really looking forward to it nonetheless. I believe that we have the makings of a fantastic side next year, although I will miss being part of it. I was so looking forward to linking up with Regan, Crimmins and McKeigue and, along with the old experienced warriors, they will take some beating in Leinster. So look out Laois, Dublin and Kildare – you have been warned!

If not next year, then however long it takes, it is just a matter of time before Meath lift some Senior silverware again. The last few years have been barren but Meath's star will rise again in the East and it will be seen over all of Ireland. When that time arrives, and even if I am not a part of it, as a Meathman I will be so proud, reawakening and stirring the emotions of glorious times past.

From a young gaping Geraghty, awestruck from the terraces at a mighty man Mick Lyons to an old O'Rourke warrior, black bandaged but brilliantly brave to the last. Buoyed up by brilliant Boylan, the gallant galloping Giles and fantastic Fay – it only remains for me to say a huge 'thank you' to all supporters and fans who at the end of the day make it possible for us to play.

Fond memories take over, and the hair stands on the back of my neck, when I look back on my Meath career. From Minor days under Paul Kenny and Pat O'Neill right up through the years and the gears to the Senior ranks. The magnificent men I have lined up with, under the legend that is Sean Boylan, make me feel like a privileged passenger. A passenger carried along through the throngs of loyal Royals by mighty men to glory. To glory and the inevitable immortality that comes from the scriptures of Sam Maguire.

# Index